THE LIFE AND
THOUGHT OF
FRIEDRICH ENGELS

The Life and Thought

of Friedrich Engels

A REINTERPRETATION

J. D. Hunley

Yale University Press • *New Haven and London*

Designed by Mary Mendell
Set in Trump Medieval type by Marathon Typography
Service, Inc., Durham, North Carolina.
Printed in the United States of America by BookCrafters,
Inc., Chelsea, Michigan.
The paper in this book meets the guidelines for perman-
ence and durability of the Committee on Production
Guidelines for Book Longevity of the Council on Library
Resources.
10 9 8 7 6 5 4 3 2 1

Library of Congress Cataloging-in-Publication Data
Hunley, J. D., 1941–
The life and thought of Friedrich Engels : a reinterpreta-
tion / by J.D. Hunley.
p.   cm.
Includes bibliographical references (p. 173)
Includes index.
ISBN 0–300–04923–4
1. Engels, Friedrich, 1820-1895.   I. Title.
HX274.7.E53H89   1991
335.4'092—dc20   90–13105 CIP

For Cheryl, Kelly, and Michael
—with thanks for your indulgence over the years

Contents

PREFACE

This study is essentially the by-product of a project I began about fourteen years ago: a full-scale interpretive biography—not just an interpretation—of Friedrich Engels. At that time, there was no interpretive life of Engels in English, although an abridged translation of Gustav Mayer's monumental work was available, and the competent but rather perfunctory biography by L. F. Ilychov and colleagues had appeared in translation. W. O. Henderson's useful but hardly interpretive two-volume biography had also just been published.

As I began to read these works, Marx's and Engels' own writings, and what I have called the "dichotomist" literature on their ideas,[1] it became increasingly apparent to me that the emphasis on significant differences between Marx's and Engels' thought in that body of writings was not at all compatible with my understanding of the two men's works and correspondence. I had already reached this conclusion when I first read Alvin W. Gouldner's *Two Marxisms*, but his excellent book, which dealt with many other matters besides the falsity of the dichotomist thesis, seemed to do nothing to stem the tide of scholarly support for dichotomism. So I decided to write this book, which provides more evidence and more concentrated argument for the essential agreement of Marx's and Engels' ideas than Gouldner could furnish.

It also provides, in chapters 1 and 2, something of an interim report on Engels' life. The more I have studied it, the more impressed I have become with the enormous scope of his interests and writings. This and his impressive grasp of the many different disciplines in which he wrote require expertise from a biographer that I have yet to acquire. In part because of this, I do not attempt to cover all facets of Engels' life. Instead, I focus on the range and depth of his intellectual achievements. In seeking to drive a wedge between the ideas of Marx and Engels, the dichotomists not only have emphasized differences that do not exist but have tended to belittle Engels' very real achievements as a thinker. Chapters 1 and 2 attempt to right the balance and show that Engels, like Marx, was an accomplished intellectual. These chapters present little new evidence about Engels' life, but they do, I think, provide a rather different interpretation of his achievements than has been available before.

I am under no illusion that this study will convince the dichotomists of the inaccuracies that I find in their portrayal of Engels as the scapegoat for all that they dislike in Soviet Marxism. I suspect their convictions are too strong to be reached by mere argument based on textual citation. As Sir Edward Grey wrote in 1925 about the "war generation," I fear they "have formed opinions that nothing will modify, and are dominated by predilections and prejudices that have become an inseparable part of their lives. With such people mental digestion ceases to be able to assimilate anything except what nourishes convictions already formed; all else is rejected or resented; and new material or reflections . . . are searched, not for truth, but for fuel to feed the flame of pre-conceived opinion."[2] I hope, however, that they will prove me wrong and show themselves to be open to the arguments I present below. In any case, the primary audience I seek to reach with this book is the larger group of scholars who may have been convinced by the dichotomists.

To this end, in chapter 3 I trace in some detail the most important assertions of the major dichotomist writers. I had originally intended this part of the book to be simply a review of the literature, but I found it impossible to resist the temptation to refute some of the dichotomist charges right on the spot, as it were. I follow this up in succeeding chapters with a marshalling of the evidence for my view that Marx and Engels were fundamentally in agreement, as Marx's daughter Eleanor and son-in-law Paul Lafargue asserted near the end of Engels' life.

The significance of this issue seems too obvious to me to need pointing out, but it may not be equally apparent to all readers. Communist governments—or at least governments calling themselves communist—ruled until very recently over roughly a third of the world's population in sixteen different countries, among them the Soviet Union and China. The heads of the Communist parties in these countries professed to base their methods of governance ultimately upon the writings of Marx and Engels, as variously interpreted by such leaders as Lenin, Stalin, and Mao Zedong. The dichotomists have stated that Engels' alleged misinterpretations of Marx's writings served as a basis for the repressive nature of communism in the Soviet Union and that Soviet communism in turn overlooked the humanistic elements in Marx's writings.

Obviously, no serious student of communist society would use this as a monocausal explanation for communist repression, but Marx's and Engels' responsibility (or their separate responsibilities) for the nature of communism is nevertheless a significant issue. It underlines the importance of understanding whether or not there were noteworthy divergences in the thinking of the two founders of modern communism. The following pages seek to refute what has become the dominant scholarly interpretation of this issue while at the same time developing the thesis that Engels was a serious thinker whose basic ideas paralleled those of Marx.

Like anyone writing about Marx and Engels, I ought to reveal my own intellectual relationship to them. Although my admiration for much that both of them wrote will be apparent in what follows, I am in no sense a Marxist. I share Marx's and Engels' distaste for the evils of early industrialism and am far from believing that our present age has solved those problems. But although Engels in particular was a remarkable prophet, it has long been apparent that the route the two men expected the larger course of history to follow has been almost totally set aside by subsequent events.

Both men would, I am convinced, have deplored the sort of communism practiced in the Soviet Union and all other countries that profess to follow the Marxist-Leninist road to a classless, stateless society. Both Marx's and Engels' responsibility for this state of affairs can, of course, be debated. But although I think all of us should combat exploitation and injustice wherever they raise their ugly heads, I see no evidence that human beings will ever succeed in overcoming their prejudices, greed, and other like infirmities sufficiently to be able to dispense with the need for some sort of state, however minimal, to protect the weak from the strong. Indeed, the very belief that a revolution can lead to a stateless society seems perversely to lead to exactly the sort of repression the revolution was expected to end forever.

I dislike state power as much as Marx and Engels did and would like to see it reduced as far as is compatible with the welfare of the citizenry, wealthy and poor alike, but I see no prospect of its ever being totally eliminated. Certainly, it seems to me, a revolution is the least likely event to bring about the fundamental changes in human nature that would be required for an abolition of the state. Which brings me to another basic disagreement I have with Marx and Engels: it seems to me they were entirely too prone to condone the use of violence as a means of promoting their admirable ends. In short, I disagree with the two men's methods, and I fear their goals were utopian. These views do not, I trust, prevent me from judging their works impartially.

In researching and writing this book I have, of course, incurred many debts of gratitude. Most of the research and all of the writing for it have occurred since I left the academic world. I have had to do it outside of normal working hours while living and working at a considerable distance from an academic library. I am therefore deeply grateful to the libraries of the universities of Colorado, Oklahoma, New Mexico, and California (at Davis and Berkeley) for extending me the privilege of borrowing books. In addition, I have used the collections of the Manchester Public Library in England and the University of California at Los Angeles and Irvine. The libraries of Allegheny College and Travis and Randolph Air Force bases have obtained books for me through interlibrary loan.

Although I believe I have developed the thesis of this book primarily through reading Marx's and Engels' writings, a number of secondary works have helped give it shape and focus or have provided some of the details of my argument. The most important of these was probably Jerrold Seigel's masterly *Marx's Fate.* In addition, I have benefited greatly from the books and articles of Iring Fetscher, Philip J. Kain, Walter L. Adamson, and David MacGregor, although I have not always agreed with everything they wrote.

John E. Toews offered some useful criticism of a much briefer version of my arguments at a session of the German Studies Association's annual meeting in 1986. My father, (medical) Dr. Henry Cleveland Hunley, provided me with expert information leading to the diagnosis of Engels' malady in 1857–1858 as scrofula. I would like to thank my friends Drs. Timothy Keck, David MacGregor, Philip Kain, and Thomas E. Schott for reading all or parts of the book in draft, encouraging me that it was publishable, and offering me the benefit of their comments and criticisms. No doubt it would be a better piece of work if I had had the learning and skill to implement all of their suggestions, but those I have succeeded in incorporating immeasurably improved it. My wife, Cheryl, helped out immensely by proofreading the manuscript. Finally, I want to express my heartfelt appreciation to Jeanne Ferris, formerly philosophy editor at Yale University Press, for her exceptionally gracious initial handling of my manuscript and its author; Harry Haskell, for his expert editing of the draft; and Charles Grench for suggesting the slightly revised title of the book.

I regret that Terrell Carver's insightful and useful *Friedrich Engels: His Life and Thought* (London: Macmillan, 1989) came to my attention only after my book was already in press. In his biography, Carver attempts a balanced appraisal of Engels' life and ideas but overemphasizes, in my view, the influence on the adult Engels of his Young Hegelian outlook. Carver lacks a proper appreciation for the reasoned and broad eclecticism of both Marx and Engels. Thus, although I find Carver's book valuable, it is not consistently convincing. Had it been available to me earlier, no doubt I would have handled some topics in my own book a little differently, but I would not have altered my overall interpretation.

THE LIFE AND
THOUGHT OF
FRIEDRICH ENGELS

CHAPTER I

Engels' Early Years

Marx's youngest daughter, Eleanor, captured the essence of Engels' character in 1890, when he was seventy: "Next to his youthful freshness and kindness, nothing is so remarkable about him as his many-sidedness. Nothing remains foreign to him," she wrote, "natural history, chemistry, botany, physics, philology . . . political economy, and last not least, military tactics."[1] Theodor Cuno—founder of the Milanese section of the First International, later active in the American Knights of Labor, whose life Engels had saved when Cuno could not make it back to shore while swimming in the sea for the first time in 1872—commented similarly that in talking to Engels, a person gleaned much that was "new and instructive. His brain was a treasury of learned knowledge."[2] The German Social Democrat Karl Kautsky also referred to his encyclopedic knowledge and called him a laughing philosophe.[3]

Not just these intimates but—according to Paul Lafargue—Marx, too, "was proud of Engels. He took pleasure in enumerating to me his moral and intellectual qualities." Lafargue also related that "Marx appreciated Engels's opinion more than anybody else's. . . . I have seen him read whole volumes over and over to find the fact he needed to change Engels's opinion on some secondary point that I do not remember concerning the political and religious wars of the Albigenses. It was a triumph for Marx to bring Engels round to his opinion." According to Lafargue, Marx regarded him as "the most learned man in Europe" and "never tired of admiring the universality of his mind which allowed him to pass with ease from one subject to another." Lafargue recounted also, however, that Marx reproached Engels for studying so many subjects for pleasure instead of working for humanity. (Engels' reply was that he would gladly burn the Russian agricultural studies that Marx had been reading instead of finishing *Capital*.)[4]

Even the English socialist Ernest Belfort Bax, not always a sympathetic witness,[5] called Engels "one of the most remarkable men of his time—a man of encyclopaedic reading and of considerable up-to-date knowledge in all branches of science."[6] Similarly, Edward Aveling, the companion of Eleanor Marx, put Engels alongside Marx, Darwin, and the famous, learned actor Sir Henry Irving as one of the most impressive people he had ever met. "Everyone who had some special subject of his own found that Engels knew it better than himself," Aveling commented.[7]

Origins

This man of such impressive and wide-ranging knowledge came from an unlikely background. Engels was born on 29 November 1820 in the Rhenish town of Barmen. It and its twin city of Elberfield on the Wupper River today make up the core of the large city of Wuppertal. The best description of it at the time of Engels' youth still comes from his "Letters from the Wupper Valley," published anonymously in the *Telegraph für Deutschland* when he was eighteen. His father was one of the staunch Pietists who dominated local society, leading the younger Engels to call it the "Zion of the obscurantists." His already well-developed descriptive skill is apparent in some of the opening lines of the letters, depicting the Wupper itself: "The narrow stream, now swift, now stagnant, discharges its crimson billows between smoky factory buildings and yarn-bedecked bleaching grounds; but its bright red tint stems not from a bloody battle, because here only theological pens and long-winded old wives dispute about trifles. Also not from shame about the doings of mankind, although there is plenty of cause for that, but purely and simply from the many Turkey red dye-works."[8]

Engels complained that a "vigorous, hearty life of the people," with its accompanying folk songs, was hardly present here the way it was almost everywhere else in Germany. Instead, drunks sang vulgar ditties before they passed out and had to sleep off their inebriation in the gutters for want of a roof over their heads. The reason for this state of affairs was "factory" work—begun as early as age six—in low rooms where the workers breathed in more coal fumes and dust than oxygen. This deprived them of all strength and joy in life. And the cottage industry weavers, who plied their own looms at home, sat bent over them from morning into night, drying up their spinal fluid in front of hot stoves.[9]

Those who did not become subject to mysticism, Engels said, were ruined by drunkenness. "This mysticism, in the impudent and offensive form that it exhibited there, necessarily produced its opposite extreme, and for that reason the *people* there principally consisted of the 'refined' (as the mystics were called) and the immoral rabble," Engels wrote. Terrible poverty prevailed among the lower classes, especially the factory work-ers, many of whose children grew up in factories. But "the rich manufac-turers have an ample conscience, and to let a child more or less go to ruin does not doom a Pietist's soul to Hell, especially if he goes to church twice every Sunday." In fact it was a given that among the manufactur-ers, the Pietists treated their workers the worst and paid them the least on the pretext of taking away the wherewithal to get drunk.[10]

Engels claimed that the real center of Pietism and mysticism was the Reformed community of Elberfeld. It had long been characterized by a strong Calvinist spirit, "which in recent years has developed into the harshest intolerance through the appointment of highly bigoted preach-ers," who held what amounted to trials of heretics in their assemblies. They accused people of reading novels, and even if the title pages pro-claimed them Christian novels, Pastor Friedrich Wilhelm Krummacher —the leading local divine—had condemned all novels as godless books. Seemingly God-fearing persons who had the misfortune to be seen at a concert caused people to "throw up their hands in horror at the heinous sin." And if a preacher got the reputation of being a rationalist—meaning that he did not exactly agree with his detractors—they watched him to make sure that his coat was completely black and his trousers of com-pletely orthodox color. Woe to anyone seen in a blue-tinted coat or a rationalist vest. Any skeptic about predestination was immediately branded "almost as bad as a Lutheran." And a Lutheran was not much better than a Catholic. Catholics and idolaters were, of course, among the eternally damned. People who spoke that way were ignorant folk, Engels wrote, who scarcely knew whether the Bible had been written in Chinese, Hebrew, or Greek and who judged everything according to the words of a recognized orthodox preacher.[11]

Regarding the doctrine Krummacher taught, Engels opined that it was im-possible to understand how anyone could believe it, since it directly con-tradicted both reason and the Bible. But Krummacher had defined the doc-trine so sharply, followed and adhered to it in all its consequences to such a degree that no one could refute any of it once the fundamentals had been accepted—namely, the incapacity of people to desire, much less to do, what was good. So God had to instill this ability in mankind. From the free will of God there followed the arbitrary bestowal of salvation. The few elected became, willy-nilly, blessed; the rest were therefore necessarily damned.[12]

It was further written, Engels went on: "No one comes to the father except through me." But heathens could not come to the father through Christ because they did not know him. Hence, they existed solely to fill up Hell. Among the Christians, many were called but few were chosen. And lots of those receiving the call experienced it only apparently. God took care not to call them so powerfully that they obeyed—all to the glory of God and to ensure that they had no excuse. Because it was also written that the wisdom of God was foolishness to the clever people of the world. This was a mandate for the mystics to develop their beliefs in a nonsensical direction in order to ensure the fulfillment of this passage. How all that agreed with the teachings of the apostles, who spoke of the rational service of God and the rational milk of the Gospel, was a mystery too great for human understanding.[13]

The region, Engels said, was so filled with this Pietist spirit that it permeated and corrupted virtually every feature of life. But it exerted its principal power upon education, especially in the elementary schools. The religious schools were totally under the control of the Pietists. They taught only the catechism in addition to reading, writing, and arithmetic. The civil administration had more influence over other elementary schools, even though they, too, came under the supervision of clerical school inspectors. Since these schools taught the beginnings of a few sciences and also some French, many students were stimulated to seek further education even after they had left school. But the religious schools had a greater attendance because they were much less costly.[14]

There were three secondary schools in Wuppertal. The municipal school in Barmen, which Engels had attended, was poorly financed, thus badly staffed. It did everything it could, however. Most of the teachers were Pietists. Engels claimed that Dr. Philipp Schifflin, the second senior assistant master, was the most capable teacher in the school. Perhaps no one in Germany had penetrated so deeply into the grammatical structure of modern French as he had. He began, not with the old Romance languages, but with the classical tongue of the previous century, especially as written by Voltaire. From this, he proceded to the style of the most recent authors. He had published a textbook on how to learn French, which he divided into three courses. Engels claimed (on what basis he does not say) that next to one by H. Knebel, it was undoubtedly the best one available and had a wide distribution throughout Germany and even in Hungary and Russia's Baltic provinces.

Engels had a lower opinion of a history teacher named Ewich, who had also published several textbooks. He said most of the other teachers were fresh out of training school, which did not give good training to some. The best of the lot was H. Köster, a friend of the poet Ferdinand Freiligrath, who was then working in a business house in Barmen and who later gave up a pension from the Prussian king to embrace liberalism and revolution. (Besides serving as an inspiration to the young Engels in the late 1830s, Freiligrath contributed poetry in 1848–49 to the *Neue Rheinische Zeitung*, the newspaper Marx and Engels together wrote and edited.) Köster had recently written an article on styles of poetry and had been offered a job in Düsseldorf. Since the Barmen school board knew he was opposed to Pietism, it very willingly let him go. His exact opposite was a teacher Engels did not name (Rudolf Riepe), who, when asked who Goethe was, replied: "A godless man."[15]

According to Engels, the Elberfeld *Realschule* (modern or scientific secondary school), which he did not attend, was better financed and so could offer more qualified teachers. But it made use of the dreadful system of filling out exercise books, which could make a student dim-witted in half a year. The *Gymnasium* (grammar school with a classical bent) in Elberfeld (which Engels did attend) he described as in difficult circumstances but recognized as one of the best in Prussia. It belonged to the Reformed community but suffered little from its mysticism because the preachers did not concern themselves with it and the school inspectors understood nothing of its affairs. It did suffer all the more from the community's stinginess, however, as the city provided the Realschule with everything and reproached the Gymnasium with failing to cover its expenditures out of school fees. The school inspectors were responsible for selecting the teachers; yet they knew nothing of Greek, Latin, or mathematics. The chief principle they used in guiding their selections was: Better a Reformed bungler than a qualified Lutheran or, more especially, a Catholic. But since Prussian philologists were much more often Lutheran than Reformed, the inspectors had almost never been able to put their principle into practice.

Dr. Johann C. L. Hantschke, royal professor and provisional headmaster, who had taught Engels Latin, wrote that language in a Ciceronian style in both prose and verse. He was the author of a number of sermons, pedagogical writings, and a Hebrew textbook. He would long ago have become permanent headmaster but for the fact that he was a Lutheran. Dr. Karl J. L. Eichoff, from whom Engels took both Greek and Latin, had written a Latin grammar together with a younger colleague, but the *Allgemeine Literatur-Zeitung* had not given it a favorable review. Dr. Johann Christoph Clausen, from whom Engels had taken German, history, and geography, was undoubtedly the ablest man in the whole school. He was proficient in all disciplines, distinguished in history and literature. His delivery possessed a "rare charm," Engels wrote. "He is the only one who knows how to awaken a sense for poetry in the students, a sense that otherwise would languish miserably among the philistines of the Wuppertal."[16]

Of course, this portrait of the two cities—which enraged many Wuppertalers—was somewhat one-sided, if by no means inaccurate. For example, Wolfgang Köllmann has found that in this period the leading families like the Engels felt a duty to look after the public welfare. (On the other hand, Köllmann also reported that bread, potatoes, and coffee were the most important, at times the only, fare of the poor, whiskey their only luxury.)[17] Also, Johann Caspar Engels, Sr., the founder of the family fortune, had arranged for his workers to be able to acquire a house and garden through weekly payments from their wages. His son—Friedrich's grandfather—set up a school for the children of workers in his concern in 1796, and in the lean year of 1816 he headed a charitable organization that provided cheap food to the poor.[18] Thus, not all Pietists were quite as unconcerned about the plight of the poor as Engels suggested, but certainly the working classes in the twin cities suffered considerable deprivation. And Engels' witnessing of their circumstances together with his obvious distaste for the less generous aspects of Pietism help to explain his later conversion to communism.

Engels' father, also named Friedrich, had inherited the family textile firm jointly with his two brothers. It did not prosper, so the three of them agreed to determine by lot who should run it. Engels' father lost the draw, and in 1837 or 1838 he founded a cotton spinnery in Manchester with Godfrey and Peter Ermen. By 1840 they had expanded the business to locations in Barmen and nearby Engelskirchen. The older Friedrich Engels was dogmatically orthodox and conservative. He held high positions in the church community and contributed generously to charity. He inculcated in his children a literal belief in the Bible but, despite his orthodoxy, was not narrowly prejudiced by Wuppertal standards. He played the cello and even went to the theater when he was away from the Wupper Valley, for example.[19]

That he was a strict and not very broad-minded parent, however, is evident from a letter he wrote to his wife in 1835 when she was visiting her sick father in the neighboring province of Westphalia. He reported that young Friedrich had become "more polite, outwardly," but despite "severe chastisements" he could not seem to learn "unconditional obedience." His father had been "distressed to find in his desk a greasy book" on thirteenth-century knights borrowed from a lending library. "The careless way he leaves such books about in his desk is remarkable. May God watch over his disposition," his father wrote, for he was "often fearful for this otherwise excellent boy."[20]

Student Days

Young Friedrich was a good but not a brilliant student. He did write a poem in Greek that he recited at a school function in September 1837.[21] But his certificate upon leaving school that very month mixed praise with some criticism. It referred to his *"very good behavior, . . . modesty, frankness and good-natured disposition"* as well as his "commendable *endeavor*, supported by good talents" and his gratifyingly conspicuous" progress. He had "no difficulty in understanding" Livy, Cicero, Vergil or Horace and could translate them skillfully into German. But he had been less successful in mastering Latin grammar. In Greek, he had "acquired a satisfactory knowledge of morphology and the rules of syntax, in particular good proficiency and skill in translating the easier Greek prose writers," as well as Homer and Euripides. And he was skillful in understanding and explaining Platonic dialogues.

His essays in German "showed gratifying progress," particularly during his last year in school. They "contained good, independent thoughts and were for the most part correctly arranged," their expression "perceptibly" approaching "correctness." He showed "commendable interest" in the German classics and the history of German literature. In religion, he understood the doctrines of the Evangelical Church and "the chief elements of the history of the Christian Church." He was also "not without experience in reading the New Testament (in the original)." He possessed "sufficient lucid knowledge" in history and geography and had "on the whole attained gratifying knowledge" of mathematics and physics. Finally, he followed "the lectures on empirical psychology with interest and success."

Dr. Hantschke signed the certificate, referring to Engels as "a dear pupil who . . . endeavored to commend himself by his religious feeling, purity of heart, agreeable habits and other prepossessing qualities." He said that Engels was going into business, "which he found himself induced to choose as his outward profession in life instead of the studies he had earlier intended."[22]

Apprenticeship

Presumably, it was Engels' father who "induced" him to choose this "outward profession" (which remained merely outward until he retired) and leave the Gymnasium three-quarters of a year before the final examinations. He worked in his father's office for almost a year and then went to the northern seaport of Bremen in the summer of 1838 to gain further experience in the export firm of Heinrich Leupold.[23] If his letters to his sister Marie are any indication—and probably they contain some exaggerations for effect upon a younger sibling—he devoted himself less to his duties than to drinking beer, smoking cigars, resting in a hammock set up in the loft, and writing her letters on company time. In these letters, incidentally, he displayed considerable skill at drawing.[24]

While in Bremen he also found an outlet in the German press for his poetry, literary criticism, and other writings, such as the "Letters from the Wupper Valley." It is interesting to note in this connection that Marx, two and a half years older than Engels, was also something of a poet. Yet the older man's first and last published poems did not appear until 23 January 1841,[25] when he was almost twenty-three, whereas Engels began publishing poems on 16 September 1838, when he was not yet eighteen.[26] Not counting articles that were continued from previous issues, during the roughly two and a half years he was living in Bremen Engels published seven poems, five pieces of literary criticism, and eighteen miscellaneous articles.[27] One of the poems appeared not only in a literary periodical but also in an anthology entitled *Lieder der Zeit*.[28]

Opinions differ about these early writings. Peter Demetz emphasized their imitative character and lack of original ideas, hardly surprising traits in one so young. Věra Macháčková, on the other hand, referring to his writings in general from 1839 to 1844, credited his literary talent and gift for satire and humor. Regardless, these youthful writings were at least good enough to get published. And they certainly reveal Engels' wide-ranging interests and his extensive acquaintance with contemporary German literature, especially that of Young Germany and particularly of Ludwig Börne.[29]

His work in the shipping company and this literary activity by no means exhausted the young Engels' pursuits in this period. He made excursions in the vicinity of Bremen, rode horseback, swam, skated, fenced, frequented taverns, and generally exhibited that extraordinary zest for life that characterized him up until the time of his death. He joined a choral group, attended concerts and the theater. He considered Beethoven's compositions to constitute the apex of German music, his especial favorites being the *Eroica* and Fifth symphonies. He even tried his own hand at composing during this period.[30]

Engels also translated some of Shelley's poems and mentioned Shakespeare—later a favorite of his as well as the whole Marx family—among his readings. More importantly for the development of his thought, he displayed a serious interest in religious and philosophical questions. He was influenced by Friedrich Schleiermacher and mentioned reading the Pietist Heinrich Leo's *Hegelingen* and several works refuting it.[31] He also discussed reading, among others, the Pietist theologian Friedrich August Tholuck, the orthodox Lutheran theologian Ernst Wilhelm Hengstenberg, and the Protestant church historian and Pietist August Neander. With the possible exception of Börne, however, undoubtedly the greatest influences on his thinking in this period were David Friedrich Strauss and Georg Wilhelm Friedrich Hegel. He read Strauss's *Life of Jesus* and a lesser-known work by the same author that he also praised, entitled *Characterizations and Criticisms* (1839), as well as Hegel's *Philosophy of History*.[32]

Under the influence of such reading, he gradually lost his religious faith. In April 1839 he wrote to his former schoolmate Friedrich Graeber, son of a Barmen preacher and later himself a clergyman, that he had never been a Pietist although for a time he had been a mystic. Now he was a liberal supernaturalist and hoped to remain one, if inclining more or less to rationalism.[33] Whether or not it is true that he had never been a Pietist, he now faced a real struggle with his religious conscience.

He wrote Friedrich Graeber at the end of April 1839 that he occupied himself a great deal with philosophy and critical theology. An eighteen-year-old, he wrote, first become acquainted with Strauss, the rationalists, and the *Evangelical Church Times*, either had to read them all without thinking or begin to doubt his religious beliefs. He did not understand how the orthodox preachers could be so dogmatic in view of all the manifest contradictions in the Bible. How, he asked, could anyone reconcile the two genealogies of Joseph, Mary's husband; the different statements at the Last Supper ("This is my blood"; "This is the New Testament in my blood"); the two accounts of the individual possessed by a demon (the one saying the demon simply left, the other that it possessed some swine), and so forth, with the literal truth of the Gospel writers?

Christ's very words, upon which the orthodox set great store, were different in each Gospel. Where did even one apostle say that everything he related was direct inspiration from God? What the orthodox demanded was not surrender of reason in obedience to Christ; it was destruction of the godly in man in order to replace it with the dead letters (of the Bible). For that reason, Engels said he remained a good supernaturalist but had broken with orthodoxy. He could never believe that a rationalist who sought with his whole heart to do good as much as possible would be eternally damned.[34]

In July 1839, Engels wrote that he could not accept his friend's attempts to explain the contradictions in the Bible, but he did say that God's spirit gave him testimony that he was a child of God. He recognized his own strong inclination to sin but could not accept the idea that someone else could wash away his sins. He agreed with the new theology that man's sinfulness resulted from the necessarily incomplete realization of the idea (of God); that therefore every individual had to strive to realize the idea of mankind, that is, to be like God in spiritual completeness.

He said that he recognized his culpability and that if God wanted to punish him, he could do so. But an eternal separation even of the smallest part of the spirit from God was completely impossible for him to imagine or believe. "Can you believe," he asked Graeber, "that a person who strives after unity with God should be forever repudiated by God? . . . Not to be able to doubt, you say, is spiritual freedom. It is the greatest spiritual slavery."

Graeber knew, Engels said, how serious he had been about religion, but he had never experienced the ecstatic bliss that he had so often heard about from the Barmen pulpits. His religion had been and still was blessed peace, and if he could have that after his death, he would be satisfied. He had no reason to believe that God would take that away from him. He prayed daily for truth and had done so ever since he began to doubt. And still he did not return to his friend's faith, despite what was written: "Ask and it shall be given unto you." He searched after truth but could not recognize Graeber's truth as eternal. Yet it was also written, "Seek and ye shall find."

Engels said that tears came into his eyes as he wrote these lines. He felt that he would not be lost, that he would come to God, for whom his whole heart yearned. But he knew from experience that dogmatic belief had no bearing upon inner peace.

He had written these words and many others on 12 July. On the 27th, before he posted the letter, he added that according to his friend's Christianity, nine-tenths of the people were eternally unfortunate and only one-tenth blessed. Was that the endless love of God? How small that made God seem, if that was what his love meant. Graeber lay comfortably in his belief, as in a warm bed (a metaphor of which Engels was fond). He knew nothing of the struggle about whether God existed or not. But Engels asked him to consider whether he wanted to send his correspondent to Hell. He should write back soon with his judgment.[35]

By October 1839, Engels had given in to his doubts. On the eighth he wrote to Wilhelm Graeber, Friedrich's older brother who later also became a preacher, to proclaim he was now an enthusiastic follower of Strauss. "*Adios* religious faith!" he said, "it is as full of holes as a sponge. . . . If you can refute Strauss—*eh bien*, then I'll become a Pietist again." A month later he announced to Wilhelm that he was on the point of becoming a Hegelian. Strauss, he said, had shed light on Hegel that made his views plausible.[36]

Such an apparent search for something or someone to believe in led Gareth Stedman Jones to conclude that the young Engels could not abandon his beliefs but only move from one to another. According to Stedman Jones, the impact of Hegel upon him was like a religious conversion. Consequently, Stedman Jones claimed, Engels never subjected Hegel to the same critique that Marx provided.[37] Such a view of Engels might easily be applied backwards to his relationship with Börne and Strauss, forward to that with Marx himself. Engels' early life then becomes a series of searches for some faith to believe in. This interpretation is seductive in view of his sudden espousal of Strauss as well as the many later assertions that he had been honored to play second fiddle to Marx.

This partly putative conception of Engels' life, however, fails to take into account the complexities of his character. It also suggests a lack of self-confidence on his part that Stedman Jones has attributed to him in a different context.[38] In fact, though, Engels displayed a great deal of self-confidence in the letters to the Graeber brothers quoted above. He was not simply abandoning one set of beliefs for another. He was subjecting his beliefs at each succeeding stage in their evolution to searching examination. This pattern prevailed with each of the thinkers who influenced him.

Börne's works, for example, especially the *Letters from Paris* and *Menzel der Franzosenfresser* (Menzel the French-eater), strengthened his natural inclination toward freedom and independence (seen, for instance, in his relations with his domineering father) and affected his style. He also took from Börne a belief in the importance of acting over speaking. But he did not accept everything Börne said, and he criticized that political writer and satirist for being too purely political in his thinking and for believing that freedom was only the absence of tyranny.[39]

Engels felt at one point that it was his appointed task to link up the thinking of Börne and Hegel, showing that he maintained some distance from both and was not blindly a disciple of either.[40] With respect to Hegel alone, he showed this further in "The State of England: The Eighteenth Century," published in August and September 1844 in *Vorwärts* (Forward), a twice-weekly Paris journal edited by Marx. *Pace* Stedman Jones, Engels wrote there that Jeremy Bentham committed the same error with his empiricism that Hegel did with his theory: he was not serious about overcoming contradictions; he made the subject into the predicate, the whole subject into the part, and thereby turned everything upside down.[41] (Here, of course, Engels displayed the same Feuerbachian influence that characterized Marx's criticisms of Hegel in this period, but he chided Feuerbach as well for his abstract handling of mankind.)[42]

As I will discuss in more detail below, Engels also possessed enough confidence and detachment to criticize Marx's writings in their private correspondence. And, particularly late in his life, Engels showed enormous flexibility in his interpretation of his own and Marx's views about the influence of material factors upon history. The self-confidence such flexibility suggests belies the notion that Engels went through life searching for a messiah whose disciple he could become. At the same time, his thought did not diverge significantly from that of Marx, with whom, alone among Marx's early acquaintances, he maintained a close working relationship and friendship up to the time of the older man's death.

Berlin Period

Meanwhile, at the end of March 1841 Engels had returned from Bremen to Barmen, where he remained—except for a trip to Switzerland and Italy—about six months before enlisting in the army as a one-year volunteer in the artillery. Apparently, he took his military training no more seriously than his apprenticeship in business,[43] so presumably he enlisted primarily to audit courses at the University of Berlin.[44] In any event, he did get stationed in the Prussian capital, where he attended the lectures of Philipp Marheinecke on Hegel's religious philosophy, of the liberal Hegelian Ferdinand Benary on the origins of Christianity, and of the old Hegelian Leopold von Henning on Prussian financial policy, as well as those of two other followers of Hegel, Georg Andreas Gabler and Karl Friedrich Werder.[45]

Engels continued to publish articles and poems at first,[46] but from June to September 1842 he renounced all literary activity to study philosophy.[47] While in Berlin, he read Hegel's *Phenomenology, Science of Logic,* and *Encyclopedia*; Kant's *Critique of Pure Reason, Prolegomena,* and *Perpetual Peace*; and Feuerbach's *The Essence of Christianity.* He also established close relations with the Young Hegelian circle with which Marx had associated from the spring of 1837 to that of 1841—although some of its personnel had changed in the interim.[48]

Unlike the majority of the Young Hegelians, Engels had come through the influence of Börne to believe in acting as well as criticizing,[49] but this did not prevent him from becoming the principal defender of the left Hegelian position against the attacks of Friedrich W. J. Schelling. In 1848 the Prussian authorities had appointed this German philosopher as a privy councilor and member of the Berlin academy to counterbalance the influence of the Young Hegelians. He lectured at the University of Berlin, with Engels among his auditors.[50]

Under what had become his usual pen name, Friedrich Oswald, Engels wrote an article in two installments entitled "Schelling on Hegel" in which he reproduced Schelling's comments from notes he had taken during the lectures. He said that what these comments boiled down to—when divested of their courtly language—was that Hegel had no system of his own but had made his living off the by-products of Schelling's thought. While Schelling had concerned himself with positive philosophy, Hegel had developed the negative and tried to make that half into the whole of philosophy. Engels conceded that everyone had the deepest reverence for Schelling as Hegel's forerunner. But as Hegel's successor he could hardly expect dispassionate treatment from those who were standing up for the dead thinker.

Engels then expanded the criticism of Schelling with comments like: "Kant freed rational thinking from space and time. Schelling takes away existence as well. What, then still remains to us?" Schelling might develop a school of thought, he concluded, but Engels did not yet believe this was possible, although some of the audience had at least progressed to the point of indifference (instead of hostility) toward him.[51]

Engels followed this article with an anonymous pamphlet entitled *Schelling and Revelation* that appeared at Leipzig early in 1842. As the title suggests, he compared Schelling's teachings to a new revelation that would destroy the godlessness of Hegelianism. Hegel's style, Engels conceded, had been strongly scientific, almost thorny, but Hegel had rejected everything "imaginary, fantastic, emotional" in favor of grasping "pure thought in its self-creation." His world view had been completed by 1820 and bore the impression of the Restoration. Thus, he exemplified his own proclamation that every philosophy contained the thought-content of its time. His principles were independent and liberal, but his conclusions were occasionally restrained and illiberal. Some of his pupils held to the principles and rejected the conclusions. The left wing thus arose, with Arnold Ruge creating its mouthpiece, the *Hallische Jahrbücher*.

Meanwhile, Engels went on, as "Hegel's thought-creating power showed itself to be increasingly energetic, lively and active," Schelling increasingly doubted he could achieve the great results he desired by the path he had been following. He sought, Engels said, as early as the beginning of the first decade of the century, to achieve the absolute directly through assuming a higher revelation. He left the path of pure thought and burrowed in mythological and theosophical fantasies, holding his system at the disposal of the king of Prussia.

Engels accused Schelling of attempting to smuggle belief in authority, sentimental mysticism, and gnostic fantasies into the free art (*Wissenschaft*, usually translated as "science") of thinking. He said that Schelling sought to justify his incapacity to grasp the universe as rational and whole by arguing that reason was powerless to prove the existence of anything and therefore had to accept the testimony of experience as adequate. There followed a lengthy discussion of Schelling's ideas in relation to Hegel's that would require too much space here to summarize in any meaningful way.[52]

It is, of course, possible to criticize some of the arguments Engels advanced against Schelling,[53] but the significant point to be made about the pamphlet is the understanding of Hegel's and Schelling's thought its twenty-one-year-old author exhibited. The penetration of Engels' commentary is remarkable for so young a man, who had not graduated from Gymnasium and had spent his working hours since leaving school as an apprentice in an export firm and then a trainee in the army. The pamphlet received considerable attention at home and abroad. An article the Russian intellectual Vasily Botkin wrote in the January 1843 issue of *Fatherland Notes* contained a summary and some translated passages from it. The Polish democrat Edward Dembrowski praised it in an article on Schelling's Berlin lectures that appeared in the October 1842 issue of a Polish journal.[54] And Ruge, thinking the author of the pamphlet was Michael Bakunin, commented: "This promising young man is outstripping all the old donkeys in Berlin."[55]

Conversion to Communism

In October 1842, Engels' year of military service ended and he returned to Barmen by way of Cologne, where he stopped to meet the staff of the *Rheinische Zeitung* in which he had been publishing articles since March. On 15 October, Marx became the editor of the paper, but Engels apparently did not meet him on this trip. He did meet another editor, Moses Hess, who claimed to have converted him to communism. Hess's belief that social revolution would first occur in England may have influenced Engels to accede to his father's desire that he accept employment in the Manchester office of Ermen and Engels to complete his commercial training. On the way there in November 1842, he stopped again at Cologne and met Marx. By then, Marx had broken with the left

Hegelians to whom Engels had been close in Berlin. He was therefore cool toward his future friend and partner but did not discourage him from continuing to write for the newspaper.[56]

From December 1842 until August 1844, Engels served as a clerk in the cotton firm his father partly owned.[57] During that time he did continue to write for the *Rheinische Zeitung* and also published articles in other papers including the *Schweizerischer Republikaner*, Robert Owens's *The New Moral World*, Ruge's and Marx's ill-fated *Deutsch-Französische Jahrbücher*, and the previously mentioned *Vorwärts*.[58]

Undoubtedly, Engels's most important work during this period in England was his "Outlines of a Critique of Political Economy," written in late 1843 and January 1844 and published in the *Deutsch-Französische Jahrbücher* in the latter year. There he dealt with the classic writers in the discipline—Adam Smith, David Ricardo, J. R. McCulloch, J.-B. Say, James Mill, and Thomas Malthus, among others. He made comments such as "The 'national wealth' of the English is very great, and yet they are the poorest people under the sun" and "In a word, trade is legal fraud," but he also said that the economists formed a link in the chain of the progress of mankind. He criticized the economists' treatment of value and capitalism's separation of mankind into capitalists and workers—a separation that he said grew and had to grow as each day passed. He also predicted that when private property disappeared, so would this unnatural division.[59]

There is not room here to follow all of Engels' arguments in this seminal article, but clearly he displayed a grasp of contemporary economic thought that is surprising in someone who had recently occupied himself primarily with literature and philosophy. Equally clearly, not everything he wrote in this essay squared with Marx's mature economic doctrines. On the other hand, it was a brilliant piece—one that Marx admired and that prefigured his life's work. In Terrell Carver's words, "Marx's *Capital* was in effect a much elaborated specification of the contradiction discussed by Engels in his 'Outlines'."[60] Other scholars, too, have noted the significant impact Engels' article had on Marx's intellectual development. David McLellan, for example, said that Marx's reading of it "marked the real beginning of his lifelong interest in economic questions."[61]

Quite apart from this article and the reading he did for it, Engels' stay in England had a formative influence upon his life. It was there that he met his future common-law wife, whom he never formally married —Mary Burns, then apparently a domestic servant. Mary was the daughter of an Irish dyer. According to Marx family gossip later reported by Eleanor Marx, who never knew Mary, she was "a very pretty, witty and altogether charming girl (in her twenties)." She was "quite uneducated" and had earlier worked in a factory. She appears to have helped introduce Engels to proletarian circles in Manchester.[62] These contacts, of course, formed part of the background for his book *The Condition of the Working Class in England*. It was in the process of gathering further materials for this study that Engels met George Julian Harney, the Chartist leader and editor of the *Northern Star*, with whom he maintained a friendship off and on through the rest of their lives. Harney has left us a description of Engels in 1843 as "a tall, handsome young man with a countenance of almost boyish youthfulness, whose English in spite of his German birth and education, was even then remarkable for its accuracy."[63]

It was on his way back to Barmen from Manchester in 1844 that Engels stopped in Paris and began his remarkable friendship with Marx. While living at home, he then wrote *The Condition of the Working Class*,[64] which David McLellan has called "a pioneering work in the relatively modern fields of urban geography and sociology."[65] That, of course, is but one of many views of the book, pro and con.[66] Whatever one thinks of it, there is no doubt that it is not exclusively a work of pure or original scholarship and that Engels painted a one-sided picture of the conditions of the English working classes at the time, overemphasizing the well-being of the workers before industrialization and the subsequent impact of the machine upon them.[67] Similar criticism can be made of Marx's writings, of course,[68] and in any event, Engels' work was noteworthy despite its flaws from the standpoint of modern scholarship.[69]

Particularly in the sections on London and Manchester, Engels presented vivid accounts of what he himself had observed. Perhaps no other book but Elizabeth Gaskell's *Mary Barton* provides so graphic a depiction of the real evils the English working classes suffered in this period. Take, for example, Engels' description of a court near the Irk River in Manchester:

> In one of these courts, right at the entrance . . . there stands a privy that has no door and is so filthy that the inhabitants can only enter or exit the place through a stagnating pool of putrid urine and excrement that surrounds it. It is the first court above Ducie Bridge, if anyone should desire to examine it. Below on the river are several tanneries that fill the whole region with the aroma of decomposing animals. . . .
>
> Further down, the Irk flows, or rather stagnates—a slender, pitch-black, stinking stream, full of refuse and offal that wash up on the less steep right bank. In dry weather there remains on the bank a

long series of the most loathsome black-green pools of slime, out of whose depth bubbles of miasmic gases continually rise and produce a stench that even on the bridge, forty or fifty feet above the surface of the water, is still intolerable. . . .

One proceeds on an uneven bank, between poles and wash-lines through a chaos of small, one-floor and one-room cottages, most of which have no flooring—kitchen, living- and bedrooms all combined into one. In such a hovel, scarcely six feet long and five feet wide, I saw two beds—and what bedsteads and bedding!—that, together with a doorstep and hearth, filled the whole room. In several others I saw *absolutely nothing*, although the door was open and the inhabitants leaning against it. In front of the doors, debris and garbage were everywhere. . . . The whole agglomeration of cattle stalls for human beings was bordered on two sides by houses and a factory, on the third by the river, and except for the small path along the bank of the river, there was only a narrow archway out of the place—into another almost as poorly built and wretchedly maintained labyrinth of dwellings.

Enough of this! The entire side of the Irk is similarly constructed, a planless chaos of houses thrown together, whose uninhabitability is more or less equivalent and whose unclean interiors fully match the filthy surroundings. How can the people be clean! . . . There are so few privies here that they are either full all day long or are too far away for most people. How can the people wash, when they have only the filthy water of the Irk nearby and there are water piping and pumps only in the respectable neighborhoods. Truly, one cannot blame these helots of modern society if their dwellings are no cleaner than the pigsties that here and there stand in their midst.[70]

Even before he had written these lines and the rest of the book, Engels had composed three short chapters and sections of four others for *The Holy Family*, jointly written with Marx. Then, in April 1845, he joined Marx in Brussels. Later that year, they began work on *The German Ideology*. In early 1846 they founded a Communist Correspondence Committee.[71] Engels moved to Paris in August of that year to spread his and Marx's ideas among the members of the League of the Just. As this organization metamorphosed into the Communist League, Engels and Marx gradually converted its "Confession of Faith" into the *Communist Manifesto*.[72]

The Revolutions of 1848

When the revolutions of 1848 broke out, Marx and Engels returned to Germany. With Marx as editor-in-chief and Engels among a number of other editors, they organized and published the *Neue Rheinische Zeitung: Politische-ökonomische Revue*, the first issue of which appeared on 31 May 1848. Engels did most of the writing the first month, after which they divided the labor but also often collaborated on individual articles.[73]

Engels was evidently the sole or principal writer of articles on such varied topics as "The Frankfurt Assembly," "The Most Recent Heroic Deed of the House of Bourbon," "The War Comedy," "The New Partition of Poland," "The Berlin Debate about the Revolution," "The Armistice with Denmark," "The Italian Struggle for Liberation," "The Uprising in Frankfurt," "The New Authorities—Progress in Switzerland," "The Personalities of the Federal Council," and "The War in Italy and Hungary" (one of many pieces on the campaigns in southern and eastern Europe).[74]

On 19 May 1849, the last number of the paper appeared in red ink. It contained, besides a "Word of Farewell" from Ferdinand Freiligrath, an article by Marx on the suppression of the paper, and among others, a long summary of the situation in Hungary by Engels.[75] Next, the two friends headed south. Marx went to Paris on 3 June, while Engels took part as a soldier in the last stand of the democratic revolutionaries in Baden against Prussian soldiers, for whom they were no match. Engels participated in four battles as adjutant to a former Prussian lieutenant, August Willich. He later wrote to Jenny Marx (Karl's wife) that he had found "the much-celebrated courage to attack is the most ordinary attribute that a person can have."[76]

Manchester Years

Over the next few months, Engels and the Marx family went into exile in England where, except for trips abroad, they were to spend the remainder of the two men's lifetimes. Engels stayed in London, where the Marxes lived, until November 1850, when he began working again for Ermen and Engels in Manchester. Although at first he did not earn a great deal, he was able to support himself and supplement Marx's meager income while also helping to write or translate the articles published under Marx's name (see chapter 8). Later, as his own income rose, Engels' support of Marx became quite substantial.[77]

Engels started as a clerk at an annual salary of £200, roughly the same income that Freiligrath received as manager of the London branch of the Banque Générale Suisse in this same period.[78] Engels actually worked, not for the Manchester firm itself, but as the representative of the German branch thereof. In 1852 his father negotiated a new contract with the Ermens, making the younger Engels responsible for work in the office, especially the correspondence. His remuneration changed to £100 per year salary plus a sliding percentage of the firm's profits—5 percent the first four years, 7.5 percent the next four, and 10 percent the following four. He was not financially responsible for losses, if any occurred. The firm apparently prospered, however, because according to Mayer, Engels' share of its earnings came to £168 in 1854, £163 in 1855, £408 in 1856, £837 in 1857, £840 in 1858, and £978 in 1859, the last year for which information is available.[79]

Paul Lafargue reported that Engels worked weekdays at Ermen and Engels from ten until four, his "main occupation" being "to deal with the firm's correspondence in several languages and to attend the Exchange."[80] If correct, these working hours would help to explain how he was able to research and write as much as he did during his Manchester years. In fact, however, there is evidence that his hours at the firm were not always so limited. On 6 July 1852, for example, he wrote to Marx that he was up to his ears in work. It was seven p.m. and he still had eleven business letters to compose. If possible, he would still write an article that night or the next night at the latest[81] for Marx to send to the *New-York Daily Tribune*.[82] Earlier that year he had written that he was working until seven or eight at night, and he faced the same schedule at least once in 1853. Likewise, in 1854 he reported that he had neglected some work for his father and had to work particularly hard at the counting house for a couple of weeks to catch up.[83] He did sometimes write private letters at the office, but in one of them he commented that it was six o'clock, closing time.[84] This suggests that in fact even his regular hours were longer than Lafargue, who knew Engels mostly after he had retired and moved to London, had conceived to be the case.

If that is so, the explanation for the amount of work—and play—that Engels engaged in outside of his hours at the counting house is solely the one Marx gave to Adolf Cluss, a former member of the Communist League who had emigrated in 1849 to America, where he helped to spread Marx's and Engels' ideas. Marx wrote to him in October 1853 that the only person Cluss could count on for articles to appear in *Die Reform*—a German-language, working-class newspaper published in New York from 1853 to 1854—was Engels. He was really overworked, but he was a true encyclopedia, capable of working every hour of the day and night, quick as the devil in comprehending and writing.[85]

Engels wrote most of his major works either before he moved to Manchester or after he retired from business, but he did put together numerous articles during the Manchester period both to help Marx earn money and to support working-class newspapers like the Chartist journal *The People's Paper* and the Lassallean *Social-Demokrat*. In the same timespan, Engels also undertook a serious study of military history and current developments in the art of war.

He began this endeavor in mid-1851 in consultation by mail with his friend Joseph Weydemeyer, a former Prussian lieutenant who had emigrated to America. But he soon passed beyond the point where Weydemeyer was any help as a tutor, even though that gentleman later became a colonel in the Union Army during the American Civil War.[86] Engels quickly found a ready market for his military writings, the proceeds from which, of course, went to support the Marxes. Charles A. Dana, whom Marx had met in Cologne in 1848, had commissioned him to write a short piece on European armies for *Putnam's Monthly*, for which he was to be paid ten pounds. Marx turned to Engels for assistance, and Engels ended up writing much more than Dana had bargained for.[87] Three lengthy articles appeared between August and December 1855 dealing not just with the armies of major powers but with those of such secondary ones as Bavaria, Saxony, Turkey, Sardinia, Portugal, and the Netherlands.[88]

A couple of years later he began writing some sixty-three articles on such topics as "Army," "Fortifications," "Alma," "Military Bridge," and "Cavalry" for *The New American Cyclopaedia*, which came out in sixteen volumes under the editorship of Dana and George Ripley between 1858 and 1863. Again, Dana had approached Marx alone to contribute, but Engels did most of the work despite his full-time employment and a severe bout with scrofula during the last half of 1857 and early 1858.[89] Marx wrote ten biographical articles on military figures and collaborated with Engels on eight others. Marx had also collected some data at the British Museum for Engels' articles on European armies,[90] a sort of activity that prompted Martin Berger's wry comment, "In a history of the nineteenth century compiled by a truly single-minded military buff, Marx would figure only as Engels' research assistant."[91]

Meanwhile, Engels had written some sixty-two articles on the Crimean War (1853–1856), not counting contributions to joint articles with Marx. Most of these appeared in the *New-York Daily Tribune*, but some were reprinted or appeared solely in the *Neue Oder-Zeitung*.[92] During the fighting and turmoil leading up to Italy's unification, Engels wrote two pamphlets dealing with strategic but disputed borders, *Po and Rhine* and *Savoy, Nice and the Rhine*.[93] He and Marx covered other military conflicts, including the Indian Mutiny, in various forums including the *Manchester Guardian*. Then in 1870–1871 he penned a series of fifty-nine articles on the Franco-Prussian War that appeared in the *Pall Mall Gazette*.[94] Thereafter, a period of comparative peace lasting the rest of his life restricted the scope of his military writings.

Although one expert has commented on the conventionality of Engels' military thinking,[95] other students of the subject have underscored the brilliance and prescience of his observations. Jehuda L. Wallach, for example, noted that in *Po and Rhine* he foresaw the German route of march through Belgium prescribed in the Schlieffen Plan.[96] Sigmund Neumann pointed out that in the same pamphlet he had, in effect, warned the Germans against the programs of Hitler's New Order and the Rome-Berlin axis eighty years before the fact, not exactly a military observation but one that impinged on military grand strategy. Neumann also noted that in *Savoy, Nice and the Rhine* Engels had laid out the strategy for the miracle of the Marne. And he quoted Engels from the latter pamphlet, "History has yet to show that in case of war Belgium's neutrality is more than a scrap of paper." Finally, he pointed out that Engels, noting a sudden shift of the Prussian army marching on Châlons early in the Franco-Prussian War, became the sole European observer to forecast the strategy leading to Moltke's decisive victory at Sedan.[97]

Actually, the method Engels used to make this last discovery was a little more complicated than Neumann suggested. He told Marx that the decisive moment in his divination of the plan arrived when he received the news that his friend Dr. Gumpert's cousin—the commander of a company in the 77th Regiment, the advance guard of the Seventh (Prussian) Army Corps—had marched from Aachen to Trier. That revealed the entire maneuver to the alert Engels.[98] The article in which Engels made his prediction appeared in the *Pall Mall Gazette* on 2 August 1870 with "Z." for a by-line.[99] Contemporaries ascribed it to an English general, and thereafter the Marxes and other friends conferred on Engels the nickname "General."[100]

Of course, Engels' military predictions did not all pan out the way this one had. Although unlike most European military authorities he recognized the significance of the American Civil War,[101] he allowed himself to be convinced by southern successes up to 1862 that the Confederacy would win it.[102] And he predicted an Austrian victory in the Austro-

Prussian War of 1866. He had thought, incorrectly, that Prussian superiority in weaponry and its quartermaster corps would be outweighed by several Austrian advantages, including better overall leadership and more recent experience with war.[103]

But the surprising thing about Engels' military writing is not that he was sometimes wrong; it is rather that he was able to cover so many campaigns so insightfully without ever leaving Manchester. He frequently had a clearer perception of what was happening on the battlefield than did the generals on the spot—at least those on the losing side. He achieved this on the basis of official communiqués, reports of war correspondents, and his own skill in using maps and applying the lessons of military history.[104]

He succeeded so well at these techniques that others of his writings besides those on the Franco-Prussian War were attributed to generals. People credited articles of his in the *New-York Daily Tribune* to General Scott, and his brochure *Po and Rhine* to a Prussian general.[105] Engels also enjoyed the esteem of Major Otto Wachs, a member of the Prussian General Staff and, not altogether incidentally, the cousin of Gumpert whose march from Aachen to Trier tipped Engels off about Prussian plans in the Franco-Prussian War. Engels had met him in the 1860s in Manchester, and they had since corresponded. The two men disagreed in their politics, but Wachs nevertheless regarded Engels as a friend and told Hellmut von Gerlach, a fellow member of the Social Conservative Club, that he held none of his colleagues on the General Staff in higher esteem for their "expert knowledge, objectivity and clear judgement."[106]

The occasion for these comments was Gerlach's announcement of his plans to study social conditions in England. Wachs had said that if he was going to London, where Engels by that time lived, he must certainly call upon that gentleman. Gerlach did so and got a friendly reception, although he told the communist leader that he was a Christian socialist, not a social democrat. Engels invited him repeatedly to his home, one time during a gathering to celebrate a Social Democratic victory in a by-election. Engels made this aristocratic future opponent of Nazism feel right at home—but one indication among many of his usual broad-mindedness.[107]

CHAPTER 11

Engels' Later Life

Besides his military and other writings,[1] Engels also found time for a variety of activities while living in Manchester. He was an avid rider and fox hunter, and he otherwise participated in the normal social life of an English businessman. He joined the Albert Club, a social institution composed half of English and half of German members, and, to maintain appearances, he kept up a bachelor lodging where he entertained his middle-class friends and his father on the latter's occasional visits. He actually lived with Mary Burns in a series of separate dwellings elsewhere in the city. Mary's sister Lizzie lived with them, and Engels continued to live with her after Mary's death in 1863. He also became a member of the Schiller-Anstalt, a social and cultural institute of the German community in Manchester, of which he served as president from 1864 to 1868.[2]

Something of Engels' character in this period can be gleaned from his answers in April 1868 to a series of questions in a popular parlor game called "Confessions." His favorite virtue, he said, was cheerfulness. His favorite characteristic in a man was minding his own business; in a woman, not to mislay things. His own principal characteristic, he felt, was to know everything by half. His conception of happiness was Château Margaux 1848; of unhappiness, going to a dentist. The vice he forgave was excess of all kinds; the one he abhorred was hypocrisy. His disinclination was affected, stuck-up women. The person he liked the least was Charles Haddon Spurgeon, an influential Baptist preacher (1834–1892). His favorite occupation was teasing and being teased. For his favorite hero, he put "none." As to a heroine, he said there were too many to list. His favorite poets were Renard the Fox, Shakespeare, Ariosto, "etc." Among prose writers, he favored Goethe, Lessing, and a certain Dr. Samuelson. His favorite flower was the bluebell. He liked all colors but those produced by aniline dyes. Regarding favorite dishes, he gave two answers: "cold: salad; hot: Irish stew." His favorite maxim was not to have any. And his motto was to take it easy.[3]

It would be wrong, of course, to take answers to a parlor quiz too seriously, but many of these have a ring of truth about them. Concerning characteristics of women, for example, he sometimes complained to Marx about a maid's having mislaid a book or paper. Eleanor Marx wrote of his cheerful disposition that he had inherited from his mother. He dearly loved a good wine as well as a glass of beer. Eduard Bernstein recalled about him some twelve years later, when Engels was sixty, that it was no easy task to keep up with him on walks, but that was easier than keeping pace with him drinking a glass of wine.[4] Thus, it would appear that these answers pretty accurately reflected his real views.

In 1860 Engels' father died. His brothers did not want him to have any rights with respect to the family business in Ermelskirchen, so he wrote to his mother that he would give them up to spare family strife. (Unlike Marx, who was extremely fond of his father but not his mother, Engels had no particular love for his father but had a great affection for his mother.) By English law, Gottfried Ermen became the sole owner of the firm in Manchester, but Engels' brothers were willing to keep ten thousand pounds invested in the English business. Engels was able to parlay that and the threat of entering into competition with Ermen into a partnership in the firm beginning in 1864.[5]

From 1860 to 1864 he received 10 percent of the firm's profits and one hundred pounds per year for his continuing services as corresponding clerk and general assistant in the office. In 1864 his share of the profits increased to 20 percent, and he received 5 percent interest on capital for the five years of the agreed-upon partnership. He was to manage the "office department . . . now carried on at the counting house in Southgate" (near the center of Manchester) and to conduct the correspondence as before.[6] It would be highly interesting to know what Engels' relations to the workers in the factory portion of the business were, but little evidence appears to have survived. He wrote to Marx on 13 February 1865 that thanks to Ferdinand Lassalle, who had given the German working-class movement a "Tory-Chartist" character, louts in the movement would ask how he could speak in their name and say what they should do when he sat in Manchester and exploited the workers. He said that was all the same to him, but evidently he was sensitive about the matter.[7] And, of course, it is one of the more striking ironies of history that Marx's principal source of income while he wrote his scathing critique of capitalism was himself a capitalist.

Engels' end of the business, however, remained the office, not the factory floor, which was located some distance away, so he did not deal directly with the actual factory workers. But he could be a hard taskmaster to those who did work directly for him. In October 1865 he complained to Marx that "der Gottfried" had engaged three "fellows" who were worth nothing. He said he would have to fire a couple of them.[8] In November he did fire an errand-boy who had forgotten to mail a registered letter to Marx containing fifteen pounds.[9]

Perhaps in part because of the necessity for such actions, Engels relished his retirement from what he sarcastically called "noble commerce" on 30 June 1869.[10] Eleanor Marx, then fourteen, was staying with Engels and Lizzie when he retired,[11] and she recalled some twenty years later: "I shall never forget the triumph with which he exclaimed: 'For the last time!' as he put on his boots in the morning to go to the office. . . . A few hours later we were standing at the gate waiting for him. We saw him coming over the little field opposite the house where he lived. He was swinging his stick in the air and singing, his face beaming. Then we set the table for a celebration and drank champagne and were happy."[12]

London "Retirement"

With the help of Marx's wife, Jenny,[13] Engels rented a house in London and moved there on 20 September 1870 after he had completely tied up his business affairs with Ermen and Engels.[14] His house was ten minutes from the Marxes', opposite a park. Marx's health was somewhat parlous, and Engels felt the best medicine for him was exercise and fresh air. He therefore insisted on their taking a one-and-a-half-mile walk three or four times a week up and down steep hills.[15]

Lafargue remembered that the two men saw each other daily, and if the weather did not permit a walk outdoors, they walked up and down in Marx's study for an hour or two while engaged in conversation. He recalled one discussion about the Albigensians that lasted several days. Both studied the issue between sessions. He said that their "lives interwove so closely . . . they seemed to form one single life," but they also "differed from one another not only outwardly but in temperament, character and way of thinking and feeling." For example, their study rooms were in marked contrast with one another. In Engels', there was not a scrap of paper on the floor, and all his books were in their places except for a dozen or so that were on his desk. It resembled a reception room rather than a scholar's work area. Marx's, on the other hand, was always in apparent disorder. There were volumes and pamphlets of different sizes next to one another because they were arranged by content. But despite the apparent disarray, Marx could always find whatever he wanted.[16]

One indication of Engels' standing in the Marx household was that before Laura became formally engaged to Lafargue, she felt obliged to obtain Engels' consent.[17] On the other hand, his relationship with Marx's wife seems to have been rather formal, perhaps as a result of her aristocratic upbringing. She invariably referred to him in the salutations of her letters as "Dear Herr Engels" or "My dear Herr Engels" and he to her as "Dear Frau Marx."[18] Several scholars have commented on her refusal to have anything to do with Mary Burns,[19] although there is little real evidence on the subject, perhaps because Marx's daughters destroyed letters that may have contained unfavorable references to Mary.

We do know of one encounter between the two women at a banquet of the German Workers Society in Brussels at the beginning of the eventful year 1848. Engels had brought Mary back from England the year before and took her to the banquet. The couple did not sit with the Marxes, and Stephan Born, the leader of the Labor Brotherhood during the revolutions of the ensuing two years, recalled that Marx had indicated to him "through a look and a very expressive smile" that Frau Marx "rigidly rejected an acquaintance with that—woman. In questions of marriage and purity of morals the noble lady was intransigent."[20]

If the cause of the smile was, indeed, Frau Marx's ethical principles, as Born surmised, it is curious that she did not apply those same principles (or prejudices, as some might call them) to Lizzie Burns, who replaced Mary as Engels' "wife" without benefit of a marriage ceremony until she was on her deathbed. Yet Frau Marx struck up an intimate friendship with Lizzie, spending holidays at the seaside with her in 1871, 1873, 1875, and 1876.[21]

Perhaps the difference in Frau Marx's relationship to the two equally illiterate (and presumably, by her lights, immoral) sisters resulted from Eleanor Marx's friendship with Lizzie. (She had been too young to have developed one with Mary.) Perhaps it arose simply from a personality clash between Frau Marx and Mary. Or, quite conceivably, there were real moral scruples on Frau Marx's part that she overcame in Lizzie's case as a result of Engels' being grievously hurt at the comparative lack of sympathy Marx displayed on the occasion of Mary Burns's death.[22] It is even possible that only through Engels' reaction to Mary's death did the

Marxes—both husband and wife—come to realize the depth of his affection for her and therefore come to respect his relationship with her
and subsequently with Lizzie.

Be that as it may, in 1865 both Engels and Lizzie had become members
of the First International. Two weeks after his move to London, he was
unanimously elected to the General Council of that organization. Marx
served as its secretary for Germany, and Engels initially took over as
secretary for Belgium in place of the absent Auguste Serraillier. In May
1871 he became the regular secretary for Italy. In October he assumed
the secretaryship for Spain, and in 1872 for Portugal and Denmark as
well. Together with Marx, he actively participated in the struggle against
the Bakuninists and in the decision to move the General Council to
New York, which precipitated the slow demise of the International.[23]

Naturally, most of Engels' writings in this period—both those he composed individually and the ones he and Marx collaborated on—had to
do with issues confronting the International.[24] But in 1872–1873 he
published a series of articles on the housing question in the Social Democratic organ *Volksstaat*, which also appeared as three separate pamphlets and later as a single work in a revised edition of 1887. The occasion for the initial articles was the *Volksstaat's* previous publication of
an anonymous series on the subject by an obvious Proudhonist who
later turned out to be Dr. Artur Mülberger from Württemberg.[25]

This is obviously not the place to provide a detailed analysis of the
work, even though it deserves to be better known than it is. But a few
comments are in order both for that reason and because in it Engels
made some important theoretical pronouncements and at the same time
continued on a broader geographical canvas the kind of urban sociology
he had begun in *The Condition of the Working Class in England*. In the
process of attacking the views of Mülberger and the Proudhonists, on
the one hand, and those of an Austrian economist named Dr. Emil Sax,
on the other, Engels pointed out that poor living conditions for the working class were not peculiar to the present; poorly built, overcrowded,
unhealthy dwellings had housed the oppressed classes of all times. The
movement of the population into large cities had made the problem more
acute, but the only solution was to end the exploitation and oppression
of the working class by the ruling class.[26] (This comment, incidentally,
answers the criticism of the earlier book—noted in chapter 1—that he
had overemphasized the well-being of workers before industrialization.)

Contrary to what the Proudhonists thought, industrialization had constituted progress in this endeavor. Despite poverty and political griev-

ances, the hand weaver with his house, garden, and fields was satisfied with his lot. Yet he was nonetheless a slave, Engels said. By creating the propertyless worker, industrialization had also created the condition for ending the exploitation of workers. But the Proudhonists complained that it marked a step backwards for the workers to lose their houses and hearths; for Proudhon, the replacement of handwork by the machine was a hateful development. But in fact it increased productive powers to such an extent that for the first time in human existence it was possible to produce enough for all members of society to have ample consumption with enough left over for a reserve fund.[27]

By contrast with the Proudhonists, Sax would not admit that the housing shortage was a necessary condition in bourgeois society. He complained that workers spent money on tobacco and alcohol that they should have saved to buy a house. He did not recognize that in existing society, if the worker could save from his earnings, the earnings would soon fall by the amount of the savings.[28] (That is, the capitalists would lower wages to a level equivalent to the previous earnings minus the savings.)

Sax had pointed to the results of a Bonapartist commission that, on the occasion of the World Fair, had tried to portray the French Second Empire as a paradise for workers. Yet the statistics of even this corrupt tool of Bonapartism showed that of eighty-nine industrial concerns studied, thirty-one had built no dwellings for their workers. And even the houses that were built consisted almost exclusively of only two rooms for each family. Engels noted that Mülhausen had become *the* example of a modern factory city. There, after fifteen years of paying high rents, a worker came into possession of his house. He had paid forty-four hundred francs for a building that had been worth thirty-three hundred francs fifteen years before. Engels also observed that some of the worst areas in Manchester, described in *The Condition of the Working Class in England*, had since disappeared, but comparable slums had arisen elsewhere in the city, which fact he documented with a lengthy quotation from the *Manchester Weekly Times* of 20 July 1872.[29]

In 1870 and again in 1875 Engels republished *The German Peasant War*, which he had written in 1850 while in London. It had originally appeared in his and Marx's *Neue Rheinische Zeitung*. As he pointed out in the preface to the 1875 edition, the work made no claim to original research on his part. He had borrowed information extensively from Wilhelm Zimmermann's *Allgemeine Geschichte des grossen Bauernkrieges*, published in 1841–1843. What Engels added was an interpretation showing that the religious and political issues of the early sixteenth century mirrored a class struggle among nobles, urban bourgeoisie, craftsmen, and peasants.[30] This interpretation is still accepted today by many historians in both East and West, although naturally with a number of qualifications.[31]

Engels emphasized, of course, the social and economic conditions in sixteenth-century Germany and drew pointed parallels between the middle-class opposition to the patriciate then and the liberal opposition to the existing order in 1848–1849. He also saw the mixed "plebeian" faction in the sixteenth century cities as an embryonic proletarian element. In his view, the church provided a sanction for the existing feudal rule during the Reformation, so all attacks on feudalism were also attacks on the church. He maintained that the heresy of the peasants and plebeians shared some of the views of the middle-class heresy but went much further to demand the restoration of the equality that had prevailed in early Christianity. Incidentally, he pointed out that John Ball and John Wycliffe in England had earlier voiced similar demands, as had the Taborites and Calixtenes in Bohemia. Thus, Thomas Münzer and other plebeian leaders understood the realm of God as a social order in which there would be no class differences, no privileges, and no independent state power above the members of society.

Engels used the declining position of the German nobles vis-à-vis the secular and ecclesiastical princes to explain the actions of Ulrich von Hutten and Franz von Sickingen in trying to free Germany from the rule of Rome and to restore the German Empire to a position of unity, freedom, and power. He discussed the differences between England and Germany to explain why the lower German nobility did not ally with the cities to set up a middle-class, constitutional regime. He noted that the particularism of Germany's small states prevented common action throughout Germany, a problem that recurred in 1848.

Münzer, he pointed out in a memorable passage, was in the worst possible position for a leader of an extreme party: forced to take over a government with the situation not ripe for the rule of the class he represented. He was thereby compelled to represent, not his own class, but the one for which the movement was ready. There was thus a great gap that Münzer seemed to have felt between his theories and existing reality.

Engels concluded the work by pointing not only to parallels with 1848 but to differences. In 1525 and 1848 the princes had won out—in 1848 the two great princes of Austria and Prussia. But 1525 had seen a local German revolution because the English, French, Bohemians, and Hungarians had already been through their peasant wars. The year 1848 in Germany, by contrast, formed part of a great European movement, which suggested, Engels said, that 1848 could not ultimately end as 1525 had.[32]

This brief summary of some of the salient points in *The German Peasant War* can only begin to suggest its character. Without being a piece of original research, it was nevertheless an impressive achievement. Like Marx in *The Eighteenth Brumaire*, Engels displayed a wide-ranging knowledge and the ability to draw telling but qualified analogies with events in other countries and other eras. Obviously, his materialist point of view colored many of his judgments, but the work still makes stimulating reading even for non-Marxists.

In the interest of brevity, analyses of Engels' other major writings must be limited. Suffice it to note that in *Herr Eugen Dühring's Revolution in Science* (*Anti-Dühring*, 1878) he complained of having to follow Dühring into fields like jurisprudence and theoretical natural science where he could at most claim to be a dilettante. Indeed, in theoretical natural science even trained scientists had to depart from their specialties to study neighboring fields where, according to the pathologist Rudolf Virchow, they had only superficial knowledge.[33]

Despite this disclaimer, Engels was able to range with considerable success through the fields of philosophy, astronomy, physics, chemistry, biology, ethics, and politics. To give just one example, it should be somewhat startling for those who accuse Engels of being a rather narrow positivist and determinist to read his criticisms of the notion of eternal truths. He said in this connection that the theory of evolution was very recent. Therefore, undoubtedly, further research would make important modifications to Darwin's ideas on the subject. But, he said, knowledge of human history was even further in arrears than that of biology. When, exceptionally, the internal relationship of society and politics in a given period was known, it was only when the period was about to end. The knowledge was thus only about ephemeral social and political forms. Anyone who sought final, unchanging truths would find little except platitudes and commonplace ideas such as that men cannot live without work, that they have heretofore been divided into rulers and ruled, that Napoleon died on 5 May 1821, and so on.[34]

Regarding the much criticized *Dialectics of Nature*, it is important to observe not only that Engels never finished it or sought to publish it himself, but also that at the end of the often fragmentary notes and comments it consisted of, he wrote in parentheses, "All of this to be extensively revised."[35] In view of this, it is hardly surprising that the unfinished manuscript contains some views that were obsolete when Engels wrote them,[36] that he sometimes shared some of the confusion prevalent in contemporary science,[37] or even that he "did not understand [Michael] Faraday's 'lines of force' and [James Clerk] Maxwell's efforts to give these mathematical expression."[38]

Despite such problems, the manuscript contains much that is original and even striking. In it, Engels—unlike many contemporary scientists —"differentiated between the potential differences across the electrodes and the electromotive force of the cell and wondered about the relationship between them. It is a fine distinction, one not always made in physics classes." If the work had been published shortly after he wrote it, his approach could perhaps have "clarified the confusion and begun resolution of the debate" over these matters in contemporary science.[39]

Equally remarkable, "in a partial, general way, through his method of concept clarification, Engels" predicted "the formal characteristics of the discoveries in electrochemistry by [Svante August] Arrhenius (1887) and [Walther] Nernst (1889)."[40] Implicit in Engels' approach was "a call for research on the relationship between electrical potentials and chemical affinities, an ongoing research problem today." What proved "difficult for the professional scientists to see and accept" when Arrhenius published his papers in 1887—"the independent existence of ions—was 'discovered' five years earlier by the non-scientist, Engels."[41]

Thus, despite some flaws in Engels' research and argumentation,[42] caused perhaps not only by his amateur status but by the incomplete nature of *Dialectics of Nature*, he was able to develop some brilliant insights into significant scientific problems and also to demonstrate considerable understanding of complex scientific matters.[43]

Engels wrote most of *Dialectics of Nature* from 1873 to 1883, interrupting it to write *Anti-Dühring* from 1873 to 1878. Then from March to May 1884 he put together *The Origin of the Family, Private Property and the State*, adding ethnology and anthropology to the list of disciplines in which he had written. He based the theoretical part of the work on the studies of the New York lawyer, anthropologist, and politician Lewis Henry Morgan, who had investigated the Iroquois Indians. As Engels said, Morgan in his own way rediscovered his and Marx's materialist conception of history in America.[44]

Engels used Morgan's book, *Ancient Society, or Researches in the Lines of Human Progress from Savagery, through Barbarism to Civilization* (1877), Marx's notes and additions thereto, and his own separate information on the ancient Greeks, Romans, Celts, Germans, and on economic developments to write his book.[45] As the short length of time it took him to finish it suggests—and as he later admitted to Marx's daughter, Laura Lafargue—he had not bothered to consult all the available works on the subject for the first edition.[46] But the book proved popular. After releasing unrevised new editions in 1886 and 1889 (plus translations into Polish, Rumanian, Italian, Danish, and Serbian),[47] Engels made a fuller study of the relevant ethnological literature for the revised edition of 1892. He even consulted such presumably obscure articles as one by the German ethnographer Heinrich Cunow on old Peruvian villages and frontier cooperatives, which appeared in three successive editions of the weekly *Das Ausland*.[48]

In the revised edition, Engels did not hesitate to point out where more recent research had corrected Morgan on individual points.[49] But he continued in the 1892 edition to follow Morgan in tracing the evolution of the family from a primitive communism in which sexual promiscuity prevailed and the basic social organization was thus necessarily a matriarchal clan, through a patriarchally organized society, to the monogamous stage of civilization. Engels regretted both the end of the golden age of primitive communism and the decline in the status of women that resulted, but he also recognized that these developments were concomitant with progress in productive capabilities. Moreover, both he and Marx appear to have seen in primitive communism evidence that cooperation was possible in future society without the existence of a state apparatus. Engels ended the book with a long quotation from Morgan decrying the power of private wealth but expressing hope for a time when human reason would create a society in which the interests of all would have precedence over individual interests and the freedom, equality, and fraternity of the primitive clan would reappear.[50] Such, of course, was the hope and belief of Marx and Engels as well.

In places, Engels quoted Marx's comments from his notes. But he also cited not only recent ethnological sources like Edvard Westenmarck's *The History of Human Marriage* (1891) and Maxim Kovalevsky's *Tableau des origines de l'évolution de la famille et de la propriété* (1890), but classical and medieval works like Homer's *Iliad*, Thucydides' *History of the Peloponnesian War*, the Venerable Bede's *Ecclesiastical History of the English Nation*, Caesar's *Gallic War*, Tacitus's *Germania*, the Edda, and Salvian's *De gubernatione Dei*.[51] Subsequent anthropologists have naturally discovered some errors in Morgan's work that Engels accepted as accurate description,[52] but *The Origin of the Family* is nonetheless an impressively learned and coherently argued work that shows why Engels' contemporaries were so impressed with his erudition.[53] His errors, moreover, would have come as no surprise to him since he sprinkled his narrative with expressions like "so far as I know" and "as far as we know," indicating his clear recognition that his, like all human knowledge, was both limited and provisional.[54]

In 1886 Engels published the last of his own important writings in two installments of Karl Kautsky's *Neue Zeit*. Entitled "Ludwig Feuerbach and the End of Classical German Philosophy," it appeared as a separate work in revised form in 1888. In it he provided a more comprehensive discussion of his and Marx's relationship to Hegel and Feuerbach than either man had previously attempted. Among other things, he emphasized Hegel's point—which he also accepted, as just seen—that truth was not a collection of finished, dogmatic tenets but something that developed over time without ever arriving at an absolute conclusion. Likewise, history never arrived at an ideal condition but progressed from lower to higher stages in the endless development of human society. He also pointed to Feuerbach's notions that nature was independent of philosophy and constituted the basis upon which human beings, themselves products of nature, had developed; outside of nature and human beings, there was nothing, and the higher beings created by religious fantasy were simply the reflections of humans' own natures.[55]

While Engels recognized the importance of Feuerbach's pronouncements in this regard, he also noted the astonishing poverty of Feuerbach's writings compared with those of Hegel. The latter, he said, was idealistic in method but realistic in the content of his writings, while Feuerbach was the reverse: realistic in method but idealistic in treating humans as abstractions.[56]

As I will discuss below, many scholars have criticized *Ludwig Feuerbach*. Obviously, any attempt to discuss the works of two philosophers—especially when one of them is Hegel—in as short a compass as Engels chose (forty-four pages in the *Werke*) will be controversial. Any careful and open-minded reading of the entirety of this short work, however, should reveal the richness and subtlety of Engels' understanding of both Hegel and Feuerbach, his firm grasp of the fundamental thrust of their ideas.[57]

Of course, before Engels wrote either *The Origin of the Family* or *Ludwig Feuerbach*, Marx had died in 1883. He left behind the unfinished manuscripts of what became volumes 2 and 3 of *Capital* once Engels had laboriously edited them.[58] Engels also had to take over the entire responsibility for counseling the growing European socialist movements—a burden he had previously shared with Marx. Given the enormity of the task, it is amazing that he found time to write at all, let alone edit *Capital*. Yet during the twelve years that separated Marx's death from his own, Engels wrote prefaces for and often oversaw the republication of twelve of Marx's works, eleven of his own, and four written jointly. In addition, he edited translations, wrote numerous articles, and carried on a voluminous correspondence.[59]

Much of the correspondence and many of the articles, of course, concerned the activities of the various socialist movements just mentioned. His work in this regard earned him the sobriquet—bestowed by Julian Harney—"Nestor of Socialism." Harney also marveled at Engels' work habits after he had finished editing volume 3 of *Capital*: "You have done with the Marx work, but there is plenty more to do! What a glutton you are! What about the eight hours? Can we wonder at the number of unemployed when you take in hand the work of half-a-dozen men . . . ?"[60]

In his correspondence and in keeping up with developments affecting the socialist movements all over Europe and in America, Engels enjoyed the benefit of his extraordinary facility with languages. Edward Aveling recalled that every post brought letters and newspapers to his house in all European languages. It was amazing, Aveling said, how he found time to read and organize the important parts of it all in addition to his other work.[61] One emigrant from the Paris Commune of 1871, referring to Engels' pattern of speech when he got excited, said that he stuttered in twenty languages.[62] This might seem a pardonable piece of hyperbole, but in fact it underestimated his achievement. At one time or another in his life, Engels had acquired some knowledge of at least twenty-six languages.

He spoke and wrote English and French with virtually the same ease and correctness as his native German.[63] Before he reached his nineteenth birthday he had already acquired considerable knowledge of Greek and Latin, as already seen, and had at least some acquaintance with Italian, Spanish, and Portuguese besides French and English.[64] He later became considerably more proficient at the three southern European tongues, although he complained at the time of the First International of having to write many letters in Spanish and Italian, two languages he said—with excessive modesty—that he scarcely understood.[65] But Paul Lafargue recalled that people from the National Council of the International in Spain had told him in 1871 that Engels wrote perfect Castillian. The secretary of the National Council in Portugal also told Lafargue that Engels wrote impeccable Portuguese. And Lafargue related an incident at the seaside resort of Ramsgate, where Engels had encountered a bearded dwarf in the uniform of a Brazilian general. Engels spoke to him in Portuguese and Spanish but got no reply. Then the diminutive gentleman said something and Engels exclaimed that he was Irish. When spoken to in his "native dialect," the "poor fellow wept for joy," Lafargue related.[66]

In addition to these languages, Engels also developed considerable proficiency in Danish and Russian, although he frequently offered disclaimers about his knowledge of the latter.[67] And he possessed at least some knowledge of Slovenian, Sanskrit, Arabian, Persian, Hebrew, Polish, Czechoslovakian, Rumanian, Bulgarian, Old Icelandic, Provençal, Catalonian, Dutch, Old Irish, Old Nordic, and Serbian.[68] Clearly, Engels was a polyglot as well as a polymath.

Further instances of his erudition are scattered through his various writings and letters. Though probably not as accomplished a classical scholar as Marx or as knowledgeable about Shakespearian lore, he frequently used a great variety of classical and literary references in his writings. For instance, in an article entitled "The German Central Power and Switzerland" in the *Neue Rheinische Zeitung* (1848), he referred to *Reich* Don Quixotes and quoted the beginning of a Latin phrase from Horace's *Epistles* meaning "whatever folly their kings commit, the Achaeans must pay for it."[69] In another article from the same paper, he played upon a line in *King Lear* by calling the president of the German Bundesrat "every inch a provincial."[70] Still another article from the same period quoted from one of Schiller's ballads.[71]

In an article entitled "Program of the Blanquist Refugees from the Commune," he quoted a line from Heine's *Romanzero*, "Every word is a chamber pot, and not an empty one."[72] Within a few pages in *Socialism: Utopian and Scientific*, he referred to Descartes, Newton, Hegel, and Saint-Simon.[73] In an article on the Book of Revelation—for Engels even ventured into the realm of biblical criticism—he claimed that Renan was a plagiarist of German critics, although he had some good things to say, as well as that Philo was the spiritual father of Christianity and Seneca its uncle, since whole paragraphs of the New Testament came almost verbatim from his works.[74]

In an article about the German Empire in 1890, he invoked the famous story about the prediction of the oracle at Delphi: "If Croesus crosses over the Halys or Wilhelm the Rhine, a great kingdom will be destroyed—but which?"[75] As will be seen below, this was but one instance among many where Engels' predictions—while usually less ambiguous than this one—proved to be right on the mark.

Elsewhere in his writings and letters, he referred to Vergil's *Eclogues* and used Latinisms like "Habeat sibi" with easy familiarity.[76] Similarly, he often resorted to partial quotations from sources like Lucan's *Pharsalia*, ending with an "etc." This assumed that his reader (usually Marx) could readily recall the rest of the passage.[77] In Marx's case, at least, the assumption was undoubtedly valid, but the practice puts most modern readers at a disadvantage and thus further underlines the extensive learning of both men.

Engels wore his learning lightly and unpedantically. In fact, he frequently made fun of it by employing puns. He and Marx were particularly fond of this form of humor, but it is impossible to determine which of the two was ultimately responsible for most of the in-jokes they passed back and forth in their letters. In any event, Engels continued the practice after Marx's death.

For example, in a letter to Laura Lafargue in 1888 he sincerely congratulated her husband, Paul, for the etymological discoveries in an article he had published in the *Nouvelle revue*. Engels said it was "something" for Paul to discover that a number of French words previously said to stem from the Latin for ox (*bos*) really came from the Greek word for the same animal (*boûs*). But to derive *bouillon* from *boûs* instead of *bullire* (to cook or boil) was, he said, a great discovery.

Turning from serious praise to joking in mid-sentence, Engels began to play upon the fact that in many languages the term *ox* also had the connotation of blockhead, as in the English "dumb ox." He said that it was too bad Paul had stopped where he did and not proceeded a little farther with the etymologies from *boûs*. For example, it was obvious that his and Marx's nickname for Napoleon III, *Boustrapa*, also derived from the Greek word for ox, as did Buonaparte (from *Boûnaparte*). (Marx and Engels had had, of course, no use for Napoleon III or his Second Empire. They had derived Boustrapa from the beginning syllables of *Stra*ssburg, where the subsequent French dictator had tried to stage a putsch in 1836, *Bou*logne, where he attempted another in 1840, and *Pa*ris, where he carried out a successful coup d'état in 1851.)

If Napoleon III was etymologically linked to an ox, with all that implied, Gen. Georges *Bou*langer had to be also. (He was then in the process of preparing a coup to overthrow the Third Republic in France but later failed to seize the right moment, went into exile, and ended up committing suicide.) And since *boulanger* meant baker in French, a then infamous Col. Valentine Baker shared the connection. He had molested a young woman in a railroad car, an event that Engels compared to Jupiter's abduction of the beautiful Europa (achieved, of course, by assuming the form of a bull).[78]

Engels did not use his extensive knowledge only for such extended puns, of course. He also made some remarkable predictions besides the ones already mentioned. For example, on 25 July 1866, the day before the preliminary peace of Nikolsburg laid out the main lines of the new organization of Germany, Engels wrote to Marx that Bismarck would be compelled by the new arrangements he was making to rely upon the bourgeoisie (for support of his policies). He would not necessarily have to do this right away, because he had the prestige of the army behind him for the moment. But ultimately he would have to make concessions to the middle classes, a practice his successors would be obliged to follow. Unification of Germany would make a revolution easier, do away with the worst local influences, and make the political parties into really national instead of merely local organizations. The principal disadvantage would be the flooding of Germany by Prussianism. In any event, the North German Confederation had to be accepted without his and Marx's agreeing with it, and it did offer the advantage of a possible national organization and unification of the German proletariat.[79] In broad outline, this is an excellent description of what happened in Germany over the next half century or so.

Even more prescient was Engels' successive harping from 1880 on upon the dangers and potentially disastrous consequences of a European war.[80] Up to the outbreak of hostilities in 1914, both soldiers and statesmen failed to recognize what effects civil war in Europe would have upon their own countries and Europe as a whole.[81] Engels was more far-sighted. On 17 November 1885, for example, he wrote to Bebel that European war was becoming a serious threat because the "wretched rubble" of former nations—Serbs, Bulgars, Greeks, "and other thieving rabble"—for which liberal philistines raved in the interests of Russia, disposed of the balance between peace and war. They fired the first round at Dragoman (the day before, in a war between Serbia and Bulgaria over Eastern Rumelia), he wrote, and who could say when and where the last shot would be fired? Such a war, Engels said, would halt the progress of the worker movement and condemn it for many years to the back burner of European history. Of course, the war could produce a revolution in Paris, but it would call six million soldiers to arms and cost an unheard of sum of money. It would produce bloodshed and devastation and, finally, an exhaustion never seen before.

Too optimistically, Engels predicted that if the war came, it would be the last and would bring with it the downfall of the class state. It would ultimately bring the worker party to power. But he confessed that he wished this could come about without the bloodshed. It was unnecessary. But if war came, he hoped his old injuries would not prevent him from mounting a horse (and participating).[82] On 5 December 1885, he wrote to another supporter of the international workers' movement, Johann Philipp Becker, that the war would massacre one and a half million men and squander a thousand billion francs.[83]

In another but related vein, on 13 September 1886 he wrote again to Bebel that if the Russian army pressured the tsar to overcome his disinclination for the French republic, Bismarck and Wilhelm I would have to oppose this, raising the prospect of a Franco-Russian alliance and a world war. Or they would have to give in to Russian demands in the Balkans and betray Austria. In any event, the opposition of Russia and Austria in the Balkan peninsula was coming to such a head that war was more probable than peace. The war, moreover, would be impossible to localize, and who would win was impossible to say.

But there was one sure outcome: mass butchery on an unheard-of scale, the exhaustion of Europe, and the breakdown of the entire old system. A direct result of all this for the worker movement would only occur through revolution in France, giving France the role of freeing the European proletariat. But Engels did not know if this would be a good thing, as it would strengthen French chauvinism. A revolution in Germany after a defeat would be helpful, so long as it led to peace with France. The most favorable outcome would be a revolution in Russia, but this could only come after a severe drubbing of the Russian army. Certainly, war would suppress the worker movement, totally so in many countries, since it would incite chauvinism and national hatred. The movement would have to begin again after the war, but on a much more favorable basis.[84]

In still another vein, on 7 January 1888 Engels wrote to Friedrich Adolf Sorge that despite the enormous military forces the powers had assembled, the war would be a long one and would bring destruction like that of the Thirty Years' War. American industry would emerge victorious during its course and place before Europeans the alternative of falling back into a purely agricultural existence (producing for their own needs because American industry would supplant that of Europe) or social transformation. He presumed for that reason that statesmen would attempt to restrict fighting to a phony war, but after the first shot, control would cease and the horse would bolt.[85]

Engels also predicted that the neutrality of Belgium and Switzerland would be the first victims of the war. He wrote to Laura Lafargue on 7 May 1889 that if the war became really dangerous, the only chance for them (presumably meaning the worker party) would be if the Russians were defeated and made a revolution. Without revolution, the war would take its course, and then the side that England joined—if it entered the war—would win.[86]

Related to all of this were his predictions about Wilhelm II, grandson of Wilhelm I. On 19 March 1888 he wrote to Paul Lafargue that if Friedrich III—the father of Wilhelm II—died, his son would not be a Wilhelm I and there would follow a change in middle-class opinion. The young man would commit blunders that people would not forgive the way they had those of his grandfather.[87] And on 12 April 1888 he wrote to Bebel that things would become crazy upon the accession to power of Wilhelm II. Germany's Bonapartism had reached its Mexican period (a reference to the armed intervention by Napoleon III in Mexico from 1861 to 1867, which preceded his fall from power in 1870). Following that would come Germany's 1866 and soon 1870 (references to France's foreign policy defeat in the Seven Weeks' War and then her military defeat at Sedan on 1–2 September 1870, which prompted the overthrow of the empire of Napoleon III). Germany's, however, would be an internal Sedan, Engels felt.[88]

Subsequent events, of course, did not bear these predictions out in every detail. But in broad outline and in many details, Engels' forecasts proved astonishingly accurate. The world in the twentieth century might have been a very different, and perhaps better, place if pre–World War I statesmen had read and heeded them. Ironically, indeed, the Russian Revolution might never have occurred, but the irony is only partial. Neither Engels nor Marx, had they lived into the 1920s and 1930s, probably would have supported Lenin's Blanquism before the war or the course the revolution took, especially under Stalin.

Besides such predictions, many of Engels' later writings contain significant historical judgments and exquisite descriptive passages. In his "England in 1845 and 1885," first published in *Commonwealth* in the latter year, he anticipated the thesis of Lenin's later *Imperialism, the Highest Stage of Capitalism*: "The manufacturing monopoly of England is the pivot of the present social system of England, [but] even while the monopoly lasted, the markets could not keep pace with the increasing productivity of English manufacturers. . . . How will it be when continental, and especially American, goods flow in in ever-increasing quantities . . . ? Answer, Free Trade, thou universal panacea."[89] He noted that the English working class had shared in the benefits of this monopoly, though unequally. That was "the reason why, since the dying-out of Owenism there has been no Socialism in England." But "with the breakdown of that monopoly, the English working class" would "lose that privileged position." Then, socialism would again appear in England, as indeed it did.[90]

In his introduction to the 1891 edition of Marx's *The Civil War in France*, he pointed out that America provided the best example of how state power became independent of the society whose instrument it was originally intended to be. Here there existed no dynasty, no nobility, no standing army besides the couple of men (the U.S. Army on the frontier) charged with guarding the Indians, no bureaucracy with permanent appointments and pension rights. Yet two great bands of political speculators (Republicans and Democrats) alternately took possession of state power and exploited it with the most corrupt means and ends imaginable. And the nation was powerless against these two great cartels of politicians, who purportedly served but in reality ruled and plundered it.[91]

In a letter to Minna Kautsky, novelist and mother of Karl Kautsky, Engels left a unique description of London that helps to explain why he chose to live there and also reveals something of his character. He readily believed she had not cared for London, he wrote in 1885. Years ago he had had the same experience.

> One accustoms oneself only with difficulty to the gloomy atmosphere and the mostly melancholy people, to the seclusion, the class divisions in social affairs, to the life in closed rooms that the climate prescribes. One has to tone down somewhat the spirit of life brought over from the continent, to let the barometer of zest for life drop from 30 to 29.5 inches until one gradually begins to feel at home. Then one finds oneself slowly blending in and discovers that it has its good side, that the people generally are more straightforward and trustworthy than elsewhere, that for scholarly work no city is so suitable as London, and that the absence of annoyances from the police compensates for a great deal. I know and love Paris, but given the choice, I would rather live permanently in London than there. Paris is only suitable for enjoyment if a person becomes a Parisian, with all the prejudices of Parisians, with interest primarily only in Parisian things, accustomed to the belief that Paris is the center of the world, is all in all. London is more ugly but also

more noble than Paris, the real center of world trade, and it offers far more diversity. But London also permits a complete neutrality vis-à-vis the whole surrounding area, a trait so necessary for scholarly and even artistic impartiality. One adores Paris and Vienna, one hates Berlin, but with respect to London one retains a neutral indifference and objectivity. And that also is worth something.[92]

A different kind of descriptive power appears in what he wrote Eduard Bernstein on 22 August 1889 about the London dock laborers' strike then in progress:

> The East End previously was sunk in a swamp of penury—the lack of power to resist of those broken down by hunger, of those absolutely without hope, was its signature. Those who landed in this swamp were physically and morally lost. Then last year came the victorious strike of the match girls. And now this giant strike of the most depraved of the depraved, the dock laborers—not the established, strong, skilled, relatively well-paid and regularly employed, but those accidentally driven to the docks, the unlucky, the people who had shipwrecked in all other trades, the starvelings, this mass of broken existences on a collision course with total ruin, about whom one can write on the dock gates Dante's words: "All hope abandon ye who enter here."[93] And this apathetically despondent mass that literally fought battles every morning at the opening of the dock gates to determine who would have precedence with the people who engaged the workers—actual battles in the competition among the surplus of workers—this accidentally thrown-together, daily changing mass achieves discipline among its 40,000 men and causes anxiety to the mighty dock companies. It gives me pleasure to have witnessed that.[94]

Declining Years

During the years when he was penning these predictions and descriptions, Engels' personal life underwent substantial change. After several years of ill health and pain, Lizzie Burns died of a bladder tumor and hemorrhage early in the morning of 12 September 1878. Actually, by the time she died she was properly called Lizzie Engels, because the night before Engels had legally married her—curiously, according to the rites of the Church of England, although she lies buried in a Roman Catholic cemetery as befits her Irish Catholic upbringing. According to Eleanor

Marx, Engels took this step, which ran counter to his own personal beliefs and previous practice, to please her.[95] He had treated her and Mary before her as his wives and had so referred to them without feeling any need for formal wedding vows. But ever kind to those he felt deserving of kindness, he evidently sacrificed his own beliefs to her comfort.

Apparently, he felt no such grief at her passing as was the case with Mary. He wrote to Friedrich Lessner—an old friend from the Communist League and later the First International—at 1:30 A.M. on the 12th, "My poor wife has just been delivered by death from her protracted suffering." That and nothing more, except a brief paragraph about some personal business. Later in the day Engels wrote a similar line to his brother, Rudolf, adding the fact that he had legally married her the night before.[96] Presumably, that information would have been a matter of indifference to Lessner but of some importance to pious relatives in the "Zion of the obscurantists."

Several years later, after Marx's death, Helene Demuth took over the management of Engels' household. It appears that there was never any question of her being either a wife or a mistress, especially as he had for many years accepted an assumption of his parenthood for Helene Demuth's son, Henry Frederick, known as Freddy. Scholars have generally accepted Marx's parentage of Freddy, and Engels clearly resented the false assumption that he was the responsible party—perhaps because he disliked dissimulation or because, as Yvonne Kapp has suggested, his generous nature was offended at Freddy's being brought up away from his mother to the deprivation of both. However that may be, when Freddy's mother died on 4 November 1890, Engels wrote to Friedrich Adolph Sorge: "My good, dear, true Lenchen gently went to sleep yesterday after a short and mostly painless illness. We have spent seven happy years together here in the house. We were the two remaining people from the old guard of before 1848. Now I am the last. If during many years Marx, and in these seven years I, found peace for work, that was primarily her doing. How things will fare with me now, I don't know. I will also sadly miss her wonderfully tactful advice in party matters."[97]

Engels did not long remain in doubt about who would manage his household. He had been quite taken with Louise Kautsky, the attractive wife of Karl, who had married her in 1882. She was an Austrian gentlewoman whose father had been Master of the Horse in the Emperor's Household Cavalry (possibly the reason for Karl's nickname, Baron).[98] When Engels learned in October 1888 that Karl intended to divorce her, he wrote Louise that the news had struck him and "Nimmie" (another nickname for Helene Demuth) "like a bolt of lightning out of a clear sky." Since he had known her, Engels said, he had esteemed her steadily higher and higher and found her increasingly charming. He and Nim regarded it as inconceivable, impossible that Karl wanted to divorce her. Karl would awaken one morning as out of a deep dream and find that he had committed the greatest piece of folly in his life.[99] Engels repeated this admonition to Karl, but he proceeded with the divorce anyway.[100]

Five days after Helene Demuth's death, Engels wrote to Louise of his loneliness and asked her to come manage his household, though, since she was a lady, he would not expect her to perform any "manual services." She would merely oversee the housework, done by maids, and have the remaining time free for whatever she wanted to do. He said that she should discuss the whole matter with her friend, the Viennese doctor and socialist leader Victor Adler. If she found the inconveniences of such an arrangement greater than the benefits, she should let him know without circumlocution. He was too fond of her to want her to make a sacrifice for him. In three weeks he would be seventy and had only a short time to live. No young, hopeful life should be sacrificed to the couple of years he had left, he insisted.[101]

Louise acceded to his request and brought some sunshine into his life, as he wrote to Sorge.[102] He explained to Adler, who had evidently expressed concern that she would have to work too hard, that she would do no housework if only because then the maids would not consider her a true lady. But she was serving as his secretary. He dictated to her or gave her things to copy so as to spare his eyes. (He suffered from chronic conjunctivitis and increasing myopia, so he could not write for more than two hours a day, and then only during daylight.) But he also worked with her on chemistry and French. She wanted to learn Latin as well, and he could help with that, too. After dinner, they napped. Then from 11 P.M. to midnight they played cards. That rested his eyes from reading, and with an empty cranium he slept better.[103]

Engels remained active. At this time, Eleanor Marx commented that he bore "his three score and ten years with great ease" and was "really the youngest man I know."[104] In January 1892 he stated to his brother, Hermann, that the previous summer he had spent four weeks on the Isle of Wight and then two in Scotland and Ireland, most of the time on the water. He had to restrict his smoking (of cigars) severely because it, good wine, and unfortunately also pilsner beer brought his "heart nerves somewhat into disorder" and disturbed his sleep. If he could ride horseback in the winter and sail the seas in the summer, that would bring him around.

(He had always had great faith in the restorative powers of fresh air and exercise.) But he could no longer ride, so he had to make do with climbing what he called the London Chimborasso—Hampstead Heath. Fortunately, that kept the bodily fluids flowing.[105]

On 8 August 1892 he wrote Hermann again about his health. He was suffering from a pain in the groin originally caused by a fall from a horse while fox hunting many years before. He had had no problems with it for five years, but now it had suddenly afflicted him again. Wrapping the affected area did not help. A walk of two miles a couple of days before had made him almost incapable of proceeding further. He knew what he had to do to cure it: rest completely for four weeks and abstain from beer and wine.[106]

The old injury had kept Engels from a trip to Switzerland, south Germany, and Vienna, but by 22 August he was getting better and had been moving about in his garden enjoying the fresh air. It was not until 22 October that he was able to walk up Primrose Hill, however.[107] There were reports that he was seriously ill in January 1893, but he wrote to his brother that they were false. He was healthier than in a long time, could walk an English mile, and had been able at Christmas to do too much rather than too little.[108] (Whether he meant too much activity or too much drinking is not clear from the letter.)

Meanwhile, Louise had continued to oversee Engels' household and look after his health. She kept on doing so even after her marriage to the Viennese medical doctor Ludwig Freyberger, all three of them living in his house at Regent's Park Road. When Louise had a baby, however, they all moved to a larger house closer to the park on the same street, completing the move in early October 1894.[109]

By May 1895, Engels was complaining of "rheumatic pains in the scalp" and associated sleeplessness. As a result, he was momentarily unable to work but hoped to be better in a week. Only five days later, however, he wrote to Laura Lafargue about a swelling in the right side of his throat. He hoped to have it removed surgically, but he admitted that old people like him were such slow "nags" that it was impossible to set a precise time for the operation. The problem, although he did not know it yet, was cancer of the throat.[110]

In mid-June he went to Eastbourne on the English Channel. He wrote Eduard Bernstein that the disease followed the rules of the dialectic, both positive and negative sides of it intensifying. He was stronger, had a better appetite, and ate more. But the tumor was growing, he had more pain and more trouble sleeping. As a result, his pathological stupidity also increased, as did his inability to work. Louise and her family had joined him for the weekend, but Ludwig had had to return to work in London. The next Saturday or Sunday Eleanor Marx and her lover, Edward Aveling, were coming.[111]

By 29 June, Laura Lafargue had also joined him. They, Edward Aveling, and Eleanor sent Paul a picture postcard of Eastbourne with a note saying that if the mountain (Paul) would not come to Mohammed (Eastbourne), Mohammed would come to the mountain.[112] Laura remained with him and on 2 July responded for him to an inquiry from Chicago that he was sick and at the moment not literarily active. Thus he could not authorize third parties to publish her father's manuscripts.[113]

On 21 July Dr. Freyberger reported that at Engels' age, quite apart from the tumor, he could die suddenly from heart failure or pneumonia. Otherwise, he might live for a few weeks. Engels was nevertheless hopeful and convinced he would recover. He planned to return to London on the 24th.[114] He did so and died there on 5 August, the immediate cause being, as Freyberger had anticipated and now diagnosed, bronchopneumonia. According to his wishes, he was cremated and had a private funeral. Those invited were sworn to secrecy to ensure its privacy. *Justice*, the newspaper of the English Social Democratic Federation to which Engels and the Avelings had been opposed but which Eleanor later rejoined, reported that "there was an entire absence of ceremony" at the funeral. Paul Lafargue, whom Engels had supported financially and counseled (sometimes with more frankness than Lafargue probably thought desirable or necessary), said about his departed benefactor: "Farewell dear friend. I shall never again know so lovable, so good and so indulgent a friend."[115]

Seventeen days after the funeral, on 27 August, Eleanor, Edward Aveling, Friedrich Lessner, and Eduard Bernstein went to Eastbourne, which had been Engels' favorite seaside resort, hired a rowboat, and deposited his ashes in the briny deep off of Beachy Head.[116]

Engels left £1,000 to the German Social Democratic party for electoral expenses. Ellen Rosher, the niece of the Burns sisters, whom Engels had helped to raise, received £2,230. The remaining (roughly) £24,000 of his estate he divided into eight equal parts, three of which (totaling about £9,000) went to each of Marx's surviving daughters, Laura and Eleanor, while two parts (some £6,000) went to Louise Freyberger, who also received £250 as one of the executors of the estate. Engels asked Eleanor and Laura to hold one-third of their legacies in trust for their sister Jenny's children. Louise also inherited his furniture, so she actually received a larger bequest than either Laura or Eleanor by herself, after deduction of the money for the Longuet children.[117]

Although Engels possessed rare descriptive powers as a writer and his *The Condition of the Working Class in England* deservedly ranks as a minor classic, he was hardly one of the foremost literary figures of an age that included Dickens, Thackeray, Tolstoy, Turgenev, Dostoyevski, and Gogol, among others. As a scholar and thinker, he made no really original contributions, although the synergism of his collaboration with Marx contributed significantly to the latter's discoveries. As a military critic, he was perhaps in the first rank, although purely as an amateur. But his real claim to distinction lay in the wide range of his knowledge, which he achieved without falling into the pit of dilettantism. Marx may have been right when he dubbed Engels the most learned man in Europe. For who among his contemporaries equaled his knowledge of such a diversity of disciplines as science, philosophy, anthropology, languages and linguistics, economics, history, current events, business matters, and military affairs?

Who among them could claim to have made as many accurate predictions as he did? Who had written about periods as diverse as the birth of civilization and the contemporary world, regions as far-flung as Asia and the United States of America, not to mention his own Europe from the Atlantic to the Urals? Engels was not always right. But he was a serious thinker. Like Marx, he had his biases, but neither man was an ideologue. It is simply inconceivable that so learned, wise, and flexible an intellect as Engels' could have foisted on the world the kind of narrow-minded positivism and determinism many scholars insist that he exhibited. The views of these scholars, the subject of the next chapter, contrast markedly with the facts of his life and ideas.

CHAPTER III

Engels in the Dichotomist Portrait

For more than eighty years after Karl Marx's death in 1883, the dominant view of his intellectual relationship with Friedrich Engels was one of partnership in a common venture. A representative example of this common view comes from the still respected biography of Marx by Boris Nicolaievsky and Otto Maenchen-Helfen: "From October 1844 until he closed his eyes for the last time, in victory and defeat, in the storm of revolution and the misery of exile, always struggling and always fighting, he trod by Engels's side and Engels trod by his, along the same path towards the same goal."[1]

Contemporary observers supported this perception of Marx and Engels' relationship. Paul Lafargue, who had often seen the two men together, called Engels Marx's alter ego. Wilhelm Liebknecht, their old, if sometimes exasperating, friend, used the same phrase to describe Engels' position vis-à-vis Marx. And Eleanor Marx, a zealous guardian of her father's reputation, stated that Marx and Engels' life and work were "so closely associated that they cannot be separated."[2]

Despite this testimony, over the course of the last twenty years or so it has become increasingly fashionable to reject this older view and to emphasize instead significant disparities in the views of the two friends—a view described in the title of this chapter and below as "dichotomist." This recent emphasis is not altogether new. Early in the century, some scholars had noted differences in the two men's thinking. Two of the most celebrated and earliest to perceive such differences were George Lukács and Karl Korsch. In his influential work *History and Class Consciousness: Studies in Marxist Dialectics*, written in 1922, Lukács —among other things—criticized Engels' account of dialectics in *Anti-Dühring* as following Hegel's mistaken precedent and extending the method to apply to nature as well as society. In doing this, Lukács said, Engels failed to recognize that "the critical determinants of dialectics —the interaction of subject and object, the unity of theory and practice, the historical changes in the reality of the categories as the basis of changes in thought, etc.—are not present in our knowledge of nature."[3]

Since these "critical determinants" were central to Lukács's own interpretation of Marx, he was by implication suggesting a dichotomy in the thought of Marx and Engels. Nevertheless—and this is a point that some other proponents of such a dichotomy have failed to notice—Lukács referred at several points in his work to Marx and Engels together as if they agreed with one another for the most part and formed a kind of team. Further, he quoted Engels approvingly in a number of places. Thus, his goal would appear to have been not to drive a wedge between the two men's ideas in general but merely to suggest a delimited area of disagreement.[4]

Of course, it is not impossible that Lukács inserted the references to Marx and Engels together as a sort of pious obeisance to communist orthodoxy. He was, after all, later condemned for his unorthodox views, following which he engaged in the prescribed self-criticism and remained a member of the party, something Korsch refused to do in similar circumstances. In a work entitled *Marxism and Philosophy*, published in 1923, the latter took the position—at variance with many later interpretations of Marx's thought—that "the dialectical materialism of Marx and Engels is by its very nature a philosophy through and through." Despite this coupling of the two men here and elsewhere in the work, Korsch did notice some differences in their thought.[5]

More significant, though, was Korsch's rejection of the view that Marx and Engels fundamentally disagreed. He noted that (even in 1923) it was "widely believed that the later Engels degenerated into a thoroughly naturalistic-materialist view of the world by contrast to Marx, his more philosophically literate companion." But, he said, it was "precisely in one of his last writings that Engels, in the same breath as he describes thought and consciousness as products of the human brain and man himself as a product of nature, also unambiguously protests against the wholly 'naturalistic' outlook which accepts consciousness and thought 'as something given, something straightforwardly opposed to Being and Nature.'" Later, in a work published in 1930, four years after his expulsion from the Communist party, Korsch wrote that in *Marxism and Philosophy* he had refrained from what he regarded (inaccurately, it might be added) as Lukács's one-sided view of Marx and Engels as being completely at variance with each other, just as he had refrained from the dogmatic, orthodox position that their ideas were entirely consistent.[6]

In 1936, Sidney Hook in essence repeated Lukács's criticism of Engels.

In *From Hegel to Marx* he stated that Karl Marx had never spoken of a dialectic of nature, "although he was quite aware that gradual quantitative changes in the fundamental units of physics and chemistry result in qualitative changes." Engels, however, "openly extends the dialectic to natural phenomena" in *Anti-Dühring* and the manuscript Hook curiously referred to as *Dialektic und Natur* (Dialectics and nature), although its actual title was *Dialektic der Natur* (Dialectics of nature). This, in Hook's view, betrayed a misunderstanding of the dialectic and showed that Engels had "swallowed more of Hegel than, as a naturalist, he could properly digest."[7]

Despite these early criticisms of Engels as having diverged from Marx's thought patterns, the mainstream of scholarly opinion remained in line with the views of Lafargue and Eleanor Marx. That all began to change only in 1961 with the publication of George Lichtheim's influential and impressive *Marxism: A Historical and Critical Study*. Lichtheim pointed to a whole range of differences between Marx and Engels, beginning with the views expressed in Engels' draft of the *Communist Manifesto* —called "Grundsätze des Kommunismus" (Principles of communism) —as opposed to those in Marx's finished version of the work. Lichtheim said that Engels' draft, together with his earlier writings, displayed an idea of history and a doctrine of revolution significantly different from Marx's. The tenor of Engels' argument was, in Lichtheim's view, more technocratic than that in the *Communist Manifesto*, which retained only echoes of Engels' "technological enthusiasm." Whereas Marx stressed the catastrophic nature of productive forces, Engels pointed to their liberating and progressive character. Engels' emphasis later became a key element in Leninism, according to Lichtheim.[8]

At the same time, Engels' stress on the inevitability of the sociopolitical transformation into communism—a development that would result from the industrial revolution's technological changes—became an element in the ideology of the German Social Democratic party. Oddly, then, Engels was in Lichtheim's view the "father both of Social Democratic orthodoxy and of the Leninist faith in industrialization"—despite the very real differences between those two creeds.[9]

As portrayed by Lichtheim, Engels was also a rather simple-minded determinist and positivist, in contrast to Marx, who developed a "complex dialectic of existence and essence, reality and 'alienation'" in his writings of 1843–1848. Additionally, Engels placed the accent in his writings about the future communist society upon satisfying human needs. Marx, on the other hand, stressed the transformation of human and social nature.[10]

Lichtheim admitted that there was an element of determinism in Marx's as well as Engels' thought, but in Marx this was allegedly counterbalanced by a vision of theory and practice interacting to transform the human condition. (As we have already seen, this vision was hardly absent from Engels' ideas.) Engels, the Social Democrat Karl Kautsky, and others allegedly transformed this vision, however, "into the doctrine of a causally determined process analogous to the scheme of Darwinian evolution." In Lichtheim's view, Engels began this transformation in *Anti-Dühring*, which Lichtheim accepted as having been prepared with some help from Marx. Engels' "later writings, especially *Socialism: Utopian and Scientific*"—a brochure consisting of a few revised chapters from *Anti-Dühring*—were, Lichtheim claimed, "a veritable compendium of the new positivist world-view." Even Marx had moved in that direction; he "gradually came to adopt a standpoint" that "in some respects resembled the scientism of the age, but he never quite yielded to the temptation to recast his doctrine altogether in evolutionary-materialist terms; Engels had no such inhibition."[11]

Thus, Engels' writings—not those of Marx—became the source of the doctrine known as 'dialectical materialism,' and "as a coherent system 'Marxism' came into being during the dozen years" between the deaths of Marx and Engels (1883–1895). Engels' ideas—especially those in the uncompleted and posthumously published *Dialectics of Nature* —"became the cornerstone of the Soviet Marxist edifice." In this connection, Lichtheim emphasized the "line of descent" running from Engels via Kautsky and the Russian Marxist Georgii V. Plekhanov to Lenin and Nikolai I. Bukharin. Despite their differences, these men all shared a "common faith in 'dialectical materialism' as a universal 'science'" comprehending the laws of both nature and history "as supposedly adumbrated in a confused fashion by Hegel and finally given adequate expression by Engels." (As a qualification upon the "supposedly" in the last quotation, Lichtheim admitted the ageing Hegel's attempt to "comprehend nature and history in a unified system.")[12]

The problem with Engels' position in this regard was that "if nature is conceived in naturalistic terms it does not lend itself to the dialectical method, and if the dialectic is read back into nature, materialism goes by the board." Sensing this, "Marx wisely left nature (other than human nature) alone," but "Engels ventured where Marx had feared to tread." Even so, Lichtheim admitted, Engels "cannot be held responsible for the subsequent transformation of his speculative essays into a state religion imposed upon captive audiences by doctrinaire schoolmasters scarcely more literate than their pupils"—a reference, of course, to Soviet Marxism under Stalin.[13]

Lichtheim went on to develop differences between Marx and Engels on the subject of nature. He quoted Engels at length from *Ludwig Feuerbach and the End of Classical German Philosophy*. There Engels had discussed the differences between nature and human history with regard to the operation of historical and natural laws. Nature featured "only blind, unconscious agencies acting upon one another, out of whose interplay the general law comes into operation." History, by contrast, involved conscious men "working toward definite goals." Despite this difference, history, too, was governed by "inner general laws." What men willed rarely happened. In most cases, their desired ends conflicted, producing "a state of affairs entirely analogous to that prevailing in the realm of unconscious nature." Lichtheim called this "an amalgam of Hegelian and Darwinian concepts." To it he contrasted the young Marx as envisaging "a unique historical occurrence" that enabled "mankind to comprehend history as its own creative act."[14]

According to Lichtheim, for Marx there was no nature apart from man. He quoted the young Marx: "Nature, as it unfolds in human history, in the genesis of human society, is man's *real* nature; hence nature, as it develops through industry, albeit in alienated form, is true *anthropological* nature." Thus, Lichtheim summarized, "for the early Marx—and in a measure for the mature Marx too—nature and man are complex realities whose interaction is studied in society." This was "precisely the reverse of Engels's habit of deducing historical 'laws' from the operation of a nature conceived as an independent reality external to man."[15]

Lichtheim in effect charged Engels, a man whose "very considerable erudition" and "command of philosophical metaphor" he admitted, with failure to understand the dialectical method. "When the dialectic is properly understood," he wrote, "it is seen to presuppose situations in which conscious activity realizes a possibility grounded in the nature of things—in other words, historical situations. In such cases, human action may be said to synthesize the antithetical elements by 'negating' a definite obstacle to a chosen goal. To extend this possibility to the realm of inanimate matter"—as Lichtheim said Engels did—was "to read an element of purposive striving into the structure of reality: in other words, to revert to romanticism." The only alternative to such romanticism was stretching the idea of dialectical change "to the point of tautology."[16]

Lichtheim held that Engels chose to interpret the various scientific discoveries of the age "in quasi-philosophical terms." The result was "the construction of a materialist world-view which conserved *both* the positivist outlook of the late nineteenth century *and* the language of romantic 'natural philosophy.'" For example, Engels asserted that it was the nature of matter to bring about human beings and, hence, thought—"an ingenious manner of bringing Hegel and [the Darwinian materialist Ernst] Haeckel into some sort of balance." Engels employed the principles of the transformation of quality into quantity, the identity of opposites, and the negation of the negation. "His application of these Hegelian categories preserves an outward resemblance to Hegel's procedures," Lichtheim wrote, "but necessarily lacks the consistency which permits Hegel to dispense with the customary distinction between logical and physical concepts." That is, unlike Hegel, Engels did not assume the identity of logical constructs and physical reality. Instead, he illustrated the Hegelian categories by confronting them with scientific discoveries. This resulted in "a useless duplication of the conceptual apparatus employed by science" in *Anti-Dühring* and, more extremely, in *Dialectics of Nature*. The latter went on to become "the principal source of . . . the world-view of Marxism-Leninism."[17]

In *Anti-Dühring* and "the studies published by Engels after the death of Marx"—presumably *Ludwig Feuerbach* in particular, since Engels never published or even completed *Dialectics of Nature*—"the logic of history appears as a special case of a more general logic embracing the entire universe." Engels also equated Marx's mode of reasoning with that of the empirical sciences. This constituted a "radical inversion of the Marxian approach," according to Lichtheim. In the *Grundrisse* (1857–1858) and *A Contribution to the Critique of Political Economy* (1859), Marx had not made historical materialism "depend on a general theory of evolution, let alone a universal logic of enquiry."[18]

Lichtheim also pointed to what he said was Engels' "singularly unsuccessful attempt to come to grips with the Kantian theory of knowledge, which is dismissed in a very cavalier fashion on the grounds that its assumptions have been invalidated by positive science." Actually, this was not quite Engels' contention, as a glance at Lichtheim's own footnote to this assertion reveals. There, Lichtheim quoted Engels from *Ludwig Feuerbach*: "If we are able to prove the correctness of our conception of a natural process by making it ourselves, bringing it into being out of its conditions and making it serve our own purposes into the bargain, then there is an end to the Kantian ungraspable 'thing in itself.'"

Lichtheim called this a "naive display of positivism" and "a line of reasoning quite irrelevant to the subject," but he said Engels' "excursion into epistemology" was significant because "it set the tone for the idealist-materialist controversy" around 1900 in Germany and later in Russia. Engels' "muddled presentation" of the whole epistemological issue was "yet another aspect of that materialist-monist outlook which is Engels's peculiar contribution to Marxism."[19]

Following the publication of Lichtheim's study, the emphasis on the differences rather than the similarities in Marx's and Engels' views quickly shifted from a minority to a majority view among scholars. In the same year Lichtheim's book came out (1961), Robert Tucker published his *Philosophy and Myth in Karl Marx*. There he stated: "The concept of a 'dialectical materialism' dealing with nature apart from human history takes its rise from some of the later writings of Engels," although he admitted that Plekhanov had introduced the phrase itself.[20]

Engels' "doctrine of dialectics in nature," as set forth in *Anti-Dühring* and *Dialectics of Nature*, "was a *mélange* of Hegel at his worst and the materialism of such nineteenth-century writers as Haeckel." Here, Tucker was at one with Lichtheim, but he also noted Engels' continuing emphasis on the Marxian theme of human activity changing nature. At the same time, he pointed out a new area of difference between Marx and Engels. In the article "On Authority" that Engels wrote in 1872 to combat Michael Bakunin and his followers in the First International, he had stated: "The automatic machinery of a big factory is much more despotic than the small capitalists who employ workers have ever been. . . . Wanting to abolish authority in large-scale industry is tantamount to wanting to abolish industry itself." In quoting this passage, Tucker noted: "There is clearly some inconsistency between this position and Marx's." What Tucker meant by this rather vague assertion is evident from a comment in one of his later works: "A nonauthoritarian existence in the factory was integral to communism in Marx's understanding of it, and this was a central message of his political philosophy."[21]

In 1962 the German scholar Alfred Schmidt provided a somewhat different perspective on the question of the differences between Marx's and Engels' ideas. He did this in a study of the concept of nature in Marx's theory. There he said, for instance, that in Engels' writings on nature the younger man—unlike Marx—fell back into a dogmatic metaphysics by dialecticizing natural science. But, Schmidt added (in partial contradiction of Lichtheim's general emphasis, if not of anything he said specifically), Engels was not a reductionist since he made no effort to recommend the dialectics to the natural scientists as a direct method of research. On the other hand, Schmidt agreed with Lichtheim that in the late Engels man seemed only a product of evolution—a passive reflection of the process of nature, not a productive force. This constituted a fall from Marx's position into a naive realism.[22]

At one point, Schmidt claimed that for Marx nature and history were indissolvably interwoven. For Engels, they were two different realms. Here, Schmidt basically agreed with Lichtheim. But elsewhere in his treatment—in seeming contradiction to his own view—Schmidt criticized the idea that for Marx nature had no meaning without man. He also noted Marx's comment to the Hannoverian physician Ludwig Kugelmann: "Natural laws generally cannot be repealed [aufgehoben]. What can change in historically different circumstances is only the form in which these laws are carried out." Schmidt compared this with Engels' not dissimilar statement in Anti-Dühring that freedom lies not in dreamed-of independence from natural laws but in the knowledge of those laws and the resultant possibility of letting them work according to plan for given ends. Schmidt also quoted Engels favorably from Dialectics of Nature: "But precisely man's transformation of nature, not just nature itself, is the fundamental and immediate basis of human thinking," a point very close to Marx's views on the subject as portrayed by both Schmidt and Lichtheim.[23] Thus, it would appear from Schmidt's own evidence that man was not for Engels simply a product of evolution but an active transformer of nature and that Engels' views of nature were not notably different from Marx's.

Schmidt further supported this point (unintentionally?) by noting Engels' definition of socialism in "Outlines of a Critique of Political Economy" (1844) as "reconciliation of mankind with nature and with itself" and by quoting from Marx's Economic and Philosophic Manuscripts of the same year to similar effect. On the other hand, Schmidt also noticed a difference in the way Marx and Engels described the transition to socialist society. For Engels, socialization of the means of production would allow men to become, for the first time, real rulers of nature. This would constitute the leap of mankind from the realm of necessity into the realm of freedom. For Marx, too, freedom would result from socialized mankind's bringing the economy under common control instead of being ruled by it. But Marx was more skeptical and dialectical than Engels. There remained for him a realm of necessity upon which the realm of freedom rested.[24] On balance, then, although Schmidt certainly emphasized a number of divergences between Marx's and Engels' thought, some of them in contradiction of his own statements, he also noted several points of agreement.

These three scholars foreshadowed most of the basic themes and characteristics that subsequent dichotomists have emphasized or exhibited to this day. First of all, they contradicted one another and sometimes even themselves. Second, they stressed to one degree or another the technologism, determinism, and positivism in the writings of Engels, the supposed founder of dialectical materialism. This they contrasted with the humanism of Marx, although both Tucker and Schmidt also pointed to humanistic elements in Engels' thought. Third, although this was a more minor theme, they noted the allegedly muddled epistemology of Engels.

Perhaps the strongest subsequent emphasis on technologism in Engels' writings came from the pen of Shlomo Avineri. In *The Social and Political Thought of Karl Marx*, he repeated Lichtheim's charge that "Grundsätze des Kommunismus" was more "technologically oriented" than Marx's final version of the *Communist Manifesto*, where technology was a mere "side issue." Avineri said Engels influenced Marxism in both a mechanistic and deterministic direction. "Both the cruelty and harshness of Bolshevism and the intellectual wastelands of Social Democracy" grew "directly from this mechanistic twist Engels gave to Marxism, emasculating its specific intellectual achievement."[25]

Somewhat similarly, Norman Levine accused Engels of converting Marx's "naturalistic humanism" and "negative *praxis*" into "mechanistic materialism, social positivism, instrumental rationality and the morality of the Puritan work ethic . . . in the dress of socialist productivity."[26] In Levine's account and those of other dichotomists, the supposedly mechanistic element in Engels' writings was less important than the alleged positivism, however.

Z. A. Jordan was typical of the school in charging Engels with believing that a single set of laws governed the physical universe and the human world, a view that he said Marx did not share.[27] In much the same vein, Avineri claimed that where Marx sought the human meaning of the natural sciences, Engels looked for a scientific methodology to apply to the human world.[28] And Terrell Carver accused Engels of espousing a materialism that was "close in many respects to being a simple reversal of philosophical idealism *and* a faithful reflection of the natural sciences as portrayed by positivists."[29]

By contrast, Carver tried to dissociate Marx from any taint of positivism. He had to admit that in *Capital* Marx had written "that the molecular theory in chemistry" illustrated "Hegel's analysis of the transformation of quantity into quality." But he insisted that Marx never claimed there were "dialectical laws of *matter* in motion forcing their way through these transformations." He was "endorsing neither a metaphysics of Hegelian laws nor the 'scientific' *Weltanschauung* of Engels."[30]

The most blatant example of the attempt by the dichotomists to tar Engels with the brush of positivism while wiping any residue of the gooey stuff off of their portrait of Marx comes from a later book by Norman Levine than the one cited above. Unlike Carver (see below), Levine was not uncomfortable associating Marx with Hegel. Thus, he said that Marx's *Grundrisse* was Hegelian in tone and language, whereas he had to admit that *Capital* used the language of natural science.

But he attributed this to the growth of the natural sciences in the interim between the two works, not to any positivistic leanings on Marx's part. Hence, when Marx "repeatedly spoke of 'laws,'" this was "because he made a linguistic adjustment to a mode of rhetoric which was fashionable in an age of accelerating scientific advances." Levine then quoted several undeniably positivistic and deterministic passages from volume 1 of *Capital* and proceeded to deny that they were positivistic. He quoted Marx as speaking, for example, of "the social antagonisms that result from the natural laws of capitalist production. It is a question of these laws themselves, of these tendencies working with iron necessity toward inevitable results." Marx also said, "The laws that regulate the division of labor in the community act with the irresistable authority of a law of value," and, "Capitalist production begets, with the inexorability of a law of nature, its own negation."[31]

According to Levine, a "careful reading" of these quotations shows "that Marx did not 'impute,' did not state that laws existed 'in' society in the same way laws existed 'in' nature." Had he done so, he would have been a positivist "in the manner of Engels." Instead, "Marx used the word law as an 'analogy.'" For him, "the structural regularities of social totality operated 'like' a law of nature." In each of the quoted passages, Levine stated, "Marx used the preposition 'with,' not the verb 'is.'"[32] Such linguistic quibbles hardly dispel the positivistic implications of Marx's statements. More importantly, though, this is but one of many examples that could be provided of Levine in particular and the dichotomists in general applying a double standard to the writings of Marx and Engels. They never suggest such arguments where Engels used similar language.

Another example of Levine's application of this double standard occurred in his discussion of the changes Engels introduced into volume 2 of *Capital*—undoubtedly the most important contribution of his most recent book despite the flaws in its argument. There he wrote that "Engels's conception of the manuscripts Marx left were [*sic*] positivist from the beginning." He cited as his proof Engels' claim in a letter that book 2 was "purely scientific."[33] This ignores the fact that Marx, too, frequently referred to his work as scientific. He did so twice, for instance, in a letter of 27 June 1867 that Levine cited in another connection.[34] Yet Levine dismissed Marx's words as merely a "linguistic adjustment" to a fashionable mode of rhetoric, while he castigated Engels' similar phraseology as positivist.

While Levine made other unfair charges against Engels,[35] he did succeed in showing that Engels had made some changes to Marx's manuscripts for what became volumes 2 and 3 of *Capital* that he failed to annotate in footnotes. Although Levine saw these unacknowledged changes as distortions that made the volumes more deterministic and positivistic than the Marxian manuscripts from which Engels worked,[36] in fact they hardly seem that significant. This appears particularly to be the case when one considers the difficulties Engels labored under to convert Marx's unfinished manuscripts into publishable prose—difficulties that Levine completely ignored in his commentary.[37]

But interestingly enough, some unacknowledged changes that Jerrold Seigel found in volume 3 of *Capital* altered Marx's original argument in an antipositivist direction. Seigel discovered that Engels had reordered some sections of chapters 13 and 14 in such a way as to give the factors working against the law of falling profits a more independent place than they enjoyed in Marx's manuscripts. This weakened what Marx had conceived as an economic law affecting capitalist society. Seigel therefore found that the changes Engels introduced in volume 3—including his unacknowledged writing of a chapter that Marx had left unwritten—far from making the work more positivist, actually operated in the opposite direction. It was Marx who proposed the law of falling profits. Engels, by his editorial changes, emphasized the contradictions in that law, contradictions that Marx had recognized but tended to downplay.[38]

In apparent ignorance of Seigel's important book, Levine used Engels' very changes—which he did not recognize as such—to argue against *Marx's* positivism. Levine had admitted that although in chapter 13 Marx had dealt with the law of the tendency for the rate of profit to fall, "this chapter was immediately followed" by chapter 14 discussing "counteracting influences." Then, Levine said, in chapter 15 "Marx went on to catalogue those inherent contradictions which destroyed any pretense that there was a 'law' for the rate of profit to decline."[39]

But it was precisely from chapter 13, as Seigel showed, that Engels had extracted the material for chapter 14 from the middle of Marx's exposition of the law itself. Thus, it was Engels, not Marx as Levine assumed, who made Marx's confidence in the operation of the law seem less strong than it had appeared in the original manuscript. Seigel also pointed out that the title for chapter 15, "Development of the Internal Contradictions of the Law," was Engels'. Marx, he said, never spoke of contradictions in the law, only contradictions in capitalist society.[40] Therefore, ironically, it was *Engels'* changes that provided the basis for Levine's argument that *Marx* did not, like Engels, believe in laws for society. In contradiction to the whole thrust of Levine's book, Marx appeared more positivistic in at least some of his original manuscripts than he did in the version that emerged from Engels' editing.

Other dichotomists besides Lichtheim and Levine saw Engels as being, unlike Marx, not only positivistic but deterministic. Frederick L. Bender, for example, asserted that Engels assimilated dialectical materialism into the natural sciences and believed it demonstrated "the formal laws of a deterministic universe."[41]

Not a few dichotomists repeated Lichtheim's charge that it was Engels, not Marx, who had founded dialectical materialism. Jordan was among those who echoed the assertion, adding that Lenin and Plekhanov, rather than Engels, had coined the term. Jordan claimed that after Marx's break with Hegel, he was uninterested in academic metaphysics or the theory of knowledge, but Engels presented him as a supporter of dialectical materialism.[42]

Avineri chimed in with the rest of the chorus: "Much of what is known as 'Marxist materialism' was written not by Marx but by Engels, in most cases after Marx's own death." Marx, he said, never used terms like 'historical materialism' or 'dialectical materialism' to describe his "systematic approach."[43] And so it went, with numerous other such assertions in the scholarly literature.[44]

The obverse side of all of this was the emphasis on the part of many scholars upon the humanism or naturalism in Marx's writings.[45] Here Jordan was typical. He characterized Marx as a naturalist who left "the priority of external nature unassailed" but "abolished the distinction between man and nature" by emphasizing man's creation of the world as it had come to be.[46]

Similarly, Levine saw man in Marx's view as a being who "modified the natural world," thereby humanizing it for human purposes. Unlike Engels, the "metaphysical materialist" who held that "the elemental forces in the universe . . . were matter and motion," Marx saw communism as an end to human alienation and dehumanization, the beginning of freedom, a condition allowing man to "live harmoniously and in accordance with his naturalistic essence." Engels, by contrast, "placed the agency of change or activity outside the human being."[47]

In very much the same fashion, Frederick L. Bender claimed that Engels, having "lost his awareness of the proletariat's *revolutionary* role, apparently conceived communism largely in terms of equality, leisure, sufficiency of goods, and the rational planning of production—without the emphasis on freedom and self-creation" on the parts of the individual and society that had "so motivated Marx."[48]

Besides not being a humanist in the view of most scholars in this school, Engels also differed from Marx in his epistemology, as already noted in the case of the early dichotomists. According to Jordan, Engels had a copy theory of knowledge that Marx did not accept.[49] Bender made much of the same point.[50] Philip J. Kain agreed in part but developed a much more sophisticated argument about the epistemology and method of both Marx and Engels.

Brief summary hardly does justice to Kain's treatment of these points, but his essential arguments were as follows. Unlike Carver, who saw no break in Marx's ideas but a distinct turning point in Engels',[51] Kain found several significant changes in Marx's epistemology and method over the course of his life. In the *Economic and Philosophic Manuscripts*, written in 1844 but not published during his lifetime, Marx had seen sense perceptions and theoretical paradigms as reciprocally determining one another, Kain explained. Then, in *The German Ideology* a year or two later, Marx shifted radically to a basically empiricist conception of how ideas were formulated, with sense perceptions determining theoretical formulations—an overreaction from the earlier method of 1844 and not the basis of Marx's mature method.[52]

According to Kain, Engels remained trapped in the methodological outlook of *The German Ideology*, but Marx advanced beyond it in the *Grundrisse* and *Capital*. In those two works, he rejected the earlier notion of 1844 that the investigator constructed the plethora of sense perceptions he experienced. What he created instead, according to Marx's mature view, was only a theoretical paradigm, but this was still quite different from mere empirical gathering of evidence.[53]

In Kain's view, this shift in Marx's thinking also affected his notion of praxis (or practice), on which scholars since Lukács had laid such great stress. In the "Theses on Feuerbach" (1845), Marx had said that all knowledge involved a practical transformation of the object known. In the *Grundrisse*, according to Kain, Marx rejected this position in favor of theoretical knowledge. This became Marx's standard view, contrary to the interpretations of many other scholars. Theoretical knowledge was thus the result of investigation and analysis, not of praxis, although Kain did concede to scholars who emphasized the latter that for Marx technical knowledge did change natural objects.[54]

Partly in line with Kain's views, Carver complained that in an anonymous review of Marx's *A Contribution to the Critique of Political Economy* (1859), Engels had misrepresented Marx's method by claiming that it was Hegel's "logical method," which was "nothing else but the historical method, only divested of its historical form and disturbing fortuities." (Engels had added in a passage Carver did not mention that this "logical method" was "the dialectical method, stripped of its idealistic wrappings.")[55] Engels had also written that the "chain of thought must begin with the same thing that history begins with and its further development will be nothing but the mirror, in more abstract and theoretically more consistent form, of the historical development." This ran counter to the method Marx had set forth in an unpublished introduction to the *Critique*, which Carver admitted Engels may never have read.[56] There Marx had written: "It would be unworkable and false to let the economic categories succeed one another in the sequence in which they were the determining factors historically. Rather, their succession is determined by the relation they have to one another in modern middle-class society, which is exactly the reverse of what appeared naturally or what matched the order of historical development."[57]

In stressing Marx's and Engels' methodological differences, Carver was essentially in agreement with Kain. Kain also stated that Engels misunderstood Marx's method. Engels commented that Marx, like Hegel, saw the evolution of ideas as parallel to that of history, whereas Marx's position was quite the opposite, Kain asserted.[58] Carver, however, went on from this point to state that Engels "misrepresented Marx's enterprise as Hegelian in scope, and he initiated the . . . view that a study of Hegel is essential to an understanding of Marx and his methods."[59] As already seen, Levine did not accept this negative view of Marx's relationship to Hegel. He also rejected the notion that Engels ultimately believed in a copy theory of truth. Engels had given evidence of such a belief in *Ludwig Feuerbach*, Levine said, but in the *Dialectics of Nature* he had embraced a theory of reflection in which the mind functioned not as a passive mirror but as an active constructor of ideas through hypotheses. It determined the truth of these hypotheses through testing.

This was a more sophisticated view of Engels' epistemology than other dichotomists presented, but Levine still insisted that it differed from Marx's. Engels' conception was a form of pragmatism—"a process of verification"—whereas Marx's praxis was a "process of creation, . . . an interaction between concept and the surrounding universe."[60]

Besides these points, there were a couple of other noteworthy elements in the arguments of individual members of the dichotomist school. One was that Engels foreshadowed the later reformism of his and Marx's friend Eduard Bernstein. Bender, for example, considered the reformist theoreticians of the German Social Democratic party as the "heirs to the 'orthodoxy' of Engels." Engels' blunting of Marx's radical humanism was an important cause of the reformism of that party, as Bender saw it, although he recognized that the improvement of working-class living standards also contributed to this development.[61]

Finally, among the major theses of this school there was a contention that Marx and Engels were not truly partners. Avineri, among others, rejected "the collective personality image [of the two men] projected by partisan propaganda."[62] Carver made this a central element in his argumentation. He admitted Marx's debt to Engels' article "Outlines of a Critique of Political Economy" (1844), and of course he accepted that the two men had collaborated on *The Holy Family, The German Ideology*, and the *Communist Manifesto*, plus "a number of short communications and articles, jointly signed." But he rejected the notion that they "thought as one" or were, in effect, joint authors of their remaining corpus of work. Basically, he contended, they followed a program of "independent publication."[63] In their independence, according to Carver, their views diverged significantly. Engels developed a "quasi-Hegelian framework" far removed from "Marx's investigative, rigorous and independent approach to the politics of capitalist society." After 1859, Engels "invented dialectics and reconstructed Marx's life and works accordingly."[64]

Obviously, there were several points on which many of the authors discussed above agreed. But if their insistence on the divergences in the ideas of Marx and Engels were valid, one might expect to find at least near unanimity among the proponents of this view. In fact, the various scholars in this school disagreed about nearly as much as they agreed upon. Some of them contradicted themselves, as already seen. A further example of this phenomenon is the respected work of Z. A. Jordan, *The*

Evolution of Dialectical Materialism. Jordan stated on the one hand that Marx did not agree with Engels that a single set of laws governed the physical universe and the human world. Later in the book he offered the contrary view: "Marx held that human action conforms to laws in the same sense as the phenomena of nature do."[65]

Still later in the work, Jordan even went to the extreme of noting Marx's debt to the founder of positivism, Auguste Comte: "It is in his determination to apply scientific method to social life, to discover invariable laws to which social phenomena conform and to establish a science of society, that Marx is most clearly indebted to the Comtean methodological and sociological conception."[66] Jordan followed this view with the assertion that the later Marx forgot his earlier naturalistic approach stressing that history did nothing, men did everything. He became a sociological determinist, writing in the preface to *Capital* that the ultimate aim of the work was "to lay bare the economic law of motion of modern society." According to Jordan (and contrary to what most other dichotomists wrote), "Engels never forgot that men make their own history." Marx was the first to state this, but later he wrote as if men were merely the puppets of economic forces. Yet Jordan also wrote that Engels was a metaphysician, while Marx was not, contradicting his statement elsewhere in the book that Marx had a theory of historical causation that was clearly metaphysical.[67]

Still another contradiction in Jordan's work lay in his treatment of Marx's and Engels' relationship to Hegel. In one place he stated, "Marx remained a Hegelian in spite of the fact that he was a materialist and Hegel an idealist." But elsewhere he said: "The framework and particular concepts of the Marxian doctrine cannot be derived from the theories either of Hegel or Feuerbach." And for Jordan, Ferdinand Freiligrath's presentation to Marx in 1858 of some volumes of Hegel belonging originally to Michael Bakunin "did not revive Marx's interest in Hegelian philosophy." Engels, on the other hand, never lost his interest in Hegel, as Jordan saw it. "Unlike Marx, who saw through Hegel's deceptions, Engels mistook Hegel's plain abuse of language, elementary errors of reasoning, and pretentious trivialities for originality, audacity, and profundity of thought." And because Engels idealized Hegel, "dialectical materialism acquired numerous idealistic features and became permeated with speculative and irrational elements."[68]

Yet, "unlike Marx, whose point of departure was the world of Hegelian abstractions," Jordan added, contradicting himself one more time, "Engels based his view of history, conceived as the scene of the interplay and

operation of antagonistic forces, on the observation of social developments in England and on a sociological analysis of current events." Marx's
approach, by contrast, was philosophical rather than sociological.[69] To
say the least, Jordan's views on Marx and Engels were far from being
one-sided.

Other dichotomists did not contradict themselves as frequently as Jordan, but they certainly disagreed with one another. Carver, for example,
consistently maintained that Engels "misrepresented Marx's enterprise
as Hegelian."[70] Although Carver admired the young Engels, he complained
that after 1859 the formerly brilliant young man found a vocation as a
"systematizing philosopher." He became a Hegelian while Marx was an
independent student of capitalist society.[71] While this analysis agrees
with some of the contradictory points of Jordan, it differs diametrically
with others, making Engels the Hegelian philosopher (in a pejorative
sense) and Marx the empirical scholar (if not necessarily a sociologist).

Similarly, Levine reversed Schmidt's view that socialism constituted
for Engels the leap of mankind from the realm of necessity into the
realm of freedom, whereas for Marx there remained under communism
a real of necessity upon which that of freedom rested. Levine claimed
that Marx saw communism as an end to human alienation and dehumanization, the beginning of freedom—a condition where "man could
live harmoniously and in accordance with his naturalistic essence." For
Engels, on the other hand, communist society was simply "an enormous
factory. It would be regimented, highly supervised, devoted to the work
ethic, but highly productive of the necessities and luxuries of life."[72]

In a somewhat different vein, although most of what Bender had to say
squared with the fundamental dichotomist approach, he differed from
Lichtheim and most other members of the school in his appraisal of
Marx's and Engels' relationship to Hegel. He said it had to be conceded
"that Engels's enumeration of the three 'laws' of dialectics represented
with a fair degree of accuracy the dialectical elements which were
presupposed, without formal exposition, by Marx." Also, in at least one
instance he found that Marx (rather than Engels) misunderstood Hegel.[73]
Similarly, in a related area Kain disagreed with almost all the other scholars discussed here in insisting that Marx and Engels shared the belief
that there was a dialectic operating in nature. Marx admitted in *Capital*,
Kain found, that the law of the transformation of quantity into quality
applied to natural science.[74]

Levine did not quite agree with this point, stating that Marx had restricted "the dialectic to mind-dependent realms," but he did concede

that Marx's philosophy of science, if not nature itself, was dialectical. He found that Engels' *Dialectics of Nature*, one of the primary whipping boys for other scholars' charges of positivism, constituted "the same kind of working class intellectual history" as Marx's *Theories of Surplus Value*. He even said that Engels' writings on the history of science were precursors of such widely respected works as R. G. Collingwood's *The Idea of History* and *The Idea of Nature* as well as Alfred North Whitehead's *The Concept of Nature*.[75]

These sharp differences of opinion among the dichotomist commentators almost make one wonder if they were all talking about the same Marx and Engels. The reason for this lack of agreement, however, was not necessarily the perversity of individual interpreters. At least part of the problem lay in the enormous body of writing both Marx and Engels left behind. As Kain and others have observed on specific points, they did not always maintain a consistent line of interpretation over the course of their many writings, some of them composed in considerable haste. Not only did Marx sometimes differ with Engels on certain issues; he also contradicted himself. Engels did likewise. The following chapters will explore in some detail the great diversity of Marx's and Engels' points of view that have helped to lend credence to dichotomist charges. More importantly, they will also show that in most respects the two men fundamentally agreed with each other.

CHAPTER IV

The *Communist Manifesto*

The only important work (as distinguished from journal and newspaper articles) by Marx and Engels together of which Engels composed a draft that Marx then revised into a finished document is the *Communist Manifesto*. It therefore provides a good starting place for a comparative study of the two men's ideas. As noted in chapter 3 above, both Avineri and Lichtheim found Engels' draft—now known as "Grundsätze des Kommunismus" (Principles of communism)—to be more highly technological than Marx's *Manifesto*. Lichtheim also said that Marx stressed the catastrophic nature of productive forces while Engels emphasized their liberating, progressive character.[1] Interestingly, Carver found less difference between the two texts despite his more extended analysis. He did say that "Engels linked industrial development and revolution in a more straightforward way than Marx," but added that this hardly made him a determinist as some commentators had claimed. On the whole, Carver noticed "a general similarity" of views in the two documents. There were "many minor differences of emphasis and detail," but they were not necessarily indicative of "a difference of opinion between Marx and Engels on any given point."[2]

Who was right? Before this question can be answered, a few comments need to be made about the history of the two documents. They arose in conjunction with Marx's and Engels' joining the League of the Just. This had been a secret organization with branches in Paris, London, Switzerland, and Germany.[3] Its leaders had accepted the ideas of the "true socialists," who ignored class differences and preached a peaceful solution to social problems. But in February 1847 they entrusted Joseph Moll with approaching Marx in Brussels and Engels in Paris. Moll, a watchmaker and one of the leaders of the league, endorsed the correctness of Marx and Engels' doctrines and expressed a willingness to end former conspiratorial practices in favor of more democratic ones. Given such assurances, Marx and Engels joined. Marx established a new branch of the league in Brussels, and Engels endeavored to convert the existing branches in Paris to his and Marx's ideas.[4]

Engels attended a conference of the league, held in London from 2 to 7 June 1847, that Marx could not attend because of insufficient funds. There the delegates changed the organization's name to the Communist League and adopted the motto "Proletarians of all countries, unite." They also drafted a "Confession of Faith" lithographed in Engels' handwriting. This was a compromise document but showed Marx and Engels' influence on the new organization. Moses Hess later prepared what Engels sarcastically called a "splendidly [*gottvoll*] improved confession," but Engels said he had succeeded in convincing the Paris group to entrust him with writing a new one in October 1847.[5]

On 23 November Engels wrote to Marx from Paris that he would bring this confession—the previously mentioned "Principles of Communism"—with him to Brussels for joint revision. "I believe we would do best," he said, "to dispense with the form of a catechism and entitle it the Communist *Manifesto*. Because it must contain more or less history, the present form is not suitable." Engels stated that the "Principles" was "simply narrated but miserably edited in a terrible hurry." The catechism had not yet been approved by others in the league, but Engels thought that—except for a few unimportant matters—he and Marx would be able to bring it about that at least nothing contrary to their views would remain in it.[6]

Clearly, then, the "Principles of Communism" can hardly be accepted as a clear and unambiguous statement of Engels' ideas, although many scholars have treated it as such. Not only did he himself disapprove of its form and suggest the one that Marx later adopted, but he had had to draft it too rapidly to be satisfied with its wording. Nevertheless, it is instructive to compare it with the *Communist Manifesto*, whose final form evidently was largely the work of Marx.[7]

In the "Principles of Communism," Engels did lay considerable stress on the forces of technology. In answer to the question "How did the proletariat arise?" he responded: "Through the industrial revolution," which was "brought about via the discovery of the steam engine, the various spinning machines, the mechanical loom, and a whole series of other mechanical devices." These machines, he said, "changed the whole previous methods of production and supplanted the former workers."[8]

Because of the different format of the *Communist Manifesto*, Marx[9] did not specifically address the question Engels posed and answered, but he did write that "steam and machinery revolutionized industrial production" and that "the modern bourgeoisie is the product of a long process of developments, a series of revolutions in the methods of production and transportation." He also stated that "the work of the proletarian has lost its independent character and thereby all attraction for the worker as a result of the increased use of machinery and the division of labor." The worker became simply an "appurtenance of the machine, from whom only the simplest, most monotonous, and most easily learned tasks were required."[10] Here, at least, the published version of the joint effort is just as technological as Engels' catechism.

A bit further on, Engels wrote that "work is a commodity like every other, and its price is determined by the same laws that govern every other commodity." On average, this price was always equivalent to the costs of production. This economic law of worker wages would be increasingly put into effect as large industry spread to all branches of work, he said.[11]

The closest comparable passage in the *Communist Manifesto* reads: "The average price of wage labor is the minimum of worker wages, i.e., the sum of the means of subsistence absolutely necessary to maintain the worker in existence as a worker." The sense of the two passages is essentially equivalent, but Engels' wording is more reminiscent of the style of the later Marx in *Capital* with its reference to economic laws. Marx did not use such terms in the *Manifesto*, but he did write of the bourgeoisie's being "compelled" to let its slaves (the workers) sink into a situation where the capitalists had to feed them instead of being fed by them. He also stated that the destruction of the bourgeoisie and the victory of the proletariat were equally "unavoidable."[12] Thus, if Marx did not write in terms of economic laws, he at least implied the existence of something closely akin to them.

Both documents dealt similarly with trade crises. Engels wrote of a "general disorder" repeating itself every seven years, "which each time threatens the whole civilization and throws not only the proletariat into penury but ruins a large number of bourgeois as well." This had to lead either to the disappearance of large industry—an impossibility—or a new organization of society in which factory owners would not compete with one another but would follow a plan that would subordinate production to the needs of all. This would allow the production of enough of life's needs that all members of society would be able to develop their abilities in full freedom. As a result, the very characteristics of large industry that in the existing society produced abject poverty and trade crises would do away with them altogether in the future society. Competition would end and be replaced by association.[13]

Marx wrote that as trade crises periodically recurred, they increasingly threatened the existence of middle-class society. They constituted a social epidemic that in all previous epochs would have appeared to be a paradox—the epidemic of overproduction. Industry and trade appeared to be destroyed because of too much civilization, excessive means of subsistence, too much industry and trade. Middle-class relations had become too narrow to accommodate the riches they had produced. If in the future class differences disappeared, Marx wrote in another part of the *Manifesto*, and all production became concentrated in the hands of associated producers, public power would lose its political character. In place of the old middle-class society with its classes and class antagonisms would arise an association "in which the free development of each is the condition for the free development of all."[14]

Engels emphasized that the new society about to arise from the contradictions of the old would abolish private property. Now that, for the first time in history, capital and productive powers not only existed in never-before-seen quantities but these productive powers soon promised to increase unendingly—and yet were concentrated in the hands of fewer bourgeois while the growing mass of the proletariat became increasingly poorer—it was clear that the abolition of private property was not only possible but necessary.[15]

Similarly, Marx noted that "the bourgeoisie has, in its scarcely one hundred years of class rule, created a more massive and colossal fund of productive forces than all preceding generations together. . . . What previous century suspected that such productive powers slumbered in the womb of social labor?" (This hardly supported Lichtheim's point about Marx's stress on the catastrophic nature of productive forces, although Marx did, like Engels, also note the impoverishment of the workers and the lower middle class under capitalism.) Despite this increase in productive forces, however, Marx pointed out that the proletariat was propertyless and that industry's development had also done away with the property of the lower middle class and the small peasant. People were shocked that communism would abolish private property, but existing society had already done away with it for nine-tenths of its members. "Communism takes away from no one the power to appropriate social products; it takes away only the power to subjugate the labor of others through this appropriation," Marx asserted.[16] Here he made several points not raised by Engels, but the basic thrust of his arguments was in line with that of the "Principles of Communism."

A somewhat more significant difference appeared in the treatment of the necessity for revolutionary violence to achieve a communist society. In answer to the question "Will the abolition of private property be possible in a peaceful manner?" Engels wrote: "It would be desirable for this to happen, and the Communists would certainly be the last to oppose it." They knew that conspiracies were not only useless but harmful, he said—that revolutions could not be made willfully and arbitrarily but were always the necessary results of circumstances that were independent of the wills and leadership of individual parties and whole classes. "But they also see," he went on, "that the development of the proletariat is forcibly suppressed and that thereby the opponents of communism work towards a revolution with all their power." If the suppressed proletariat were forced into a revolution, the Communists would certainly defend it.[17]

This tone of reluctant acceptance of a revolution forced upon the proletariat contrasted with much greater enthusiasm for the revolutionary cause in the *Communist Manifesto*. Marx made no reference to a possible peaceful transition to communism, although he was later to do so in his famous Amsterdam speech of 1872 (on which, see chapter 6). In the sonorous passages at the end of the *Manifesto*, he asserted: "The Communists support every revolutionary movement everywhere against the existing social and political arrangements." They "disdain to conceal their views and intentions. They openly declare that their ends can only be achieved through the forcible overthrow of all prevailing social arrangements. Let the ruling classes tremble at the prospect of a communist revolution."[18]

To the question "What course of development will the revolution take?" Engels answered: "Above all, it will produce a *democratic constitution* and thereby, directly or indirectly, the political rule of the proletariat." Direct rule would occur in England, where the proletariat already constituted the majority of the people. It would be indirect in France and Germany, where the majority consisted of small peasants and burghers besides proletarians. These peasants and burghers were in the first stages of transition to proletarian status, however, and were becoming increasingly dependent on the proletariat in their political interests. They would therefore soon submit to the demands of the proletariat. This might require a second struggle, but it could only end with victory for the proletariat.[19]

Marx expressed essentially the same points more forcibly: "The first step in the worker revolution is the elevation of the proletariat to the position of ruling class, the forcible establishment of democracy." He went on to say: "The proletariat will use its power to take all capital gradually away from the bourgeoisie, to centralize all instruments of production in the hands of the state (i.e., of the proletariat organized as the ruling class), and to increase the quantity of productive forces as quickly as possible." This could only occur through "despotic inroads" into property rights and middle-class relations of production. Marx added that once the ruling proletariat had done away with the old relations of production, classes would disappear and therewith the proletariat's rule as a class.[20]

Both Marx and Engels followed these discussions with a list of measures the proletariat would take following the revolution as interim steps on the road to communism. The order of these measures differed in the two accounts, as the following tabulation shows:[21]

"Principles of Communism"	Communist Manifesto
1. Limitation of private property through progressive taxes, heavy inheritance taxes, abolition of inheritance by collateral lines (brothers, nephews, and so on), compulsory loans, and so forth.	2. Heavy progressive taxes. 3. Abolition of inheritance.
2. Gradual expropriation of landowners, industrialists, railroad and ship owners, partly through competition from state industry, partly through compensation in assignats.	1. Expropriation of landed property and application of land rents to public expenditures.
3. Confiscation of the property (*Güter*) of all emigrants and rebels against the majority of the people.	4. Confiscation of the property (*Eigentum*) of all emigrants and rebels.
4. Organization of work or employment of the proletarians on national properties, in factories and workshops, whereby the competition of workers among themselves will be ended and the industrialists, as long as they continue to exist, will be required to pay the same increased wages as the state.	No comparable passage.
5. Equal liability to work for all members of society until the com-	8. Equal liability to work for all, establishment of industrial armies,

plete abolition of private property. Formation of industrial armies, especially for agriculture.

6. Centralization of the credit system and banking in the hands of the state through a national bank with state capital, and suppression of all private banks and bankers.

7. Increase of national factories, workshops, railroads, and ships; cultivation of all available landed property and improvement of the land already in cultivation in proportion to the increase of available capital and workshops.

8. Education of all children—from the moment they can dispense with maternal care—in national institutions at the expense of the nation. Education together with production.

9. Erection of large palaces on national property as comman dwellings for communities of citizens, who engage in both industry and agriculture, thus combining the benefits of town and country living without the one-sidedness and disadvantages of either.

10. Demolition of all unhealthy and poorly built dwellings and sections of cities.

11. Equal inheritance for illegitimate as well as legitimate children.

12. Concentration of all means of transportation in the hands of the nation.

especially for agriculture.

5. Centralization of credit in the hands of the state through a national bank with state capital and an exclusive monopoly.

7. Increase of national factories, instruments of production; cultivation and improvement of landed property according to a common plan.

10. Public and free education of all children. Abolition of factory work for children in the present form. Combination of education with material production, and so forth.

9. Uniting of the operation of agriculture and industry, gradual elimination of the opposition between town and country.

No comparable passage.

See no. 3 above.

6. Centralization of all means of transportation in the hands of the state.

As can be seen, Marx was both (uncharacteristically) more laconic and, in some instances, more radical in his proposed measures, but in general the two lists were compatible.

Engels stated that communist society would make the relation of the two sexes into a purely private one that involved only the persons concerned and in which society did not have to meddle. This could be the case because of the abolition of private property and the collective education of children. These arrangements did away, he said, with the two bases of existing marriage: the dependence of the wife upon the husband and of the children upon the parents by means of private property. "Herein lies also the answer to the outcry of highly moralistic philistines against a communistic community of wives," Engels wrote. This community of wives was altogether a feature of middle-class society that presently exhibited itself in prostitution. Prostitution rested on private property and would cease to exist when private property did likewise. Communism would thus do away with community of wives instead of instituting it.[22]

Marx approached these questions somewhat more obliquely through the medium of sarcasm: "Abolition of the family! Even the most radical get aroused at this scandalous intention of the Communists," he wrote. But the present middle-class family, based on private profits, existed in complete form only for the bourgeoisie. It found its complement in the forced absence of family among the proletariat and in public prostitution. The bourgeois family and its complement would disappear with the abolition of capital. To the charge that they would end exploitation of children by their parents, the Communists pleaded guilty. Regarding the claim that Communists would replace education in the home by social education, he pointed out that this was not something new. The Communists would only change the character of existing social education by removing it from the influence of the ruling class.

The entire bourgeoisie screamed in chorus against communist plans to introduce a community of wives. The bourgeois saw in his wife a mere instrument of production, and he heard that instruments of production would be exploited in common. He thus assumed that the same would be true of wives. He did not dream that communism would abolish the position of wives as instruments of production. Moreover, the Communists didn't need to introduce community of wives. It had existed almost from the beginning of time. The bourgeois were not satisfied with having the wives and daughters of the proletariat at their disposal, not to mention public prostitution; they took great pleasure in seducing one another's wives. Middle-class marriage was in reality a community of wives. The most the Communists could be charged with was replacing a hypocritically hidden community of wives with an official, open one. It went without saying that with the abolition of existing relations of production, the community of wives proceeding from them—that is, the official and unofficial prostitution—would disappear.[23] Here Marx was the more long-winded of the two, but his message was essentially the same as Engels'.

To the question about communist attitudes toward existing nationalities and religions, Engels wrote the verb "remains." Scholars have assumed, probably correctly, that this was a reference to the answer provided in the June "Confession of Faith."[24] It stated that the various nationalities would have to mingle with one another as a result of the people's associations, according to the principle of community. Nationalities would thus disappear along with distinctions of estate and class as a result of the abolition of private property, which constituted their basis. As mere expressions of the various stages of historical development among different categories of peoples, religions too would disappear because communism would make them superfluous.[25]

Marx's comments were again more indirect. He stated that Communists were reproached for their plans to do away with the fatherland, with nationality. "The workers have no fatherland," he said. "No one can take away from them what they do not possess." Since the proletarians had to seize political power in the nation, they were still national, even if by no means in the middle-class sense. National differences were already disappearing with such developments as a world market and the uniformity of industrial production with its matching living conditions. The rule of the proletariat would make these differences disappear "more and more." To the degree that the exploitation of one individual by another was abolished, the same would occur with the exploitation of one nation by another. With the antagonism between classes internally, that among nations would also end.

Marx stated that the charges against communism in the religious, philosophical, and ideological arenas did not require detailed treatment. Did it require deep insight to comprehend that with the living conditions and social relations of men, their consciousness also changed? "The ruling ideas of a period were always only the ideas of the ruling class." As the ancient world was perishing, Christianity replaced the old religion. As Christian ideas succumbed to those of the Enlightenment in the eighteenth century, feudal society was in a death struggle with the revolutionary bourgeoisie. The communist revolution was the most extreme break with property relations bequeathed from the past; it would break more radically than past movements with traditional ideas.[26] Here Marx developed the notion that material conditions shaped ideas more fully than Engels had done, but he was in other respects somewhat more vague. Basically, however, the two treatments agreed.

To the question of how the Communists differed from socialists, Engels replied that there were three types of socialists. The first consisted of supporters of feudal and patriarchal society, which was in the process of being destroyed by large-scale industry, world trade, and the bourgeois society that both had created. This type of socialist wanted to restore feudal and patriarchal society. Communists needed to oppose it energetically despite its sympathy and hot tears for the distress of the proletariat because, for one thing, its goals were completely impossible. Also, it sought to restore the rule of the aristocracy, guild masters, and dealers in textiles, together with their retinue of absolute or feudal kings, officials, soldiers, and priests. Such a society was free from the disadvantages of existing society but had at least as many other disadvantages, besides denying the prospect of freedom for the suppressed workers through a communist organization. Further, such socialists showed their real intentions by allying with the bourgeoisie against the proletarians when the latter became revolutionary and communist.

A second type of socialist consisted of supporters of existing society, who, awakened to its necessary evils, now feared for its continued existence. They sought to retain existing society but to eliminate the evils connected with it. Communists had to struggle against these bourgeois socialists because they worked for the enemies of communism and defended the societies the Communists wanted to overthrow.

The third category of socialists encompassed democratic individuals, who wanted some of the same measures as the Communists (see the twelve proposed measures listed above) but not as a transition to communism; they saw such measures as sufficient in themselves to end distress and make the evils of present society disappear. These democratic socialists were either proletarians who were not sufficiently enlightened about the conditions for freeing their class, or they were members of the lower middle class, which had many of the same interests as the proletarians up to the achievement of democracy and the socialistic measures that would arise from it. The Communists would ally with these democratic socialists and for the moment pursue common policies with them. But only insofar as these momentary allies did not enter into the service of the ruling bourgeoisie and attack the Communists. Clearly, though, this temporary alliance did not exclude a discussion of mutual differences.[27]

Engels' treatment of this issue took up almost exactly two pages of text in the *Werke* of Marx and Engels. The corresponding section in the *Communist Manifesto* occupied over nine pages in the same volume of the *Werke*. Marx also dealt with three categories of socialists and Communists. His category of reactionary socialists, however, broke down into three subcategories. The first, feudal socialism, arose out of the need on the parts of the French and British aristocracies to arouse sympathy for themselves after the July Revolution of 1830 in France. To do this, they had to appear to attack the bourgeoisie not in their own interests but in those of the exploited workers. This feudal socialism was half echo of the past, half threat of the future. Its bitter criticism struck at the heart of the bourgeoisie, but it was always comical in its effects because of its complete incapacity to understand the path of modern history. Among the many other things that Marx said about it was that its proponents took part in all coercive measures against the working class.

Marx's second subclass was petty bourgeois socialism. Like the aristocracy, the petty bourgeois class was threatened by the bourgeoisie and modern society. Its brand of socialism acutely analyzed the contradictions in modern relations of production. It showed irrefutably the destructive effects of machinery and the division of labor, the concentration of capital and landholdings, overproduction, crises, and so forth. But it lacked a positive program. This type of socialism wanted either to restore the old means of production and exchange—and with them the old property relations and the old aristocracy—or it wanted forcibly to confine the modern methods of production and exchange within the framework of the old property relations, which those methods had burst asunder and were bound to burst asunder. (That is, structural changes in the economy had destroyed the old relations of production and were constrained by the laws of capitalist production to do so—to put the point into the kind of language Marx later used in *Capital*.) In both cases, this type of socialism was at the same time reactionary and utopian. The guild system in manufacturing and the patriarchal economy on the land were its last words.

The third subcategory of reactionary socialism was German or "true" socialism, spawned (Marx explained) by German literati who had transferred French socialist and communist ideas into a different social setting and molded them into the German philosophic point of view. In the process, they completely emasculated the ideas they borrowed. By criticizing the bourgeoisie before it rose to power, this type of socialism became a weapon in the hands of the absolute governments to use against the bourgeoisie. In addition, it represented the reactionary interests of the German philistines, the petty bourgeoisie—a hand-me-down from the sixteenth century that had ever since cropped up in a variety of forms and constituted the true social foundation for the existing state of affairs. From the rule of the bourgeoisie it feared its certain downfall, on the one hand as a result of the concentration of capital, on the other through the rise of a revolutionary proletariat. The garment of German socialists, woven out of speculative cobwebs, in which they wrapped their bony "eternal truths," served only to increase the sale of their wares. German socialism recognized increasingly its role as the bombastic representative of these philistines. It gave every one of their basenesses a hidden, higher, socialist meaning. It directly opposed the "brutally destructive" tendency of communism and announced its own disinterested elevation above all class struggles.

Regarding conservative or bourgeois socialists, Marx's second main category, he wrote that part of the bourgeoisie wanted to remedy social grievances in order to secure the continued existence of middle-class society. The socialistic bourgeois wanted all the conditions of life of modern society without the struggles and dangers necessarily following therefrom. He wanted the bourgeoisie without the proletariat. One variety of bourgeois socialism sought to disgust the proletariat with every revolutionary movement by showing that it would benefit from political changes rather than from changes in material conditions. Such changes were not intended to abolish bourgeois relations of production, which abolition could only result from revolution, but merely to institute administrative improvements that could occur on the basis of these relations of production. They would not alter the relationship between capital and wage labor but, in the best case, reduce the costs to the bourgeoisie of its rule and simplify the state budget.

Marx's third category he called "critical-utopian socialism and communism." Its proponents saw class opposition and the decomposition occurring in existing society. But they did not perceive in the proletariat any possibility of historic spontaneity, of its own political movement. They discerned no material conditions for the freeing of the proletariat and sought to create these conditions through social science, social laws. In the place of social activity, historical conditions for freedom, and the gradually developing organization of the proletariat as a class, they foresaw propaganda and the practical application of their social plans as the keys to the future. They appealed preeminently to the ruling class, feeling that if a person only understood their system, he would immediately recognize it as the best plan possible for the best possible society. They rejected all political, especially all revolutionary action. They wanted to reach their goals by peaceful means and sought to prepare the way for the new social gospel through the example of small experiments that were naturally bound to fail.

Their writings, however, also contained critical elements. They assailed all the foundations of existing society. They had thus provided the most valuable material for the enlightenment of the workers. Their positive propositions for the future society, such as the abolition of the opposition between town and country, of the family, of private profits and wage work; the proclamation of social harmony and of the conversion of the state into a mere administration of production—all of these proposals expressed clearly the abolition of class antagonisms that were just beginning to develop and were still in their first, formless indefinitude. These propositions still had, therefore, a purely utopian tendency. As the class struggle developed, they thus lost all practical value, all theoretical justification. The originators of the systems were in many respects revolutionary, but their followers constituted reactionary sects. They held fast to the views of their masters in the face of the historical development of the proletariat. Consequently, they sought to blunt the class struggle and to reconcile all opposition. Gradually, they fell into the category of reactionary or conservative socialists, from whom they differed mainly through their more systematic pedantry—through the fanatical, superstitious belief in the miracles their social science would produce. They therefore bitterly opposed all political movements on the part of the workers.[28]

This summary and paraphrase of Marx's brilliant rhetoric hardly does justice to his ringing periods and biting sarcasm, but it does suggest the basic contents of his message. It was much more developed than the mostly shorter questions and answers in Engels' catechism. Nevertheless, the fundamental thrust of both accounts was the same.

The final sections of both Engels' "Principles" and Marx's *Manifesto* dealt with how the Communists related to the other opposition parties. The treatments of this issue were of almost equal length, though Marx again was somewhat more prolix. Engels wrote that the relationship differed from country to country. In England, France, and Belgium, where the bourgeoisie ruled, the Communists had a common interest with the various democratic parties. This common interest grew the more the democrats represented the interests of the proletariat and depended upon it for support. In America, where there was a democratic constitution, the Communists had to ally with the party that turned this constitution against the bourgeoisie and used it in the interests of the proletariat. In Switzerland the radicals, although a very mixed party, constituted the only political force with which the Communists could have dealings. In Germany, finally, the decisive struggle about to begin lay between the bourgeoisie and the absolute monarchy. Since the Communists could not expect the decisive struggle between themselves and the bourgeoisie to occur until the latter ruled, it was in their interests to help the bourgeoisie to power as soon as possible in order to overthrow it again as soon as that would be feasible. The benefits victory for the bourgeoisie would offer the Communists were twofold: the various concessions that would make it easier for the latter to defend, discuss, and disseminate their principles and thereby unite the proletariat into a tightly connected, organized class ready for struggle; and the certainty that when the absolute governments fell, the struggle between bourgeois and proletariat would begin. From that day forth, the Communist policy would be the same as in countries where the bourgeois already ruled.[29]

Marx's treatment of the subject was in section 4 of the *Manifesto*. He said there that section 2 had indicated what the relationship of Communists would be to other worker parties like the Chartists in England and the agrarian reformers in America. He had not mentioned these specific parties in the earlier section but had remarked that the Communists differed from the remaining proletarian parties in only two respects: on the one hand, in the different national struggles they raised the common interests of the whole proletariat independently of nationality; on the other hand, they always represented the interests of the whole movement, regardless of the particular stage of a given struggle between proletariat and bourgeoisie.

In section 4 itself, Marx went on to state that the Communists strove to attain the immediate goals and interests of the worker class, but in the present movement they also represented the future of the class. In France they worked with the Social-Democratic party against the conservative and radical bourgeoisie, without giving up the right to criticize phrases and illusions stemming from the revolutionary traditions. In Switzerland, they supported the radicals without forgetting that this party consisted of contradictory elements, Democratic Socialists as well as radical members of the bourgeoisie. In Poland, the Communists supported the party that made the agrarian revolution a condition for national freedom.

In Germany, the Communists struggled in common with the bourgeoisie against absolute monarchy, feudal land ownership, and the lower middle class, so far as the first acted in a revolutionary way. At the same time, they made clear to the workers the antagonism between bourgeoisie and proletariat so that after the fall of the reactionary classes, the struggle against the bourgeoisie could begin. In a word, the Communists generally supported every revolutionary movement against the existing social and political order. They worked everywhere for the alliance and understanding of the democratic parties of all countries.[30] Here again, Marx's rhetoric was more developed and his language more forcible. The two men also presented somewhat different details (Engels bringing up America; Marx, Poland), but the fundamental argument in both accounts was the same.

Overall, the *Manifesto* occupied thirty-two pages in the *Werke* compared to seventeen for the "Principles." Besides the greater length and rhetorical embellishment, the *Manifesto* did exhibit a greater tendency toward radicalism, although perhaps this resulted from the fact that it made fewer concessions than the "Principles" to the ideas held by the League of the Just as distinguished from Marx and Engels' own beliefs. (Recall Engels' comment that they should be able to work it so that the *Manifesto* contained nothing contrary to their views, implying that the "Principles" did still have ideas with which they disagreed.) The *Manifesto* was not, however, either less technological or more inclined to stress the catastrophic nature of productive forces than Engels' draft. Moreover, in view of the uncertainty about the degree of Engels' participation in the composition of the *Manifesto*[31] as well as his own dissatisfaction with the "Principles," it would be wrong to attribute much significance to the differences that do exist between the two documents. In short, even though there were fewer differences between the *Manifesto* and the "Principles" than some scholars have claimed, a comparison of the two compositions leaves moot the larger question of whether there were significant disparities in the thought of Marx and Engels. To answer that question, we must turn to their other writings.

CHAPTER V

Epistemology and Method

As we have already seen, one area in which scholars have pointed to disagreement between Marx and Engels involves their views of knowledge theory and methodology. Jerrold Seigel has presented a convincing and well-documented argument about Marx's mature method that provides a good point of departure for a discussion of these issues. Like Kain, Seigel distinguished between Marx's empirical views of the late 1840s and those in *Grundrisse* and *Capital*. In the 1840s, according to Seigel, Marx had criticized Pierre-Joseph Proudhon's search for mysteries and revelations beneath the surface of economic relations. And in the *Communist Manifesto* he had spoken of "real conditions" under capitalism as if they were simple and obvious. In the *Grundrisse*, however, Marx came to regard reality as being in opposition to appearance. Likewise, in *Capital* money concealed rather than revealed the realities of economics and society.

In the *Communist Manifesto*, Seigel explained, Marx wrote that feudal society had hidden the realities of exploitation, whereas capitalist society revealed these same realities. In *Capital*, Marx reversed this perception about the two societies. Feudal society, he now held, had openly admitted relations of dependence, but he now implied that capitalist society hid them. Seigel showed how basic the opposition between appearance and reality had become for Marx's mature view of capitalist society as expressed in *Grundrisse* and *Capital*. Surface appearances were merely "illusion," "semblance," "mystification," which Marx contrasted with realities such as surplus value that were "entirely buried," forming a "concealed essential pattern." Interestingly, in view of the dichotomist argument, Seigel found this viewpoint in all three volumes of *Capital*, but most strikingly expressed in volume 3, which Engels had edited and could have revised had he disagreed with what Marx had written.[1]

Yet Seigel also noticed that in a letter to Engels dated 24 August 1867 Marx had written with reference to recent British blue books (government reports), "I was delighted to find my theoretical results fully confirmed by the facts." Thus, on the one hand, appearances ("facts") were at variance with reality, while on the other, they "confirmed" it.[2] Marx never resolved this contradiction in his thinking.

In connection with this argument, Seigel stated that Marx's method in economics did not start from an analysis of empirical data but from "abstractions evolved by economic theory." He used these abstractions, Seigel stated, to reproduce the concrete (by which both he and Marx appear in this particular connection to mean the reality behind sense experience). This was a method Marx acknowledged to be borrowed from Hegel, except that he (Marx) did not believe mind created the concrete. Instead, thought merely reproduced the concrete in the mind. This later method, Seigel said, was quite different from the one Marx had proposed in 1844, which involved beginning with "positive facts" known by the various senses.[3]

The complexity that Seigel noted in Marx's methodology is capable of further illustration. In the afterword to the second edition of *Capital*, for instance, Marx said his dialectical method was basically the direct opposite of Hegel's. For Hegel, the process of thinking—which he converted into an independent subject under the name "Idea"—was "the demiurge of the real," which constituted only its outward appearance. "With me," Marx went on, "the world of ideas is the contrary, nothing but the real transferred and translated into the human mind."[4] This quotation supports the views of Kain and others that Marx, at least at times, accepted a reflection theory of how the mind related to reality.[5] It is exactly analogous to a passage from Engels' *Ludwig Feuerbach*: "We comprehend the concepts in our heads once more materialistically—as images of real things instead of regarding the real things as images of this or that stage of development of the absolute concept."[6] As will be seen below, just as this reflection theory was not Marx's only perception of how the mind related to reality, so also with Engels. He was too subtle a thinker to believe that the mind simply mirrored existence.

In a letter to Engels on 27 June 1867, Marx further demonstrated his emphasis on the difference between appearance and reality as well as his at least sometime belief in a reflection theory of knowledge. In reference to the conceptions of the bourgeois and the vulgar economists, he wrote: "In their brains were reflected always only the direct *outward appearance* of relations, not their *internal connection*. If they perceived the latter, why would a science be necessary?"[7] Notice here, incidentally, Marx's Hegelian emphasis on totality, on the interconnectedness of individual phenomena, despite his claim that his method was the opposite of Hegel's.

Susan M. Easton has quoted Marx (from *Capital*, volume 3) to a similar effect: "All science would be superfluous if the outward appearance and the essence of things directly coincided." Yet she rejected the distinction between essence and appearance (which she called "quasi-empiricist") as the ground for his theory of knowledge. Her basis for this stand was Marx's insistence on the "social foundations of knowledge" and his "essentially transformative epistemology."

This argument simply points to a further level of complexity in Marx's method and epistemology, but certainly in *Capital* the essence-appearance distinction was basic to much of Marx's treatment, as Easton readily admitted.[8] In his discussion of the fetishistic character of the commodity, for example, he wrote: "A commodity seems at first glance an obvious, trivial thing. Its analysis shows that it is a very complex thing, full of metaphysical subtleties and theological caprices." He spoke of the "mystical character of the commodity," its "enigmatic nature," and "the mysteriousness of the commodity form." Then he launched into a famous Feuerbachian analogy: "It is only the distinct social condition of human beings that takes on here the phantasmagorical form of a relation of things. In order to find an analogy, we must flee to the misty regions of the religious world. Here the products of the human brain appear endowed with their own life and to stand in relation to human beings as if they were independent beings. So in the commodity world the products of the human hand."[9]

A couple of pages further on, Marx spoke of humans seeking "to decipher the sense of the hieroglyphics, to get behind the secret of their own social product" and of the fact that "the determination of the magnitude of value through labor time is therefore a secret hidden beneath the apparent movement of the relative commodity values. Its discovery cancels and yet preserves [*aufhebt*] the purely accidental determination of the magnitudes of value of the products of work but by no means their essential form."[10]

"Reflection [*Nachdenken*, literally: after-thinking] about the forms of human life," Marx went on, "thus also their scientific analysis, generally goes the opposite way from real developments. It begins after the fact and therefore with the completed results of the process of development. But this completed form—the money form—of the commodity world is the very thing that masks the social character of individual work and therefore the social character of the individual worker, instead of revealing it." Nevertheless, "all the mysticism of the commodity world, all the enchantment and phantoms that befog labor products based on commodity production, immediately disappear as soon as we turn our attention [*flüchten*, literally: flee] to other forms of production."[11]

Much further on in *Capital*, volume 1, Marx returned to the distinction between appearance and reality in his discussion of the concept of relative surplus value. "Scientific analysis of competition is only possible," he asserted, "once the inner nature of capital is understood, exactly as the apparent movement of heavenly bodies is only comprehensible to those who know their real movement, which is not perceptible to the senses."[12] (Notice here, incidentally, the comparison between natural science and social development and at the same time the acceptance of knowledge about nature that is not socially determined.)

In his discussion of the general law of capitalist accumulation, Marx again returned to the theme in a different context. He referred to the workers' learning the secret that to the degree they increased their work, produced more wealth for others, and added to the productive power of that work, their function as the means for the realization of capital became increasingly precarious for them. He also wrote: "The inner connection between the hunger pangs of the most industrious groups of workers and the uncouth or refinedly prodigal consumption of the rich, based on capitalistic accumulation, unveils itself only with the knowledge of economic laws." He added that it was "otherwise with housing conditions. Every impartial observer sees that . . . the quicker the capitalist accumulation, the more impoverished the housing conditions of the worker.[13] Thus, Marx himself recognized explicitly the contradiction that Seigel called attention to. In some instances the inner reality of capitalist society contrasted with appearance, just as the sun appeared to circle the earth each day when in reality the opposite occurred. Only the scientific observer trained to distinguish appearance from reality could discern the true movement of the earth around the sun or the fact that capitalists enriched themselves through appropriating surplus value from the workers. On the other hand, there were some instances like housing where any impartial observer could perceive the realities of the situation. There, appearance and reality coincided.

A considerable part of *Capital*, volume 1, was based on this simple coincidence. Marx cited blue books, factory inspector's reports, even newspaper accounts ad infinitum and quoted from them at length in exactly the same way that Engels had done in *The Conditions of the Working Class in England*, a work that Marx admired and praised for its deep understanding of the capitalist method of production even before its thesis was confirmed by factory reports, reports on mines, reports of the children's employment commission, and so forth, which all appeared after 1845.[14]

Both men in countless cases accepted the data and observations from these reports and other sources as empirically valid. Both, of course, had undertaken the research for their respective volumes with a preconceived, theoretical conception of how capitalist society operated, so neither man's method was purely empirical. But both had sought to confirm their theoretical paradigms with the "facts," as Marx expressed it to Engels in the letter of 24 August 1867 referred to above.[15] Thus to the extent that they relied on surface reality, Marx's and Engels' methods were exactly the same.

As already noted, however, Marx returned to the distinction between appearance and reality in volume 3 of *Capital*. In his discussion of the transformation of surplus value into profit, he distinguished between the capitalistic cost of a commodity, measured in terms of the expenditure of capital, and its real cost, measured by the expenditure of work. He wrote about false appearances in the capitalist economy and of how the reality of a given situation necessarily appeared inverted from the standpoint of capitalist production.[16]

He said that the difference between fixed and circulating capital with regard to the calculation of cost price confirmed the apparent origin of this cost price in the price the capitalist himself paid for the elements of production, including work. The capitalist's identification of variable or circulating capital expended on labor power with constant capital expended on production materials completed the mystification of capital's transformation into value.[17]

Profit, Marx went on, was the same as surplus value, only in a mystified form. Although in the apparent formation of cost price there was no difference between constant and variable capital to be discerned, the origin of the transformation of value that occurred during the process of production had to be transferred from the variable part of capital to the capital as a whole. While on the one hand the price of labor power appeared in the transmuted form of worker wages, on the other, surplus value appeared metamorphosed as profit.[18]

Marx continued this theme in the next chapter on profit rate. "Surplus value and rate of surplus value," he wrote, "are respectively the invisible and the to-be-discovered essence, while profit rate and therefore the form of surplus value as profit appear on the surface of phenomena." He said that "the original form in which capital and wage labor stand against each other becomes veiled by the insertion of seemingly unrelated matters; the surplus value itself appears not as a product of the appropriation of labor time, but as the surplus of the selling price of the commodity over the cost price." As a result, the latter "easily presents itself as the true value (*valeur intrinsèque*),[19] so that the profit appears as the surplus of the selling price of the commodity over its inherent value."[20] Marx went on to say:

> The manner in which surplus value is changed into the form of profit by way of transition through the rate of profit is, however, only the further development of the inversion of subject and object that already occurred during the process of production. Here we saw all the productive powers of labor—the subject—present themselves as productive powers of capital. On the one hand, value—work of the past that controls its still active counterpart—is personified in the capitalist; on the other, the worker appears inverted as pure, objective labor power, as a commodity. Out of this inverted relationship there necessarily arises already in the simple relations of production themselves the matching inverted conception—a transformed consciousness that is further developed through the transformations and modifications of the real process of circulation.[21]

Thus, Marx concluded, "profit is a transformation of surplus value, a form wherein its origin and the secret of its existence are veiled and effaced. In reality, "profit is the outward form of surplus value. The latter must be obtained out of the former through analysis by peeling off its outer layers. In surplus value the relationship between capital and labor is exposed." Yet, "the further we follow capital's process of realizing its value, the more the relations of capital mystify themselves and the less the secret of its inner organism is laid bare."[22]

Thus, although Marx was by no means consistent—even within *Capital*—in his social and economic analysis or the assumptions about knowledge and methods that underlay them, he did use the distinction between appearance and reality extensively in developing one of his most central conceptions, the theory of surplus value.[23] He pointed to the distinction repeatedly in volume 3. Since Engels spent a great deal of time pouring over and creatively editing Marx's manuscripts for that volume, it would be very surprising if he had failed to perceive Marx's emphasis on this distinction. Indeed, it would be almost equally surprising if a man of his discernment had failed to pick it up in volume 1. Yet, as already seen, many scholars have claimed that he accepted only a copy theory of perception, the simplistic assumptions behind which would seem to be at odds with an appreciation for Marx's subtle and complex social theory and methodology. As we have also seen and as Kain stated, Marx, too, sometimes accepted a reflection theory—but only at times. Was Engels more consistent—and therefore more simple-minded—than Marx in this regard?

There is, of course, no doubt that Engels wrote in *Ludwig Feuerbach* as if he believed in a copy theory of knowledge. In expressing the view of Hegel's idealism that he and Marx shared, for example, Engels wrote: "We conceive the ideas in our heads again materialistically as the images of real things, instead of regarding the real things as images of this or that stage of the absolute idea."[24] But a year before he wrote *Ludwig Feuerbach*—and also before he began editing volume 3 of *Capital*—Engels had expressed a quite different notion in a foreword to the first German edition of Marx's *The Poverty of Philosophy*. There he stated: "That thereby the form of appearance of value, price, as a rule seems different from value, which it brings to appearance, is a fate value shares with most social relations."[25] Here Engels revealed his recognition of a difference between appearance and reality that one would expect from a careful reader of *Capital*, volume 1—a recognition that is hardly compatible with a simple copy theory of perception, which would accept all data at face value and could not, by implication at least, distinguish between some data as real and others as merely apparent.

In *Anti-Dühring*, written still earlier (1876–1878), Engels expressed both a complex reflection theory of perception (as Levine noted in *Dialogue within the Dialectic*) and the notion of the difference between appearance and reality. In the introduction, he discussed the intricacies and the dialectical nature of reality. There he treated what he called the metaphysical outlook of Bacon and Locke, and said it held that a thing either existed or it did not. For these metaphysicians, a thing could not be both itself and something else. Positive and negative excluded one another absolutely. Cause and effect were in sharp contrast. This method of thinking, he went on, seemed at first glance to be highly plausible, but it was one-sided, limited, and abstract. It looked only at individual things, not their context; at being, not becoming and passing; rest, not movement. Hence, it missed the woods for the trees. (Notice, here and below, Engels' Hegelian emphasis on both a dialectic and totality: a position exactly analogous to Marx's own.)

Continuing this line of thinking, Engels said that ordinarily we knew if an animal existed or not. But the lawyers recognized how difficult it was to set a rational point at which killing a child in its mother's body was murder. It was also impossible to establish the exact moment of death, because death was not an immediate event but a slow process. Likewise, at every moment cells in the body died and new ones came into being. As a result, over a certain period the body was completely renewed. Hence, every complex organism was always both the same and different. Similarly, the poles of an antithesis, like the positive and negative, were as inseparable from each other as they were opposed. The same with cause and effect. In individual cases their separability might seem clear, but as soon as the individual cases were considered in their general context within the totality of the whole, their interconnectedness, their resolution in the universality of reciprocal action became clear. There, cause and effect continually changed place. What was one place effect became in another place, cause—and vice-versa.

Metaphysical thinking considered none of this, Engels said, but dialectics looked at things and their "conceptual images" in their context, their connectedness, their movement, their origin and passing. Nature was the test of the dialectic. In the final analysis, nature proceeded dialectically and not metaphysically. "Therefore, an exact description of the totality of the world, its development and mankind, as well as the mirror image of this development in the heads of men, can only come into being dialectically," Engels held, "with continual attention to the general interaction of becoming and passing away, the progressive or regressive changes."[26]

A few pages further on, moreover, Engels wrote about the materialist conception of history, its depiction of the capitalist method of production in its historical context and its necessity for a fixed historical period, thus also the necessity of its downfall. This method unveiled, he said, capitalism's "inner character, which was still hidden because former critics had turned their attention to the evil effects rather than the progress of the thing." This unveiling occurred through the discovery of surplus value, he pointed out—completely in line with Marx's approach to this topic.[27]

A perhaps even clearer demonstration of Engels' appreciation for the difference between appearance and reality was his revision of Marx's *Wage Labor and Capital*. As Seigel has shown, in the original work—which appeared as a series of articles in 1849—Marx had written in the straightforward terms he used in that period: "The bourgeois therefore *buys* their [the workers'] labor with money. They *sell* him their labor for money." In 1891, Engels revised this passage to show the distinction between appearance and reality that characterized Marx's thinking in *Capital*. As revised, the passage read: "The capitalist, it seems, therefore *buys* their labor for money. They *sell* him their labor for money. But this is merely the appearance. In reality, what they sell to the capitalist is their labor *power*."[28]

To return to *Anti-Dühring*, however, in the section on philosophy Engels came back to the empirical approach that seemed to assume a simple acceptance of the evidence of the senses at face value. He accused Dühring of idealism and said that, contrary to that academic's perception, "principles are not the starting point of the investigation but its result; they are not applied to nature and human history but abstracted from them; nature and the human realm do not conform to principles, but principles are only correct insofar as they agree with nature and history." Engels even argued for an empirical basis for mathematics as arising out of the needs of men to measure land and volume.[29]

These passages show the complexity and inconsistency of Engels' thinking on these matters, as did his comment on Dühring's alleged claim that the essence of all thinking lay in the fusion of consciousness into a unity. This, Engels said, was simply false. Thinking consisted as much in the decomposition of objects of consciousness into their elements as in the fusing together of correlated elements into a unity. "Without analysis, no synthesis," he asserted.[30]

The quotations in the last two paragraphs, if taken by themselves, might suggest that Engels rejected Marx's Hegelian emphasis on grasping the elements of capitalism in their totality, but his earlier comments on dialectics clearly show his understanding of the interrelation of ideas. One final passage from Engels' writing shows another facet of his thinking in this regard that further illustrates the point. In a letter to Conrad Schmidt on 12 March 1895, he criticized his correspondent's epistolary treatment of profit rate and the law of value. Engels said Schmidt had gotten so engrossed in particulars that he had lost track of the totality; he had degraded the law of value to a necessary fiction. The criticisms that he had made of it were true of all conceptions with respect to reality. The notion of a thing and its reality approached one another like two asymptotes, getting closer and closer together but never meeting.

"That an idea has the essential nature of an idea," Engels went on, "that it therefore does not exactly and at first glance coincide with reality —from which it was first abstracted" did not mean that it was merely "a fiction, unless you declare all results of thought to be fictions because reality corresponds to them only in a roundabout way and then only asymptotically." A general rate of profit existed only approximately at any given moment, he held. If two firms had exactly the same profit rate in a given year, this was pure accident. In reality, profit rates varied with different circumstances from business to business and year to year. A general rate existed only as an average of many businesses and a series of years. If we demanded that the profit rate be exactly the same, up to the hundredth decimal place, in every business, we would, Engels held, grossly misconstrue the nature of the profit rate and of economic laws in general. "They all have no other reality than in the approximation, the tendency, on average but not in *direct* actuality. That comes partly from the fact that their action is intersected by the simultaneous action of other laws, but also partly from their nature as ideas."[31]

Incidentally, this particular letter shows clearly that Engels, like Marx, recognized that laws were only tendencies as well as that he shared with Marx a Hegelian emphasis on totality. Although at times both Marx and Engels acted and wrote like empiricists, neither ever completely forgot that the totality of the capitalist process was their focus and that its particular manifestations were only aspects of the larger whole.

Of more direct relevance to the topic of this chapter, the above discussion also documents clearly that neither Marx nor Engels was consistent in his theoretical formulations concerning knowledge. Both men wrote at times as if they believed in a sort of simple empiricism, a copy theory of perception, and the implications of both. The two friends at other times—and more characteristically—recognized that appearance and reality were at odds and that it required a sophisticated methodology to get at the appearance behind the reality. In short, although Marx wrote at greater length and more pointedly about epistemology and method, in all important respects his and Engels' views were in agreement.

One area where there might appear to have been a difference between them, however, as already indicated in chapter 3, was in the comparatively minor methodological point about the sequencing of economic categories in thought. Both Kain and Carver agreed on Engels' misunderstanding of Marx's conception that—to use Kain's words—"the order in which the logical method takes up and connects the categories is *not at all* the order in which they arose historically."[32] Both scholars based their comments about Engels' misunderstanding of Marx's point on Engels' review of *A Contribution to the Critique of Political Economy*, the key quotation from which has already appeared above: "The chain of thought must begin with the same thing that history begins with and its further development will be nothing but the mirror, in more ab-

stract and theoretically more consistent form, of the historical development."[33]

This passage, taken together with others discussed above, would seem
to suggest that Engels better appreciated the part that theoretical construction played in Marx's method than Kain has allowed for. That is to
say, Engels seemed to be using the metaphor of a mirror here quite loosely.
The qualifying phrase "in a more abstract and theoretically more consistent form" suggests a shaping of sense perceptions by the mind into
something more than simple reflection (see below). And as the quotations above also show, Kain simply erred in stating that Engels refused to
accept the difference between appearance and essential reality.[34] But the
last quotation cited above does seem to corroborate Engels' failure to
appreciate Marx's point about the sequencing of categories.

Even here, however, Engels betrayed an understanding of some of the
subtleties of Marx's thought processes. In the same paragraph with the
quotation about "the chain of thought," Engels said that the critique of
economics could proceed historically or logically, but because history
often developed "by leaps or bounds and in a zigzag manner," the logical
method was the only appropriate one. (He wrote this in the abstract,
without specific reference to Marx's book, but evidently he was referring
to the method Marx chose to use therein.) This logical method, however,
was "in fact nothing but the historical, only stripped of the historical
form and the accidents that interfered with a straightforward treatment,"
he wrote. Here followed "the chain of thought" quotation, after which
Engels said that the mirror in thought of historical developments would
be "a corrected mirror image, but corrected according to laws that the
real historical process itself provided, since each moment can be regarded
at its point of full ripeness, its classicism."[35] While this comment does
not quite state Marx's perception that the order of presentation of the
categories had to be changed from the order in which they actually appeared historically, it does suggest the need to regard historical development from the vantage of its "point of full ripeness" before anyone could
reach conclusions about it. This view is not significantly different from
Marx's, even though Engels' wording in one sentence seems to betray a
view almost diametrically opposed to that of his friend.

But here, appearance once again belies reality, as a passage from *Ludwig Feuerbach* shows. There, Engels wrote about historical method:
"While, however, in earlier periods the investigation of these motive forces
behind history was almost impossible—because of the complicated and
hidden connections with their effects—our present period has so far

simplified these connections that the riddle can be solved." He went on to discuss the breakthrough of large industry and said that, at least since the peace of 1815, it was no longer a secret to anyone in England that the entire political struggle revolved around the claims to power of two classes—the landed aristocracy and the middle class. In France the same fact came into people's consciousness with the return of the Bourbons.

The historians of the Restoration—from Thierry to Guizot and Mignet to Thiers—pointed to this as the key to understanding French history since the Middle Ages. Moreover, since 1830 a third element in the political struggles in both countries had been the working class. Relations had become so simple that a person had to close his eyes deliberately not to see the struggle of these three classes and the conflicts in their interests as the driving force behind modern history—at least in the two most progressive countries.[36]

Here, Engels clearly showed a full appreciation for the point Marx made about the order in which the logical method took up and connected the categories being different from their historical order, or—to use the phraseology of *Capital* quoted above—that "scientific analysis" generally went "the opposite way from real developments." It began "after the fact and therefore with the completed results of the process of development." Once again, Marx and Engels were in essential agreement despite individual passages from Engels' writings that seem to suggest the contrary.

That point having been made, it is important to add that none of this was fundamental to Marx and Engels' thought taken as a whole. Although these points about epistemology and method were significant in their own way, as Marx wrote in the eleventh thesis on Feuerbach (1845): "Philosophers have only *interpreted* the world in different ways; what matters is to *change* it."[37] Although Engels never made this point in so explicit a fashion, it was implicit in much of what he wrote and did from the drafting of "Principles of Communism" through his counseling of the worker movements of Europe during the last years of his life. It is often forgotten, moreover, that it was Engels who first published the "Theses on Feuerbach" as an appendix to the revised edition of *Ludwig Feuerbach* in 1888. In the preface to that edition, he said that although the theses were not intended for publication, being quickly written down as mere notes for further revision, they were "priceless as the first document in which the ingenious origin of the new world view" was written down.[38]

Both men, of course, believed it was important to understand the world in order to make intelligent decisions about how to participate in changing it (see below, especially chapters 6 and 7). The entire course of their lives, their criticisms of various working-class platforms and programs, and the nature of their writings testify eloquently to that. But neither ever doubted that what did really matter was not just interpreting the world—although they did plenty of that—but contributing to the birth pangs of a new and better system, although of course, one that would develop in the womb of the existing one.

More tangentially connected to all of this is the relationship of Marx and Engels to Hegel. That is much too large and complex a topic to be treated in any detail here, but some further discussion is certainly called for. According to Seigel, who once again provides a good commentary with which to begin such a discussion, the mature "Marx's approach to economics . . . did not begin with analysis of empirical data but with abstractions evolved by economic theory." Seigel quoted Marx from the introduction to the *Grundrisse*: "The abstract determinations lead toward a reproduction of the concrete by way of thought," and went on to note that this method Marx described was also Hegel's. In Marx's view, however, "Hegel fell into the illusion of conceiving the real as the product of thought concentrating itself, probing its own depths, and unfolding out of itself, whereas the method of rising from the abstract to the concrete is only the way in which thought appropriates the concrete, reproduces the concrete in the mind. But this is by no means the process by which the concrete comes into being."[39]

As we have just seen, Engels did not speak of "rising from the abstract to the concrete"; indeed, he wrote about abstracting principles from observations of nature and history as if he were almost a pure empiricist. But a careful reading of his comments shows his little-appreciated understanding of the overall role theoretical paradigms played in the thought process. In both the introduction to *Anti-Dühring* and his comments to Conrad Schmidt, Engels once again expressed views very close to those of Marx without using his precise wording.

Both men were strongly influenced in their thinking by Hegel's ideas. Both stressed the Hegelian notion of totality, of the interrelatedness of parts to one another and to the whole, in their writings. However much they distanced themselves from what they regarded as Hegel's idealism, both also acknowledged, either explicitly or by implication, their debt to him and his ideas. Marx, for example, wrote to Engels on 16 January 1858: "In the *method* of treatment [of the issue of profit in *A Contribution to the Critique of Political Economy*, which appeared the following year], it was a great service to me that by mere accident— Freiligrath found a few volumes of Hegel belonging originally to Bakunin and sent them to me as a present—I had skimmed through Hegel's *Logic*."[40]

Again, Engels seems not to have made a precisely comparable comment about Hegel's influence on his method of treatment, but his writings contain numerous favorable (as well as critical) references to Hegel that leave no doubt about the philosopher's influence on him. For instance, in *Ludwig Feuerbach* he commented: "The great idea that the world is not to be conceived as a complex of ready-made *things* but rather as a complex of *processes*, in which the seemingly stable things no less than their images in our heads, the concepts, experience an unremitting variation of development and passing away, in which through all seeming accidentality and despite all momentary regression, finally a progressive development prevails—this great notion has, especially since Hegel, so fully passed into common consciousness that it scarcely finds any more contradiction in the general public."[41] Similarly, in the preface to the 1870 edition of *The German Peasant War*, Engels stated: "Without the previous appearance of German philosophy, especially Hegel, German scientific socialism . . . would never have come into existence."[42]

But more important than such references to Hegel were the examples of both Marx's and Engels' use of his terminology and method in their writings. Apart from the instances already noted above in this chapter, it would be possible to provide many others. But the writings of scholars like Jean Hyppolite, Iring Fetscher, and Michel Henry make it unnecessary to give more than a couple of other illustrations of the point.[43]

As Shlomo Avineri has pointed out, Marx's thinking and form of presentation in *Capital* showed the imprint of the Hegelian dialectic and the related concept of *Aufhebung* (meaning both suppression and preservation). For example, in chapter 27 of volume 3, he wrote: "The cooperative factories of the workers themselves constitute the first breakthrough of the old [new?] form from inside the old, although they naturally reproduce and must reproduce all the failings of the existing system in their actual organization. But the opposition between capital and labor within them is abolished [*aufgehoben*], if only at first in the form of the associated workers as their own capitalist, that is, by employing the means of production to turn their own work into cash."[44]

Engels, of course, wrote much less extensively and in less detail about the development of the economy under capitalism than did Marx. He is thus much better known for his application of the dialectical method to science and nature than to economics, but even so, he used dialectical concepts with reference to the economy in *Socialism: Utopian and*

Scientific, as the following passage shows: "While the capitalist method of production increasingly transforms the great majority of the population into proletarians, it creates the forces by which this transformation, on penalty of perishing, is compelled to occur. While it increasingly compels the great associated means of production to be transformed into state property, it shows the way to complete the transformation. *The proletariat seizes state power and transforms the means of production primarily into state property.* But thereby it abolishes [*hebt auf*] all class differences and class opposition, and thereby also the state as a state."[45]

Despite such clear Hegelian influences in both men's writing and thinking, as already shown in Engels' review of Marx's *A Contribution to the Critique of Political Economy* and Marx's afterword to *Capital*, the two friends agreed in viewing Hegel as an idealist who needed to be inverted or divested of his mystification in order to rescue the rational element in his thought. According to several authorities, this view was quite mistaken. J. N. Findlay maintained against Marx that there was "as much materialism in Hegel as in Marx" and that the Hegelian absolute had as its "seat or vehicle" the "experiences and decisions of particular conscious persons."[46] David MacGregor similarly held that Marx and many other critics were wrong in understanding Spirit (*Geist*) as a "suprahistorical, supra-individual" force that achieved self-realization in history. Hegel had said that individuals were ends in themselves, and the "crowning element" in his system was the "rational human individual as his or her capabilities and abilities . . . developed through work and practical action in society." According to MacGregor, "the dialectics of labour and the concept of the social individual" were "vital components of Hegel's social and political thought," just as they were in Marx's.[47]

According to John Maguire, there was "no topic in any part of Hegel's system" that he saw "as arising from any other source than man's own activity." Hegel, he said, used the concept of spirit to explain the actions of men. It was not a "superhuman process" that lived their lives for them. So strong was "Hegel's emphasis on *man* as the maker of history that it is still a matter of controversy whether he recognized the existence of any being outside man, such as God."[48]

Thus, it would appear that although both Marx and Engels had a deep understanding of much that Hegel wrote and were considerably influenced by him in their methodology, they misinterpreted him on a fundamental point—his supposedly uncompromising idealism. But even here, the important thing to notice so far as the thesis of this book is concerned is not whether they were right or wrong—a matter that is subject to debate in any event; it is rather the fact that even where they may have been wrong, they agreed with each other.

CHAPTER VI

Engels' Alleged Reformism

It has become common for scholars to consider Engels as the first revisionist of Marx's ideas. Most of them have meant this in the generic sense that he changed some of Marx's conceptions, but a few of them have also accused him of being a revisionist in the narrower sense that he foreshadowed the reformist sort of revisionism espoused by Eduard Bernstein in the years immediately following Engels' death. (Bernstein had argued that the working class could accede to political power by extending its political and economic rights within the existing state rather than overthrowing it.)[1] Lichtheim, for example, asserted that "Engels had already reformulated the revolutionary credo of 1843–8 in a manner conducive to interpretations which brought it much closer to positivism and its political corollary, democratic reformism."[2]

Similarly, Charles Elliott (referring to Engels' 1895 preface to Marx's *The Class Struggles in France*) underlined the "serious doubts of Engels about the entire nature of the class state and the need for violent revolution." These doubts, he asserted, "set the stage for 'Revisionism'"[3] To be sure, Elliott prefaced these words with a discussion of Engels' angry complaints that Liebknecht had removed "essential reservations" from the text when he published it in *Vorwärts*—reservations that in fact never saw the light of day until the publication in 1924 of the uncensored preface. (Thus, one would think, the revisionist impact of the censored preface was hardly Engels' fault.) Despite this, Elliott concluded: "It would seem that Engels' anger was not directed at any real distortion, but rather at the uncomfortable realization that, aside from a few minor modifications (those which Liebknecht had eliminated [introduced?]), his (Engels') own position was precisely that which he and Marx had denounced over the course of many years."[4]

Elliott recognized that "Marx and Engels bequeathed a highly ambivalent legacy, full of many diverse and contradictory elements." He mentioned that Marx's 1872 address in Amsterdam (on which, see below), his preface to *A Contribution to the Critique of Political Economy*, and his joint preface (with Engels) to the 1872 edition of the *Communist Manifesto* all became texts for revisionists.[5] But he did not follow these statements up with what might seem a logical conclusion, that Marx, like Engels, showed a "trend toward Social Democracy."[6]

Despite this seeming inconsistency on the part of Elliott, what his argument does have the merit of pointing out, if perhaps somewhat inadvertently, is that the truth about Engels' alleged revisionism and its relation to Marx's own statements relevant to this issue is quite complex. As already noted in chapter 4, Engels' "Principles of Communism" expressed a seemingly reluctant acceptance of revolution as something forced upon the proletariat, whereas the *Communist Manifesto* displayed much more enthusiasm for the revolutionary cause, with its emphasis on the need for a "forcible overthrow of all prevailing social arrangements." Was this possibly an early indication of Engels' greater predisposition toward a peaceful transition to proletarian rule à la Bernstein? Or was it merely a tactical concession to the ideas of the former League of the Just that Engels himself was eager to expunge from the final document? In the absence of more evidence than has yet come to light about the composition of the two drafts of the *Communist Manifesto*, only an examination of the other writings of Engels and Marx on the subject of revolution can suggest an answer to these questions.

One of the *loci classici* of Lichtheim's "revolutionary credo of 1843–8" was *The German Ideology*, where Marx and Engels had written: "Revolution is necessary, therefore, not only because the *ruling* class cannot be overthrown in any other way, but also because the class *overthrowing* it can only in a revolution succeed in ridding itself of all the muck of ages and become fitted to found society anew."[7] Here, the two men expressed an unambiguous belief that revolution was unavoidable if the new society was to come into being.

In August 1852, in one of a series of articles published under Marx's by-line in the *New-York Daily Tribune* but written by Engels, the latter expressed continued support for the idea of revolution but also reflected the sober experiences of the failed revolution of 1848–1849: "Now, insurrection is an art quite as much as any other, and subject to certain rules of proceeding, which, when neglected, will produce the ruin of the party neglecting them." These rules were "plain and simple":

> Firstly, never play with insurrection unless you are fully prepared to face the consequences of your play. Insurrection is a calculus with

very definite magnitudes, the value of which may change every day; the forces opposed to you have all the advantages of organization, discipline and habitual authority; unless you bring strong odds against them, you are defeated and ruined. Secondly, the insurrectionary career once entered upon, act with the greatest determination, and on the offensive. The defensive is the death of every armed rising; it is lost before it measures itself with its enemies. Surprise your antagonists while their forces are scattering, prepare new successes, however small but daily; keep up the moral ascendant which the first successful rising has given you; rally thus those vacillating elements to your side which always follow the strongest impulse, and which always look out for the safer side; force your enemies to retreat before they can collect their strength against you; in the words of Danton, the greatest master of revolutionary policy yet known: *de l'audace, de l'audace, encore de l'audace!*[8]

Somewhat more ambiguous with regard to the question of Engels' possible revisionism was a speech he gave at a session of the London Conference of the International Working Men's Association on 21 September 1871. He directed the speech against Bakunin and the anarchists, who opposed political action within the framework of existing states. "We want the abolition of classes," Engels said. "What is the means to achieve this? The political rule of the proletariat. And now, when everyone is united on that point, some people demand that we not get involved in politics!" Such abstentionists, he went on, called themselves revolutionaries. "Revolution, however, is the most extreme act of politics, and those who support it must also support the means—the political action that prepares the revolution, that trains the workers for the revolution." The workers had to form a party independent of the middle-class parties and pursue their own goals.

"Political freedoms, rights of assembly and association, freedom of the press—those are our weapons," Engels said; "should we fold our arms and practice abstention when others would take them away from us? Some people claim that every political action constitutes recognition of the existing arrangement. But when the existing arrangement gives us the means to protest against it, the use of these means is not an acceptance of the *status quo.*"[9]

This was by no stretch of the imagination a revisionist statement, but some interpreters might be tempted to see it as a step in the direction of revisionism. By accepting the use of political freedoms as a means of preparing for the revolution, Engels might have been walking down the primrose path leading to reformism. If so, however, Marx was leading the way.

In a speech delivered at the London conference the day before Engels', Marx said: "One ought by no means to believe that it is of little importance to have workers in parliament." When people like Bebel and Liebknecht (founders of the Social Democratic Labor party in Germany) could speak before the legislature, the whole world listened. "The governments are inimically disposed towards us; we must answer them with all the means available to us. Electing workers to parliament is equivalent to a victory over the governments, but it is necessary to select the right men."[10] In another speech the following day, Marx said further: "We must declare to the governments: we know that you are the armed powers directed against the proletariat; we will proceed against you peacefully where possible and by force of arms if necessary."[11]

As in the case of Engels' speech, these statements are not revisionist, but they do envision the use of peaceful means to promote communist goals. Moreover, they were followed a scant year later by Marx's famous speech in Amsterdam after the Hague congress of the International. As reported in *La liberté*, Marx commented that a group had formed in the International that urged the workers not to take part in political activities. We have taken it to be our duty, he said, to declare how dangerous and disastrous such principles seem for our movement. The workers have to seize political power someday, in order to set up the new organization of work, he went on. This involved overthrowing the old politics.

But we have not maintained, Marx asserted, that the path to this goal is everywhere the same. "We do not deny that there are countries, like America, England, and if I knew your institutions better I would perhaps add Holland, where the workers can achieve their goals through peaceful means." On the other hand, in most of the countries on the Continent, force was necessary to bring about the rule of labor.[12]

Here again, Marx was not preaching unadulterated reformism. He recognized two—possibly three—countries where the workers could achieve their goals peacefully. Had he lived to witness the growing popular strength of the Social Democrats in Germany during the late 1880s and early 1890s, as Engels did, he would probably have added Germany to the list. But he also noted that in most places in Europe, a violent revolution would be required to achieve the goals of the workers. The question to be answered here is whether Engels ever departed from this basic position. Up until 1872, his statements on the subject of the necessity for violent revolution were fundamentally in line with Marx's. If in 1847 he had seemed to be leaning further toward a revisionist position than Marx, in 1871–1872 it was Marx who, without abandoning an insistence on the need for revolution in many countries, appeared the more revisionist of the two.

Certainly, one place where Engels adhered strictly to the Marxian legacy in this regard was his preface to the first English translation of *Capital*, volume 1. Writing in 1886, he said that Marx's theory was "the result of a life-long study of the economic history and conditions in England." The work, he went on, "led to the conclusion that, at least in Europe, England is the only country where the inevitable social revolution might be effected entirely by peaceful and legal means. He [Marx] certainly never forgot to add that he hardly expected the English ruling classes to submit, without a 'pro-slavery rebellion' to the peaceful and legal revolution."[13] As a matter of fact, Marx evidently had forgotten to add this caveat to his Amsterdam speech, so in the preface Engels actually strengthened the revolutionary thrust of Marx's speech, where it was present but to a lesser degree than Engels intimated.

But what about Engels' statements in the 1890s? In a letter to Liebknecht of 9 March 1890, he congratulated the Social Democratic leader for receiving the largest number of votes of any candidate in the recent elections and noted the popular success of the party, which had outpolled all the others for the first time (although because of the way the districts were laid out, this translated into only a third as many seats as the Catholic Center party won). Engels predicted that in three years the Social Democrats could "have" the votes of the workers on the land, and then they would "have the core regiments of the Prussian army." The only way Bismarck and Emperor Wilhelm II could prevent this was by force of arms and the imposition of martial law.

"We must prevent that," Engels said. The party had to be careful not to hinder its enemies from doing its work. "I am, therefore, in that regard of your opinion that *for now* [Engels' emphasis] we must proceed as peaceably and as legally as possible and shun every pretext for a collision." Thus far, except for the italicized words, Engels' comments seem eminently reformist. To them, however, he added: "To be sure, I hold your philippics against [the use of] force, in every form and under all circumstances, to be inappropriate—first because no enemy believes them (they are not that foolish); and second, because Marx and I were anarchists according to your theory, since we were never disposed to proffer the left cheek if someone hit us on the right. This time you have certainly gone too far."[14] In other words, while Engels certainly supported peaceful, parliamentary tactics under the particular circumstances prevailing at the moment, he decidedly did not rule out the use of force under other circumstances. This was simply good tactics and was perfectly in accord with Marx's prescription at the London conference almost twenty years before.

More reformist in spirit was Engels' September 1890 farewell letter to the readers of the *Social Democrat*, the German Social Democratic party organ that it had published from abroad during the twelve years of the Anti-Socialist Law (when the party could not legally exist in Germany, although individual Social Democratic candidates continued to campaign and to be elected to the Reichstag). Engels noted that the party could now use legal means in its struggle, but only so long as the opposing party did likewise. If the latter sought—through new exceptional laws, through illegal judgments and court practices, through arbitrary acts by the police, or through various illegal infringements by the executive—to deprive the party of its common rights, it would drive the Social Democrats once more to resort to illegal means. Even the English, the people who loved legal means the most of all, held that the first condition for the observance of legality by the people was that all other "power agencies" did likewise. If they did not, according to English legal tradition, rebellion was the first duty of citizenship.

But if this happened, would the party build barricades and appeal to the force of arms? Certainly not, Engels answered. "Against that the knowledge of its own political power preserves it—political power that each general Reichstag election gives it. Twenty percent of the votes cast is a highly respectable number, but it also means that the opposing parties together still won 80 percent of the votes." Yet the Social Democratic vote had doubled in the last three years, Engels said, and the party could count on still greater growth in the next election (an inaccurate prediction, as it turned out, although the number of votes for the Social Democrats did double again by 1903 and still another time by 1912). In such a circumstance, the party would have "to be crazy, today with twenty against eighty, and against the army as well, to seek a putsch whose certain result would be the loss of all the political power achieved in the past twenty-five years." It had a much better, tried and true expedient. As soon as civil rights were denied it, it could start publishing the *Social Democrat* again. If that happened, "one thing is certain: the German Empire cannot hold out a second time for twelve years."[15]

Here, one might argue, Engels was establishing a new reformist precedent. Marx had held out the prospect of the workers achieving their goals through peaceful—meaning parliamentary—means, but he had never suggested that could happen in Germany. On the other hand, as noted above, he also had not lived to witness the degree of success the Social Democrats achieved in the 1890 elections. In the last election before Marx's death, the popular vote for the Social Democrats had declined significantly and showed no promise of the phenomenal growth that occurred in subsequent elections. There seems little reason to doubt that had he lived as long as Engels did he would have seconded Engels' advice to the party.

Moreover, Engels was not arguing here for reliance on parliamentary means to the exclusion of all others. He envisioned a return to illegal methods if necessary. He was merely advocating avoidance of an armed uprising when the workers still had not achieved the support of a majority of the population and when they would have to face an army equipped with superior weapons. Marx, too, had fulminated against premature putsches when conditions were not ripe for revolution.[16] So once again, Engels' advice against an armed rising at this particular time in Germany was in line with the spirit of Marx's thinking.

The complexity of Engels' relationship to reformism appears in his criticism of the Social Democratic party's draft (Erfurt) program, which he wrote toward the end of June 1891. There he took issue with the "opportunism" that he saw as prevalent in party newspapers. The opportunists held that the existing society would develop into a socialist one without asking if, in the process, it did not have to burst the framework of the old social conditions forcibly the way a crab did its old shell, he said. "One can suppose," he conceded, "that the old society could peacefully develop into the new in countries where the representation of the people concentrated all power in itself, where a person could do constitutionally whatever was desired once a majority of the people supported it: in democratic republics like France and America, in monarchies like England . . . where the dynasty was powerless against the popular will." But to proclaim such ideas in Germany, where the government was almost all-powerful and the Reichstag and other representative bodies were without real power, was to remove the fig leaf from absolutism and tie oneself to its nakedness.

This sacrifice of the future of the movement in favor of momentary success, Engels said, might be honorably intended, but it remained opportunism. And honorable opportunism was perhaps the most dangerous kind of all. The party and the worker class could only come to power under the form of the democratic republic. This was the specific form of the dictatorship of the proletariat, as the great French Revolution had shown.

Now in Germany, he wrote, it did not seem legally possible to put a demand for a republic directly into the party program, although it had been permissible under Louis-Philippe in France and was so in contemporary Italy. But the very fact that it was not permissible in Germany showed how colossal an illusion it was to believe that the party could peacefully establish a republic there, and not only a republic but a communist society. What the party could and should demand, in Engels' view, was "the *concentration of all political power in the hands of the people's representatives.*"[17]

Here—exactly in line with Marx's earlier pronouncements—Engels seemed even more negative about the prospects for a peaceful achievement of the party's goals in Germany than he had been a year before. But what about the statement that the democratic republic was the specific form of the dictatorship of the proletariat? First of all, this statement by itself is misleading unless compared with comments Engels made only three months earlier in his 1891 introduction to Marx's *The Civil War in France*. There he had repeated the familiar Marxian utterance that the state was nothing but a machine for the suppression of one class by another. This was no less true, he said, in a democratic republic than in a monarchy. Even in the best case, it would therefore be an evil that the victorious proletariat had inherited. Like the Paris Commune of 1871, it would have to reduce democracy's worst aspects as much as possible until a generation brought up in new, free social circumstances would be in a position to abolish all the rubbish of the state. Engels followed this with the famous pronouncement that the term "dictatorship of the proletariat" that so frightened the German philistines was exemplified by the Paris Commune. (His actual words were: "Look at the Paris Commune. That was the dictatorship of the proletariat.")[18]

Earlier in the introduction, Engels had said that the Commune consisted of a majority of Blanquists. He noted the irony that although Blanquists preached strong, dictatorial centralization in the hands of a revolutionary government, the Commune had urged a free federation of all French communes with Paris. The Commune had to recognize that the working class, once come to power, could not continue on with the old, centralized power of the state machinery, which had suppressed it. It declared its own representatives and officials to be removable. This, together with election by universal suffrage, ensured that unlike all previous governments, the new state and its agencies would not transform themselves from servants of society into its rulers. The provision that all public servants receive the same wages as workers promoted the same basic goal. Engels noted that Marx had portrayed this democratic state power at length in the third part of *The Civil War in France*.[19]

There Marx had indeed admiringly described the democratic practices of the Commune in exactly the spirit of Engels' comments in his later introduction. He stated that the working class could not simply take over the machinery of the state and use it for its own ends. Thus, the Commune was the direct opposite of the Second Empire. It was a republic that tried to abolish class rule. It was democratic, with responsible and removable officials. These officials received worker wages, and so forth. Marx stopped short of calling the Commune the dictatorship of the proletariat, but he did write that "it was essentially a *government of the worker class*, the result of the struggle of the producing against the appropriating class, the finally discovered form under which the economic liberation of work could complete itself."[20] Surely this was in essence what he elsewhere referred to as the dictatorship of the proletariat.[21] Once again Marx and Engels would appear to have been is essential agreement.

Further support for the notion that Marx believed the transitional revolutionary government had to have a broad basis of popular support comes from his conspectus on Bakunin's book *Statism and Anarchy*. Marx wrote this in 1874 and the beginning of 1875. In it he commented, among other things, that a radical social revolution was only possible when, alongside capitalist production, the industrial proletariat occupied an important place in the mass of the people. If it was to have any chance for victory, it had to be at least capable of doing as much for the peasants as the French bourgeoisie had done during its revolution.[22] In short, it had to garner peasant support in addition to that of its own large class by granting to the small landholders considerable concessions to their economic interests.

Similarly, in 1848 Marx had reacted to a speech by Wilhelm Weitling in which the latter had said that democracy then would lead to chaos and that what the times required was a "dictatorship of those with the most insight." Marx argued conversely that a dictatorship was not the solution to political difficulties; rather, the solution lay in a "democratic government composed of the most heterogeneous elements."[23] Recall also that in the *Communist Manifesto*, Marx had spoken of "the forcible establishment of democracy." This would result in "despotic inroads into property rights," but apparently only on the basis of majoritarian support for such inroads.[24]

Engels, likewise, did not maintain that the transitional revolution would be without repressive features. In a letter to August Bebel written between 18 and 28 March 1875, Engels complained about the Social Democratic party's draft Gotha Program. As Marx did later in his more famous "Critique of the Gotha Program," Engels rejected the term "free people's state." He noted the *Communist Manifesto*'s assertion that with the introduction of socialism, the state would dissolve itself and disappear. It was therefore a transitory institution that would be used in the revolution forcibly to suppress class enemies. So it was pure nonsense to speak of a free people's state. As long as the proletariat still used the state, it did so not in the interests of freedom but for the suppression of its enemies. As soon as it was possible to speak of freedom, the state as such ceased to exist.[25]

To return more directly to the issue of revisionism, however, what about Elliott's contention that Engels' 1895 introduction to Marx's *The Class Struggles in France* was basically revisionist even before the German Social Democratic party leadership asked him to delete various phrases from it? The first point to be noted in this connection is that Elliott did not provide all the details of the circumstances surrounding the publication of this introduction (*Einleitung*) or preface, as he translated the German. A letter from Richard Fischer to Engels of 6 March 1895 shows that the executive committee of the Social Democratic party emphatically requested that Engels soften what it regarded as the too revolutionary tone of the introduction. The committee's justification for this request was an impending new anti-socialist law. The government had introduced a bill directed against the socialists in December 1894—a bill that the Reichstag did not reject until May 1895.[26]

Engels replied to Fischer on 8 March: "I have yielded to your serious misgivings as much as possible, although with the best will I cannot understand about half of the concerns. I still cannot accept that you intend to pledge yourselves body and soul to absolute legality, legality under all circumstances, legality even in the face of laws broken by their authors—in short, the politics of proffering the left cheek to whoever has struck you on the right. . . . I'm of the opinion that you win nothing when you preach the absolute renunciation of striking hard." No one would believe such a proclamation, "and *no* party anywhere goes so far as to renounce armed opposition to illegality."

Engels added that he had to consider foreign readers of his writings, before whom he could not compromise himself as much as Fischer requested. Thus, he had accepted most of Fischer's changes but had done so with a few notable exceptions. At one place in the introduction, for example, Engels had noted that modern weaponry had changed not only warfare but conditions for the class struggle. "The time of surprise attacks, of revolutions perpetrated by small, cognizant minorities at the head of unconscious masses is over," Engels asserted. "Where it is a question of a complete transformation of the social organization, the masses must be involved and have understood in advance what is involved that they support with life and limb." Engels did not accept Fischer's unspecified rewording of the last sentence, but did agree to remove the words "with life and limb."

In the following paragraph, Engels had originally written that in the Mediterranean countries, people had increasingly realized that the old tactics had to be revised. Everywhere, they had imitated the German tactic of using the ballot box, of conquering all outposts available to them; everywhere, "the unprepared attack" had receded to the background. Fischer had evidently proposed to revise the last clause by replacing the word *attack*, but Engels said it was a catchword used in both France and Italy. He agreed instead to remove the entire clause with those words in it, making the passage appear much more revisionist than he had originally intended it to be.

Another change Engels agreed to had a similar but less significant effect. He had written: "The Social Democratic revolution, which lives at the moment by accepting the laws, can only come about through a revolution by the party of order, which cannot persist without breaking the laws." Fischer wanted him to remove the words "at the moment" (one word in German: *angeblich*). Engels refused because he said that would "change a momentary into a lasting, a relative into an absolutely valid tactic." Instead, he changed "which lived at the moment" to "which now prospered."

He went on to say to Fischer that the party needed to consider the duty to obey the law as a juridical, not a moral obligation—one that ended when the authorities themselves broke the law. That was what the Catholics had done under the May Laws (exceptional laws against the Catholic church in Germany during the *Kulturkampf* of the mid-1870s), for example. The Social Democrats needed to make clear to the government that they waited only while the army remained only partially contaminated by an infiltration of Social Democrats into its ranks, Engels suggested. Who knew, he asked, how soon the time would return when people had to be serious about abolishing the tactic of legality? It ought to be pursued only so long as it suited the movement, Engels concluded, but not "at any price, even in our words" (as distinguished from actions).[27]

This clearly was not revisionist language, but what about the remainder of Engels' introduction, both before and after he had allowed it to be revised by the party leadership? In it, he noted that the *Communist Manifesto* had proclaimed the fight for general suffrage, for democracy, to be one of the most important duties of the valiant proletariat. When Bismarck introduced it, the workers sent August Bebel to the Constituent Reichstag. Since then, they had used their suffrage in a manner that served as a model to the workers of other countries.[28]

The bourgeoisie and the government had come to fear the legal more than the illegal actions of the worker party—the results of elections more than rebellion, Engels wrote. Street fighting with barricades became largely obsolete. In this matter, there should be no illusions. A true victory over the army in street fighting was a rarity. The troops might be mellowed by moral influences. Otherwise, the military had the advantage of training, weapons, and so on. Thus, it was no wonder that in Paris in June 1848, Vienna in October 1848, and Dresden in May 1849, the army won. Earlier, in Paris during July 1830 and February 1848 and in most of the Spanish street fighting, a militia had stood between the military and the intransigents. It had either sided with the uprising or aided it by indecisive behavior. In all cases, victory came to the insurgents because the troops declined to fight or because their leaders either could not or would not act.[29]

Even in the classic period of street fighting, the barricades were more effective morally than materially, Engels stated. They were a means of reducing the tenacity of the military. If they held out until this occurred, victory followed; if not, defeat was the result. Engels concluded this analysis with a sentence that the party leadership removed from the printed introduction: "This is the key point to keep in mind in analyzing any future possibilities for street fighting"[30]—a sentence clearly showing that, despite his pessimistic but realistic comments about revolution (comments that Marx certainly would have seconded), Engels was not a revisionist. He obviously foresaw some potential circumstances in which the party might resort to armed uprising. The sentence's removal from the published text, however, made his analysis appear revisionist.

Engels went on to expound further the advantages that had accrued to the military since 1848. Paris and Berlin had experienced fourfold growth, but their garrisons had expanded even more than that. Railroads allowed them further to increase in size rapidly. These larger concentrations of troops had incomparably more effective arms than before. In 1848 they carried smooth-bored muzzle loaders; now, small-calibered breech loaders with magazines, which fired four times as far, ten times as accurately, and also ten times as quickly. Then, the artillery had only round shot and grape-shot; now, percussion shells, one of which sufficed to demolish the best barricades. Then, the army had only the pickaxe of the pioneer to break through fireproof walls; today, the explosive shell.

On the insurgents' side, however, conditions had worsened. Even an uprising with which all social classes sympathized could hardly succeed. But in a class struggle the middle strata of society would not support the proletariat so strongly that the party of reaction would disappear. Even if numerous trained soldiers supported the uprising, arming them with proper weapons would be difficult. Also, the new, wide and straight streets in the big cities were as if made for the new artillery and rifles.

This continued pessimistic appraisal of the chances for a successful revolution—reflecting Engels' long and fruitful study of the military art—remained in the version of the introduction published in 1895. The paragraph that followed it in Engels' original manuscript, however, did not. There, Engels had asked if the developments he had described meant that street fighting would play no role in the future. "Absolutely not," he responded. A future street fight could lead to victory for the proletariat only when the developments unfavorable to the insurgents were counterbalanced by other factors. Thus, street fighting would less frequently appear at the beginning of a great revolution than at its subsequent stages, and it had to be undertaken only from a position of greater strength. The revolutionaries would then prefer open attacks to barricade tactics.[31]

Here again, Engels obviously had not become a revisionist who supported only parliamentary means for achieving socialist ends. Rightly or wrongly, he clearly foresaw a need for the use of force at some point in the revolution, which evidently might begin in a legal, even a parliamentary manner. Once more, however, the fears of party leaders in Germany emasculated his text and made him appear to be revisionist when he was not.

Even despite Fischer and company, however, some traces of the true Engels did appear in the published version of his introduction. After mentioning the point discussed above about the Mediterranean countries imitating the German example of using the ballot box, he wrote:

"Self-evidently, our foreign comrades do not renounce their right to revolution. The right to revolt is after all the only *really* 'historical right,' the only one upon which all modern states without exception rest. This includes Mecklenberg, whose revolution by the nobility ended in 1755 with the 'hereditary arrangement' [*Erbvergleich*][32]—the glorious charter of feudalism that is still in effect today."[33]

Whatever might happen in other lands, Engels went on, German social democracy had a special position by virtue of its two and a quarter million voters. Its principal duty—and here we return to the bowdlerization of Engels' text by Fischer and the others—was to keep the growth of the Social Democratic electorate in being until it became too much for the existing system of government. To this, by itself seemingly reformist sentence, Engels had originally added an elaborative clause that the party leadership expurgated. It qualified the growth of the Social Democratic electorate by calling it "this daily intensifying mass of power" (*Gewalt*, which also means force, violence, might, authority, and dominion) that the party should not fritter away in small skirmishes by the advance guard but hold intact until the day of decision.[34]

Further in the same paragraph, the party again eliminated a similar clause emphasizing the struggle that, in Engels' view, lay ahead. Engels wrote that all of the repeating rifles in Europe and America were inadequate to kill off ("aus der Welt schiessen") a party counting its voters in the millions. But, he said, an armed confrontation with the military would retard the party's normal development. In the long run, the ill effects of such a confrontation would be repaired. But "the mass of power would perhaps not be available at the critical moment, the decisive struggle would be delayed, protracted, and attended by heavy sacrifices." Here, the party removed the clause beginning with "the mass of power" and replaced the words "decisive struggle" in the next clause with "decision."[35]

No doubt unwisely, Engels had agreed to these changes. On 30 March, however, *Vorwärts*, the Social Democratic party newspaper edited by Liebknecht, published an editorial entitled "How One Values Revolution Today." This quoted passages from Engels' introduction.[36] On 1 April, Engels read this article and complained in a letter to Karl Kautsky, then editor of the *Neue Zeit* (The New Times, or Modern Age), another, more theoretical party paper: "To my astonishment I see today in *Vorwärts* an extract from my 'Introduction,' *printed without my knowledge* and chosen in such a way as to make me appear a peace-loving worshiper of legality under all circumstances. I am all the more desirous that the entire piece appear in the *Neue Zeit* so that this slanderous impression

may be effaced. I will express my opinion about this very decidedly to
Liebknecht and anyone else who . . . has given him this occasion to dis-
tort my views, and that without saying a word about it to me."[37]

Two days later, Engels wrote to Paul Lafargue in a similar vein but with
other details:

> Liebknecht has played a really nasty trick on me. He has taken ev-
> erything from my introduction to Marx's article about France from
> 1848 to 1850 that could serve him in shoring up tactics of peace at
> any price and disavowal of any application of force—tactics that he
> has for some time been inclined to preach, especially now when the
> government in Berlin is preparing an exceptional law. I, however,
> support this tactic only for *Germany today*, and then still *with con-
> siderable reservations*. For France, Belgium, Italy, Austria these tac-
> tics are not appropriate in their entirety, and for Germany they can
> already become inapplicable tomorrow. Please, therefore, await the
> complete article before you judge. . . . It is regrettable that Liebknecht
> can see only black or white. Nuances do not exist for him.[38]

Obviously, Engels' position here was in no sense revisionist. It is easy
to see why at the time this misleading article and the bowdlerized introduction caused some people to regard Engels as supporting a revisionist
position, but his original text in its entirety, together with the letters
to Kautsky and Lafargue, show that he was neither reformist nor at odds
with the position that Marx had outlined in the 1870s. As he wrote
to Laura Lafargue on 28 March 1895 (before finding out about the ex-
tracts that appeared in the *Vorwärts* editorial), his text "had suffered
somewhat from the, as I think, exaggerated desires of our Berlin friends
not to say anything which might be used as a means to assist in passing
the Coercion Bill in the Reichstag. Under the circumstances, I had to
give way."[39]

Further support for the position that Engels was not a reformist in his
last years comes from a letter he wrote to Kautsky on 3 November 1893.
"You say yourself," he asserted, that "barricades are obsolete (they can,
however, become serviceable again as soon as the army is ⅓–⅖ socialist and therefore inclined to give in), but the political strike must either
immediately win—purely through the threat . . . —or end in a colossal
disgrace or finally *lead directly to the barricades*." Even here, however,
Engels did not advise a general strike everywhere. He did not think it
likely to succeed in Austria, for example, because industry was relatively weak, the large cities were not numerous or close together, the

nationalities were hostile to one another, and the socialists constituted less than 10% of the population.[40]

A letter to Paul Lafargue almost a year earlier displays the same nuanced and well-informed but by no means revisionist thinking. Engels said the ballot box was slower and more tedious than the call to revolution but ten times surer. More importantly, it showed "with absolute exactitude the day on which one must take up arms for the revolution." It was ten to one that general suffrage, used cleverly by the workers, would force the ruling circles to abrogate legality and put the socialists in the most favorable situation for carrying out the revolution.[41]

In short, unlike Liebknecht, neither Marx nor Engels saw the world in only black and white. At different times, both men placed different emphases on the value and need for revolutionary or parliamentary tactics. Engels lived twelve years longer than Marx and adapted his position to the changed circumstances of the late 1880s and early to middle 1890s—as Marx surely would also have done had he lived that long. None of the positions Engels took after Marx's death, however, were fundamentally at variance with those Marx had supported in the 1870s. Neither man ever abandoned the idea of revolution; both, in the years after 1848, simply redefined the conditions under which it would take place.

CHAPTER VII

Humanism, Positivism, and Determinism

If Engels was not a reformist, what about the claims by many scholars that he was a positivist and determinist, unlike Marx, the humanist?[1] The problem with such labels is that Marks and Engels were much more complex thinkers than they would suggest. The writings of both men present an extreme tension between humanism and positivism. Since the humanist pronouncements of especially the young Marx are well known, there is no need to repeat them here.[2] Hence, the discussion of humanism will be restricted to pointing out the numerous instances of humanist emphasis in Engels' writings.

First, however, it would perhaps be useful to some readers to have the term defined more fully than it has been above, since the literature about Marxism uses it in a rather peculiar and restricted sense. Humanism is interchangeable in much of this literature with naturalism. According to Easton and Guddat, both terms are to be differentiated from materialism and idealism, but somehow the concept they represent unites the truth of both. They incorporate elements of subjectivity and "'the immediate' in sense perception and feeling" plus a warning against establishing society as "an abstraction over and against the individual." The two authors quoted Marx as saying that for socialists, "world history is only the creation of man through human labor and the development of nature for man." This last element appears to have been the key one for most scholars who emphasize Marx's humanism. They view Marx as stressing the role of men in the creation of history, as distinguished from impersonal forces such as nature, technology, and the operation of scientific laws. Engels, in their view, emphasized these outside forces and was therefore a determinist and a positivist.[3]

Both of these portraits are accurate to a degree but incomplete. Engels did frequently stress the role of impersonal forces in history, but he also underscored man's role in shaping his own fate. For example, in his "Outlines of a Critique of Political Economy," he wrote in a humanist spirit:

"But the economist does not know what cause he serves. He does not know that with all his egoistic reasoning he constitutes only a link in the chain of the general progress of mankind. He does not know that with the dissolution of all special interests, he paves the way for the great revolution the century is heading for, the reconciliation of mankind with nature and with itself."[4]

To be sure, in this essay as elsewhere Engels spoke of natural laws as applying to society, but as he did so with reference to crises in the trade cycle, he also wrote: "If the producers as such knew how much the consumers needed, if they organized production, if they divided it among themselves, the changes in competition and the inclination to crisis would be impossible. If they produced with consciousness, as men rather than dispersed atoms without species consciousness, they would be beyond these artificial and indefensible contradictions."[5] Thus, even though Engels wrote positivistically of natural laws dictating the trade crises, he believed that men could change the effects of these natural laws through conscious action. He even used a term, "species consciousness," that was reminiscent of much of Marx's most humanistic writing, such as the Paris manuscripts of 1844.

Of course, an important element in Marx's humanism was his acceptance of the Feuerbachian view that religion was a false projection of what was best in man onto a godhead. As Easton and Guddat expressed it, atheism for Marx implied an "affirmation of man."[6] This element of humanism was also very much present in Engels' writings and thinking. In his essay on Thomas Carlyle's *Past and Present*, written in 1844 and entitled "The Condition of England," he stated: "We want to transform [*aufheben*] the atheism as Carlyle portrays it by returning to men the ingredients they have lost through religion; not as a divine but as a human capacity, and the entire restitution limits itself simply to the awakening of self-consciousness. We want to remove all that passes for the supernatural and the superhuman. Thereby, we will eliminate dissimulation, for the pretension that the human and natural are superhuman and supernatural is the root of all falsehood and lies. For that reason, we have once and for all declared war on religion and religious conceptions."[7]

We do not need, Engels said, to call in the abstraction of a god and ascribe to it everything beautiful, great, sublime, and truly human in order to see the glory of the human condition, "in order to know the development of the species in its history, its irresistible progress, its consistently certain victory over the irrationality of the individual, . . . its hard but successful struggle with nature up to the final achievement of the free, human self-consciousness, the understanding of the unity of man with nature, and the free, spontaneous creation of a new world grounded in a pure, human, moral condition of life."[8]

Another place where the young Engels gave clear expression to his belief in the role of man in history was in one of the portions of *The Holy Family* that he wrote. There he stated: "*History* does *nothing*. It 'possesses *no* huge wealth,' it 'fights *no* battles!' It is rather *the human being*, the real, living human, who does all of that, possesses and struggles; it is not 'history' that uses people as a means to bring about *its* ends—as if it were a person; rather, history is *nothing* but the activity of people following their own ends."[9]

Lest one suppose that Engels allowed Marx unduly to influence (or to edit) what he wrote here in this joint work, the younger man expressed similar views in a speech he delivered in Elberfeld in February 1845. He said that the only way to avoid the violent and bloody overthrow of the existing social order was peacefully to introduce communism—or at least make preparations for it. People had to take actions to humanize the lot of the modern helots in the depressed lower classes. They needed to create conditions of life for all humans such that they could freely develop their human natures.[10] In this passage Engels did not juxtapose an impersonal entity, history, with individual humans, but he clearly asserted that human beings could shape the course of history by their actions.

Following the emphasis of some scholars on the later Engels' alleged revisionism of Marx's views, one might be tempted to suppose that he abandoned his youthful humanism as he grew older. In fact, he did not. In *Socialism: Utopian and Scientific*, written in early 1880, he expressed a highly humanistic vision of future society:

> With society's seizure of the means of production, commodity production ceases and with it the rule of the product over the producer. The anarchy inside social production will be replaced by a planned, conscious organization. The struggle for individual existence ceases. Thereby for the first time, man, in a certain sense, steps out of the animal kingdom, out of the animal conditions of life into the truly human. The circumference of conditions of life around human beings, which until now controlled them, now comes under their control; they become for the first time conscious, effective rulers of nature while and because they are rulers of their own socialization. The laws of their own social actions that previously operated as con-

trolling natural laws will then be employed by humans, and thereby controlled, with full, expert knowledge. Men's own socialization, which until now faced them as something forced upon them by nature and history, now will become their own free deeds. The objective, hostile powers that until now controlled history come under the control of humans themselves. From then on, for the first time, men will make their own history with full consciousness. . . . It is the leap of humankind out of the realm of necessity into the realm of freedom.[11]

Notice here, incidentally, in addition to Engels' humanistic vision of the future, his understanding of Marx's concept that under capitalism the commodity structure caused relations of people to take on the character of things in an antihumanistic fashion. At the same time, Engels clearly recognized that this situation would change when capitalism ended in such a way that the "laws" in effect in the capitalist period would no longer apply when his vision of communism emerged into reality. This view, of course, matched that of Marx who, on many occasions, had emphasized that in previous existing societies people could not choose the forces of production that formed the basis of their whole history.[12] And of course Marx, too, believed that such a restrictive situation would change with the emergence of communism.

Similarly in *Anti-Dühring*, even as Engels was writing positivistically that socially effective forces worked just like forces of nature, he added that once understood, they could be transformed by "associated producers" from "demonic rulers into willing servants. It is the difference between the destructive power of the electricity in the lightning of a storm and the tamed electricity of the telegraph and electric lighting." As the capitalist method of production increasingly converted the majority of the population into proletarians, it created the power the proletariat could use to seize state power and convert the means of production into state property. But thereby (as already quoted above from *Socialism: Utopian and Scientific* in another connection), it abolished itself as a proletariat, did away with class differences and class opposition, and abolished the state as a state.[13]

Even the unfinished *Dialectics of Nature*, Engels' most positivistic work, contains a humanistic passage: "Man is the only animal that can extricate itself from its purely bestial condition—its normal condition —[to] one adapted to his consciousness, *to be created by himself.*"[14]

Likewise, in *Ludwig Feuerbach*, Engels mixed an emphasis on "inner, hidden laws" governing history with an insistence on man's role in the process. What differentiated society from nature, he noted, was that in the former, humans followed their own goals—"nothing happens without conscious design, without intended goals," he wrote. Individual goals worked at cross purposes, however, and the effects of all the different intentions appeared to be chance but actually resulted from the hidden laws. Nevertheless, he said, "humans make their own history, however it turns out, while each follows his own, conscious, intended goals."[15] Thus, Engels even recognized a certain degree of human control over the destinies of the race under capitalism and during preceding periods of human history. This control and the freedom that would come with it would increase greatly after the proletarians ushered in communist society.

This kind of humanist emphasis comes through clearly in a retort, written in 1890 and directed against Paul Ernst, a member of the Jungen (Young Ones, an opposition group within the Social Democratic party). Engels criticized Ernst for following Dühring in claiming that Marx viewed history as occurring automatically, "without the involvement of humans (who still caused it) as if these humans were moved about like chess pieces by economic relations (which are still themselves the works of humans!)." Engels went on to say that someone else might help "a man who is capable of throwing together the misrepresentations of the Marxian theory by an enemy like Dühring with the theory itself—I give it up."[16] This brief comment shows unambiguously that Engels not only appreciated Marx's humanist emphasis but shared it.

Similarly, Engels gently criticized English novelist Margaret Harkness in 1888 because her *City Girl* was "perhaps . . . not quite realistic enough. Realism, to my mind, implies, besides the truth in detail the truthful reproduction of typical characters under typical circumstances." Her characters were typical enough but their circumstances perhaps not equally so. In *City Girl* the working class figured as "a passive mass, unable to help itself and not even making an effort at striving to help itself. . . . All attempts to drag it out of its torpid misery come from without, from above." This might have been a correct portrayal about 1800 or 1810, but not in 1887. In the latter year, "the rebellious reaction of the working class against the oppressive medium which surrounds them, their attempts—convulsive, half-conscious or conscious—at recovering their status as human beings, belong to history and must therefore lay a claim to a place in the domain of realism." (Against those who would foist on Engels the responsibility for the later narrow-mindedness of socialist realism, incidentally, be it noted that he added: "I am far from finding fault with your not having written a point-blank socialist novel, a *Tendenzroman*, as we Germans call it, to glorify the social and political views of the author. That is not at all what I mean. The more the opinions of the author remain hidden, the better the work of art.")[17]

Also at least partly humanistic was Engels' letter to Joseph Bloch of 21 September 1890. After discussing his view—which he also attributed to Marx—that the production and reproduction of life were only *"in the last instance"* the deciding factors in history and that the elements of the superstructure also played a role, he stated: "We make our history ourselves, but only under very fixed prerequisites and conditions. Among them, the economic ultimately decide. But the political, etc., indeed even the tradition rattling around in men's heads, play a role, even if not the deciding one."

From this emphasis on men's making their own history, however, Engels returned to a more deterministic and positivistic thrust, though only for history up to the point it had reached at that moment. He said that it would be laughable to explain everything in history by economic factors. On the other hand, history worked in such a way

> that the result always issues from the conflicts of many individual wills, of which each, once more, is made what it is through a number of particular life conditions; there are thus countless forces counteracting one another, an endless group of parallelograms of force out of which one resultant—the historical outcome—issues, which itself can be seen as the product of an, as a whole, *unconscious* and involuntary working power. Because what each individual wants is hindered by another, and what results is something no one desired. So develops the history until now in the fashion of a natural process, and it is also essentially subject to the same laws of movement [as a natural process].

But, Engels added, because individual wills were fused together into a common average, one should not conclude that they had no effect. "By contrast, each contributes to the resultant and is to that extent included in it."[18]

This passage illustrates the extreme tension that existed in Engels' thought between humanistic elements and positivistic/deterministic ones. Like Marx, Engels never abandoned his youthful belief in the role human beings played in making their own history. But the positivistic and deterministic element in Engels' thought was likewise present as early as his youthful essay "Outlines of a Critique of Political Economy"

—a work that Marx called a "brilliant sketch."[19] Before expressing the humanistic views quoted above, Engels said that trade crises confirmed the law of supply and demand. He even called it a natural law. But then he asked, "What shall a person think of a law that can only operate through periodic revolutions? It is in fact a natural law that rests on the unconscious of all concerned." He followed that comment by noting that if producers organized production, they could make swings in the trade cycle impossible, as quoted above.[20]

Here again, Engels was qualifying his positivism significantly, saying in effect that such natural laws applied only to the capitalist age and not to the period of communism that he believed would follow it. He was even stating that the capitalists themselves could abrogate such laws. A similar implication is present in comments later on in the essay where he called centralization of ownership (that is, the growth of big business at the expense of small shops and landholdings) a law immanent in private property. "The middle classes," he said, "must increasingly disappear, until the world is divided into millionaires and paupers, large landowners and poor day laborers." He stated that "this result must and will come unless forestalled by a total transformation of social relations, a fusion of opposed interests, an abolition of private property."[21] So here, at least, Engels' positivism and determinism contrasted significantly with the alternative path he postulated for society, in which men would have much greater control over their destinies and where deterministic laws would be notably absent.

His commentary in "The Condition of England" displayed a more unadulterated determinism, but only as it applied to the present age as distinguished from the future. "The Christian state is but the last possible form of appearance of the state in general, with whose fall the state as such must fall. The dissolution of humanity into a mass of isolated, antipathetic atoms is in itself already the abrogation of all corporative, national and indeed special interests and the last necessary stage toward the free joining together of humanity. The completion of alienation in the rule of money is an unavoidable stage if humanity, as it is about to do, is to come again to itself."[22]

An exactly parallel form of determinism is present in one of Marx's sections of *The Holy Family*. There, he noted that the abstraction of all humanity, even the appearance of humanity, was practically complete in the developed proletariat. In its conditions of life were summed up the conditions of life of today's society in their most inhuman extreme. Mankind was compelled to revolt against this inhumanity, and therefore "the proletariat can and must free itself." Marx added: "It is therefore a question of *what it* [the proletariat] *is* and what it will be compelled to do historically in conformity with its *true nature."*[23]

Similarly, in a much more famous passage from *The Poverty of Philosophy,* Marx said: "The hand mill produces a society with feudal lords; the steam mill, a society with industrial capitalists." To be sure, he went on to soften the determinism of this statement by speaking of humans shaping their social relations in accordance with their material productivity,[24] but that simply serves to highlight the point already made that Marx, like Engels, continually shifted from determinism to humanism —and vice-versa—without recognizing any sense of contradiction between the two positions as they applied to the period of capitalism. However uncomfortable some students of their thought might be with such ambiguity, Marx and Engels rightly appear to have experienced no comparable discomfort, for as they recognized, reality—which they were describing—exhibited exactly the same ambiguities and contradictions.

In 1852 in an article for the *New-York Daily Tribune,* Marx wrote about "the necessary results of modern manufacturing industry" and "the social revolution prepared by it."[25] This basically deterministic idea reappeared at much greater length in the foreword to *A Contribution to the Critique of Political Economy,* where he spoke of his earlier economic studies and then commented:

> The general result that yielded itself to me and, once obtained, served as a guide to my studies, can briefly be formulated as follows: In the social production of their lives, human beings enter into definite, necessary relations, independent of their wills, relations of production that match a fixed stage of development of their material powers of production. The entirety of these relations of production constitutes the economic structure of the society, the real basis upon which a juridical and political superstructure arises and that matches fixed social modes of consciousness. The manner of production of material life conditions the social, political, and intellectual process of life in general. It is not the consciousness of human beings that determines their being, but their social being that determines their consciousness. At a certain stage of their development the material powers of production of a society come into conflict with the existing relations of production or, what is only a juridical expression of the same thing, with the property relations within which they had previously moved. From forms of development of the pro-

ductive powers these relations turn into their fetters. Then begins an epoch of social revolutions.[26]

Not only did Marx write in this period about social determinism, however; he also wrote in a positivistic vein. In an introduction to *A Contribution to the Critique of Political Economy* that he decided not to include in the published work,[27] he stated: "Production is determined by general natural laws."[28]

This, of course, is exactly the sort of language that the dichotomists criticize Engels for using. There is no question that he did employ it. In the foreword to the third edition of *Anti-Dühring*, for example, he asserted: "In nature the same dialectical laws of motion prevail in the jumble of countless transformations that also in history govern the seeming contingency of occurrences."[29] Likewise, in the text of the work itself he made the same point: "The dialectic is, however, nothing but the science of the general laws of motion and development of nature, human society, and thought."[30]

Later in the same work, however, he gave a humanistic twist to this positivistic notion. "The socially efficacious forces operate exactly like natural forces: blindly, forcibly, destructively, so long as we do not recognize and reckon with them. But if we once have recognized them, their action, their directions, understood their operations, then it depends on us to subjugate them to our will and by means of them to reach our goals."[31]

The same humanism was at least implicit in *The Origin of the Family, Private Property and the State*, as was, again, Engels' recognition —sometimes attributed solely to Marx—that different periods operated under different economic laws. "These economic laws of commodity production change with the different stages of development of these forms of production; by and large, however, the entire period of civilization comes under their dominion," he stated. "And still today the product rules over the producer; still today the entire production of society is regulated, not by a plan developed in common, but by blind laws that make themselves valid with elemental force, in the last resort in the tempest of periodic trade crises."[32]

Elsewhere, however, Engels wrote of laws governing society without adding any hint that men could modify them or use them to their own ends. In "England in 1845 and 1885," published in *Commonwealth* on 1 March of the latter year, for example, he asserted: "The law which reduces the *value* of labour-power to the value of the necessary means of subsistence, and the other law which reduces its *average price*, as a rule, to the minimum of those means of subsistence, these laws act upon them [the workers] with the irresistible force of an automatic engine which crushes them between its wheels."[33]

Even more positivistically, in his introduction to the third edition of Marx's *The Eighteenth Brumaire of Louis Bonaparte*, also written in 1885, Engels claimed:

> It was precisely Marx who had just discovered the great law of motion of history, the law according to which all historical struggles, whether they take place in the political, religious, philosophical, or any other ideological arena, are really only the more or less clear expression of struggles involving social classes, and [which states] that the existence and thereby also the collisions of these classes once more are conditioned by the degree of development of their economic situation, by the manner of their production and their in-that-way-conditioned exchange. This law, which has the same importance for history as the law of the transformation of energy has for natural science—this law gave him here, also, the key to understanding the history of the second French Republic.[34]

The first quotation at least notes that the law operates only "as a rule." The second one has no such qualification. The points to be made in connection with such statements as this one are twofold. On the one hand, although it and others like it are clear and unambiguous by themselves, they are not—as already seen—Engels' only position on such matters. We have already looked at many of the numerous humanistic statements Engels made at various times in his life. These do not directly contradict his positivistic assertions, perhaps, but they do show a very different thrust to his thinking that is difficult to reconcile with any straightforward positivism. Late in life he also made a number of comments that strongly qualify both his positivism and the economic determinism implicit in the long quotation just cited and explicit in much else that he wrote.

For example, in a letter to Conrad Schmidt of 5 August 1890, Engels commented on some assertions attributed to the philosopher and sociologist Paul Barth by the writer Moritz Wirth. He said that while the material mode of existence may have been the *"primum agens"* (roughly, principal agent), that did not exclude the sphere of ideas from exerting "a reacting but secondary influence upon it in return." If Barth had not grasped this, he had not really understood what he wrote about the material conception of history. Of course, all of this was at second hand, and "Moritzchen" was an unfortunate friend, Engels said. But the materialist conception of history had a multitude of disciples for whom it served as a pretext for *not* studying history. Then Engels quoted what Marx had said in reaction to the French Marxists of the 1870s: "All I know is that I am not a Marxist."[35] This was hardly the commentary of a simple-minded positivist and determinist.

Engels showed a similar flexibility of mind in his 21 September 1890 letter to Joseph Bloch, a student and like Schmidt, later an editor of socialist newspapers. "According to the materialist conception of history," Engels wrote,

> the production and reproduction of real life is, *in the final analysis*, the deciding factor in history. More have neither Marx nor I ever maintained. If someone distorts that to the effect that the economic factor is the *only* determining influence, he transforms the sentence into a meaningless, abstract, absurd phrase. The economic situation is the basis, but the various factors in the superstructure —political forms of the class struggle and its results; constitutions established after a victorious battle by the triumphant class, etc.; legal forms—. . . exert their influence upon the course of the historical struggle. . . . It is a reciprocal action of all of these factors, wherein finally through all the endless multitude of accidents (that is, of things and events whose inner connection among themselves is so remote or so undemonstrable that we view it as nonexistent, as something that can be ignored) the economic movement asserts itself as necessary. Otherwise, the application of the theory to a particular period of history would be even easier than the solution of a simple equation of the first degree.[36]

In another letter to Conrad Schmidt of 27 October 1890, Engels added: "The economic movement by and large prevails, but it has to endure a reaction from the political movement that it has itself set in motion and that is endowed with relative independence." He asserted further: "It would be hard to prove that, for example, in England absolute testamentary freedom, in France the considerable restrictions in all particulars of such matters have only economic causes." With regard to philosophy he said that the economy created nothing new but did determine the kind of change and further development the substance of thought met with, and that, too, mostly indirectly, because it was the political, juridical, and moral reflections that exerted the greatest direct influence on philosophy.

"What all the gentlemen lack is dialectic. They always see here only causes, there effects," he said. "That that is an empty abstraction, that in the real world such metaphysical, polar antitheses exist only in crises, that the whole, great process occurs in the form of a reciprocal action—if also of very unequal powers, of which the economic movement is by far the strongest, most primordial, and most decisive—that here nothing is absolute and all is relative, they fail altogether to see. For them Hegel never existed."[37]

Elsewhere, Engels wrote of conflicts being decided by "personal accidents";[38] of at least the possibility that Russia could avoid the capitalist path of industrial development occurring in the West;[39] of Marx's theses being only relative, not absolute, valid only under certain conditions and limitations;[40] of "so called 'economic laws'" being *not* eternal natural laws but historical laws that arose and disappeared with the passage of time;[41] of economic laws being approximations, tendencies;[42] and of Marx's way of conceiving things as method rather than doctrine.[43]

In his own criticism of the Gotha Program, Engels had asserted that in *Capital*, volume 1, Marx had shown in detail how the laws governing workers' wages were highly complicated and—far from being iron (as Lassalle had claimed)—were highly elastic.[44] Similarly, on at least one occasion Engels spoke out *against* simple-minded Darwinism, *against* the possibility of applying laws about animal societies to human ones, and *against* the proposition that the conception of history as a series of class struggles was a variation on the Darwinian notion of the struggle for life.[45]

Comparably, in a letter of 1893—in contradiction to the places where he wrote of the same laws governing nature and history—he differentiated markedly between the two spheres: "Nature is sublime," he said, "and as a change from the movement of history I am always glad to return to it, but history seems to me still more sublime than nature." Nature had required millions of years to bring forth conscious life. Conscious living beings had needed thousands of years to act together, cognizant not only of thair acts as individuals but of their being able to act together in pursuit of a common goal. "Now we have nearly reached that stage." This process, the development of something that had never yet existed on earth, seemed to Engels "a spectacle worth watching." It could also be tiring, however, especially for someone who felt called to participate. Then the study of nature became a great alleviation and cure, "because finally, nature and history are the two components through which we live, move, and have our being."[46]

Other quotations could be added to the list, but these will suffice to demonstrate the point. Although many individual statements Engels made, taken in isolation from the rest of his writings, were undoubtedly positivistic, a close examination of the whole corpus of his writings shows enormous flexibility and nuance in his ideas. Undeniably, he was not a consistent thinker or writer, but he certainly was far from being a one-dimensional positivist and determinist.

This brings us to the second point to be made about Engels' positivism: that it was not peculiar to Engels. As already seen in part, Marx, too, made many positivistic statements. Besides the passages cited above in the present chapter, he wrote in the foreword to the first edition of *Capital*, volume 1, that "it is the final goal of this work to unveil the economic law of motion of modern society." There, he also spoke of "my standpoint, which conceives the development of the economic formation of society as a natural historical process." And he stated that "when a society is on the track of the natural laws of its movement . . . , it can naturally neither skip phases of development nor decree their disappearance. But it can shorten and alleviate the birth pangs."[47] Here Marx was saying almost exactly the same thing as Engels did in the passages quoted above from *Anti-Dühring*. Indeed, Engels' formulation was more humanistic in that it spoke of men's ability to subjugate the "socially efficacious forces" to their will—an ability Marx here largely denied in favor of mere shortening and alleviating of birth pangs.

In the body of *Capital* itself, Marx referred to the "fortuitious and always changing exchange relations" as forcibly exerting their influence like a ''determining law of nature," which he specifically compared to the law of gravity.[48] *Capital* also contained his comparison of the transformation of a master craftsman into a capitalist with the law in natural science, discovered by Hegel, "that at a certain point purely quantitative changes became qualitative differences." In the same work, he compared the scientific analysis of competition with the study of heavenly bodies, as discussed in chapter 5.[49]

Further on in volume 1 of *Capital*, he referred to an "absolute law" governing the introduction of machinery and its reduction of the total quantity of work embodied in the production of a given quantity of merchandise. He also discussed an *"absolute, universal law of capitalist accumulation."*[50]

Carver placed considerable emphasis on Engels' graveside comparison between Darwin's discoveries in organic nature and Marx's in human history as demonstrating Engels' positivism.[51] Yet Engels had good authority for making this comparison. Marx had written him on 19 December 1860 about his reading "Darwin's book on 'natural selection.' Although clumsily developed in the English manner," Marx had commented, "this is the book that contains the natural historical foundation for our view."[52] (Notice, by the way, that he called it "our" rather than "my" view; he, at least, had no doubt that he and Engels shared the same outlook.) The following month, Marx expressed a similar appreciation of Darwin to Ferdinand Lassalle: "Darwin's book is very important and strikes me as the natural historical foundation for the historical class struggle."[53]

In a letter to his friend, the Hannoverian physician Ludwig Kugelmann, finally, Marx wrote of natural laws operating in history.[54] Also, in this connection Marx complained in his afterword to the second edition of *Capital* (written in January 1873) that the method he had used had been little understood. After quoting several other reviews, he noted that the writer of a Russian commentary—I. I. Kaufman, we now know, although Marx did not name him—had said that the outer form of the presentation was idealistic but that in fact Marx was infinitely more a realist than any of his predecessors in economic criticism. Marx said that the reviewer quoted from the foreword to *A Contribution to the Critique of Political Economy*, "where I discussed the materialist basis of my method."

There followed more than a page of quotation from the review, including: "For Marx only one thing is important: to discover the law of phenomena . . . the law of change, development, that is, transformation from one form into another." Marx, Kaufman said, "demonstrated with the necessity of the present arrangement at the same time the necessity of another arrangement into which the first must pass." Kaufman stated that Marx denied the existence of abstract laws governing economic development in the past and present, believing instead that each historical period had its own laws. Economic life, in a word, presented developments analogous to biology. On all of this, Marx commented: "While the author describes what he calls my real method so pertinently and so far as my own use of it is concerned, so kindly, what else has he depicted but the dialectical method?"

Marx went on to differentiate his dialectical method from that of Hegel,[55] as he so often did, but the point to be made here is twofold. On the one hand, notice that Marx made no objection to Kaufman's analogy between economic life and biology, or to the Russian reviewer's description of Marx's major work as both discovering a *law* of development and as being deterministic (that is, as demonstrating the necessity of both the present arrangement of society and impending changes thereto). Second, notice that Marx himself had specifically identified with a materialism that was dialectical. He may not have joined the two terms into one phrase, but he clearly described his method as both materialist and dialectical. Thus, Engels was *not* the first to develop the concept of dialectical materialism, with Plekhanov later coining the term itself; Marx himself used the very terminology to describe his own ideas.

Here and elsewhere, then, the record is clear. Marx, like Engels, sometimes wrote about laws operating in history in the same way that they did in nature, and he endorsed the notion that his method was dialectical and materialist. By quoting selectively from *either man's* writings, it would be easy to characterize him as either a positivist or a humanist. But in fact, *both* men emphasized—at least at times—the difference between appearance and reality, as discussed in chapter 5. This certainly was incompatible with the positivist denial of the existence of a reality other than that derived from observations and the scientific laws based thereon. Neither man was sufficiently empiricist to pass the true litmus test of positivism. Both, however, made frequent positivist and determinist statements, just as they both significantly qualified these statements at other times. In this as in most other respects, the two men thought very much alike. Neither was altogether either a positivist or a humanist, but both incorporated elements of each manner of thinking into their complicated patterns of thought. Both, also, were much more fundamentally humanist than positivist. Where they saw laws and deterministic forces operating in human society was preeminently in the capitalist age. Rightly or wrongly, they both foresaw a succeeding period in which people could humanistically control their own fates to a much greater degree than heretofore. As Engels put it, this would constitute humankind's leap from the realm of necessity into that of freedom.

CHAPTER VIII

The Intellectual Partnership

If, then, Engels was no more a positivist and determinist than Marx, what about Carver's claim that the two men did not collaborate significantly after the publication of the *Communist Manifesto* and were therefore not really intellectual partners thereafter? He, of course, admitted their collaboration on that and earlier works—*The Holy Family, The German Ideology*—plus "a number of short communications, jointly signed."[1]

He forgot about *The Great Men of Exile*, admittedly a minor work that the two friends wrote in May and June 1852.[2] Moreover, by the phraseology just quoted, he also excluded the many articles on which they collaborated for the *New-York Daily Tribune, Putnam's Monthly*, and *The New American Cyclopaedia* that Marx alone signed.[3] At first, this peculiar sort of collaboration occurred because Marx had been invited to contribute to the *Tribune* (and desperately needed the money he earned thereby) but did not have sufficient command of English to write in that language. Even after he had mastered it, however, he continued to ask Engels for articles, particularly on his specialty, military affairs.[4]

One especially interesting article that Engels wrote in March 1862 illustrates well the pattern this collaboration often took. On 3 March, Marx asked Engels for an article on the American Civil War to be submitted to the *Tribune*. Engels dutifully mailed it to him from Manchester five days later, promising a sequel the next week. On the fifteenth, Marx asked that this follow-up be conjectural in nature, making an attempt to look into the future. When the *Tribune* failed to publish the first installment, Marx translated both of them into German, making a few revisions in the process, and sent the result to *Die Presse*, a Viennese newspaper, which published it in two segments on 26 and 29 March.[5]

Meanwhile, Engels had sent the first installment to the *Volunteer Journal for Lancashire and Cheshire*, where it appeared on 14 March.[6] Unfortunately, he seems not to have done the same for the second and more interesting part of the article. Without Engels' version, it is impossible to know the extent of Marx's revisions to it, but given Marx's usual reliance on the military expertise of what he referred to as "the War Office in Manchester,"[7] it is more than likely that the substance of the article was Engels' work alone.

He began the piece with a discussion of the recent Union capture of forts Henry and Donelson in Tennessee. Turning to the seizure of Nashville, he went on to project the strategy the North should employ from that point in the war:

> Following the complete conquest of Tennessee by the Union, the only route that connects the two sections of the slave states [those on the Atlantic coast and those along the Gulf of Mexico] goes through Georgia. This means that *Georgia is the key to Secessia* [the South]. With the loss of Georgia, the Confederacy would be cut into two sections with all communications between them severed. . . .
>
> In a country where the communications, especially between distant points, depend much more upon railroads than upon roads, the seizure of the railroads is all that is needed. The southernmost railroad line between the states on the Gulf of Mexico and those on the Atlantic coast goes through Macon and Gordon near Millidgeville. The seizure of those two points would therefore cut Secessia in two and enable the Union troops to defeat one part after the other.[8]

What makes this article so interesting is Engels' strategic conception. It happens to coincide very closely with the one arrived at over two years later by generals Ulysses S. Grant and William Tecumseh Sherman and then carried out in Sherman's famous march to the sea.[9] (Sherman followed a route swinging south-southeast from Chattanooga through Atlanta along the railroad line. Then his army divided, with one arm going southeast above Macon and Gordon while the other went between those towns, again along the railroad. Both arms followed roughly the line of the railroad to Savannah, cutting the South in two as Engels had recommended.)[10] That, of course, is only a historical curiosity, incidental to the present purpose, although it illustrates Engels' strategic vision. What is relevant here is Marx's unhesitating call upon Engels—something he repeated on many other occasions—to write an article that would appear under his by-line. This makes it seem less unusual than would otherwise be the case that Engels would do the same in reverse with the economic section of *Anti-Dühring*, something Carver was reluctant to accept.[11]

Engels also made important contributions to Marx's more significant writings. Carver recognized the important influence Engels' "Outlines of a Critique of Political Economy" had on Marx's life and work.[12] But Engels' contributions did not stop there. He evidently suggested to Marx the ideas for the brilliant opening lines of *The Eighteenth Brumaire of Louis Bonaparte*. On 3 December 1851, the day after Louis Napoleon's coup d'état in France, Engels wrote to Marx:

> The history of France has entered the phase of the most consummate comedy. Can one imagine anything more gay than this travesty of 18 Brumaire carried out in the midst of peace with discontented soldiers by the most unimportant men in the whole world without any opposition, so far as one can judge, until now? . . . If one had toiled away a whole year, one could have developed no finer comedy. . . . It really seems as if the old Hegel in his grave is directing history as world history and with the greatest conscientiousness is allowing everything to occur twice, once as great tragedy, and the second time as lousy farce: Causidière for Danton, L. Blanc for Robespierre, Barthélemy for Saint-Just, Flocon for Carnot, and the moon-calf with the first, best dozen debt-laden lieutenants for the little corporal and his round table of marshals.[13]

Compare this with Marx's comments from the *Eighteenth Brumaire*: "Hegel remarks somewhere that all great, world historical facts and people occur, as it were, twice. He forgot to add: one time as tragedy, the other as farce. Causidière for Danton, Louis Blanc for Robespierre, the Mountain of 1848–1851 for the Mountain of 1793–1795, the nephew for the uncle. And this same caricature appears in the circumstances under which the second edition of the eighteenth Brumaire takes place."[14] Marx obviously recast Engels' conception and added some touches of his own, but the basic ideas were Engels'. And since the notion of a farcical repetition of the eighteenth Brumaire formed the title of Marx's acute analysis, perhaps the latter would never have written it without Engels' unacknowledged suggestion of the idea. Nevertheless, with his characteristic modesty and self-effacement before Marx's unquestionably great abilities, Engels did not even mention in his preface to the third (1885) edition of the work that he had suggested its formative idea to Marx.[15]

The two men also collaborated in developing their notion of the peculiarities of the Asiatic mode of production that Marx wrote about first in an article for the *New-York Daily Tribune*.[16] Later, of course, Marx discussed the conception in *A Contribution to the Critique of Political Economy*, the *Grundrisse*, and *Capital*, and it became an issue of major importance in the history of Marxism.[17] Apparently, during Marx's visit to Manchester from 30 April to 19 May 1853, the two men had talked about the expansion of Islam by the Arabs in the seventh century A.D. In a letter to Marx on 26 May, Engels discussed Charles Forster's *The historical geography of Arabia; or the patriarchal evidences of revealed religion* (London, 1844).[18]

In turn, on 2 June Marx quoted extensively from the *Voyages, contenant la description des états du Grand Mogul . . .* (1670) of François Bernier, who had been a doctor for nine years with the Mogul emperor Aurangzeb in India. Bernier had observed that the king was the sole proprietor of all lands of the kingdom. Marx commented that Bernier rightly found the "basic form for all phenomena in the orient" to be the nonexistence of private property. "This is the true key," Marx said, "even to the oriental heaven."[19]

Marx thus was the first of the two friends to discuss what became in their parlance the Asiatic mode of production. Engels, however, formulated the concept more fully in his letter of 6 June 1853:

> The absence of landed property is indeed the key to the whole orient. Therein lies the political and religious history. But how does it happen that the Orientals never introduced landed property, or even feudal relations? I believe it lies principally in the climate, allied with the nature of the soil, especially the great tracts of desert that stretch from the Sahara through Arabia, Persia, India, and Tartary all the way to the Asiatic uplands. Artificial irrigation is here the first condition of agriculture, and this is the concern of communes, provinces, or the central government. The government in the Orient has always consisted of only three departments: finance (pillage of the interior), war (pillage at home and abroad), and public works [written in French, *travaux publics*], concern for reproduction. The British government in India has regulated nos. 1 and 2 somewhat narrowmindedly and has cast no. 3 completely aside, and Indian agriculture is ruined. There, free competition is completely at fault. This artificial fructification of the soil, which immediately ceased with the decay of the water supply, explains the otherwise curious fact that now whole tracts are fallow and desolate, which earlier were brilliantly cultivated (Palmyra, Petra, the ruins of Yemen, X locations in Egypt, Persia, and Hindostan); it explains the fact that a

The Intellectual Partnership 131

single war of devastation can depopulate a country for centuries and divest it of its whole civilization. Therein, I believe, lies the explanation also of the annihilation of south Arabian trade before Mohammed that you very correctly see [in the letter of 2 June] as a principal factor in the Islamic revolution.[20]

Marx returned to the theme in a letter to Engels of 14 June. He said that the stationary character of South Asia resulted from the public works tended to by the central government and the division of the kingdom into villages. On the second score, he quoted from a parliamentary report of 1812 that described the structure of village government in India: "Under this simple form of municipal government the inhabitants of the country have lived from time immemorial. The boundaries of the villages have been but seldom altered; and although the villages themselves have been sometimes injured, and even desolated by war, famine and disease; the same name, the same limits, the same interests, and even the same families, have continued for ages. The inhabitants give themselves no trouble about the breaking up and division of kingdoms, while the village remains entire, they care not to what power it is transferred, or to what sovereign it devolves. Its internal economy remains unchanged." On this, Marx commented: "I believe that one can imagine no more solid basis for Asiatic despotism and stagnation."[21]

Meanwhile, on 10 June 1853 Marx had penned an article for the *Tribune* in which he made use of Engels' material as well as his own. Entitled "The British Rule in India," it read in part:

There have been in Asia, generally, from immemorial times, but three departments of Government; that of Finance, or the plunder of the interior; that of War, or the plunder of the exterior; and, finally, the department of Public Works. Climate and territorial conditions, especially the vast tracts of desert, extending from the Sahara, through Arabia, Persia, and Tartary, to the most elevated Asiatic highlands, constituted artificial irrigation by canals and waterworks the basis of Oriental agriculture. . . . This prime necessity of an economical and common use of water, which, in the Occident, drove private enterprise to voluntary association, as in Flanders and Italy, necessitated, in the Orient where civilization was too low and the territorial extent too vast to call into life voluntary association, the interference of the centralized power of Government. . . . This artificial fertilization of the soil, dependent on a Central Government, and immediately decaying with the neglect of irrigation and drainage, explains the otherwise strange fact that we now find whole territories barren and desert that were once brilliantly cultivated, as Palmyra, Petra, the ruins of Yemen, and large provinces of Egypt, Persia, and Hindostan; it also explains how a single war of devastation has been able to depopulate a country for centuries, and to strip it of all its civilization.

Now the British in East India accepted from their predecessors the department of finance and war, but they have neglected entirely that of public works. Hence the deterioration of an agriculture which is not capable of being conducted on the British principle of free competition, of *laissez-faire* and *laissez-aller*.

After discussing the British destruction of the Indian handicraft industry, Marx turned to the village system and included the quotation from the parliamentary report of 1812, considered above. About it he commented: "we must not forget that these idyllic village-communities, inoffensive though they may appear, had always been the solid foundation of Oriental despotism, that they restrained the human mind within the smallest possible compass, making it the unresisting tool of superstition, enslaving it beneath traditional rules, depriving it of all grandeur and historical energies. . . . We must not forget that this undignified, stagnatory, and vegetative life, that this passive sort of existence evoked on the other part, in contradistinction, wild, aimless, unbounded forces of destruction and rendered murder itself a religious rite in Hindostan."[22]

Another instance of collaboration between Marx and Engels occurred in connection with Engels' brochure "The Prussian Military Question and the German Worker Party," written between the end of January and 9 February 1865, during the course of the constitutional conflict in Prussia. The impetus for the piece came from Liebknecht via Marx. Marx wrote to Engels on 25 January that Liebknecht had sent him a note pressing him for an article by Engels to appear in the *Social-Demokrat*, the Lassallean newspaper. The topic was to be the "Yankee War" or the Prussian military reform that had led to the constitutional conflict. Marx said that Engels had already told him the war was not a suitable topic for the *Social-Demokrat*, but he felt that the army reform was. The only question was, would such an article lead Engels into an undesirable, one-sided conflict with the Progressives (who opposed Bismarck and the king on both the military reforms and the constitutional issue over appropriations for them), or could Engels handle the question so as to attack both them and the reactionaries?[23]

In his reply, Engels answered the second part of the question affirmatively but raised the further issue of whether such an article could be published in Germany. Marx then wrote that he (Engels) must say in a short foreword that he was elucidating the issue from a military point of view; also that he was criticizing the middle class; "and thirdly, the reactionaries etc. and the position of the worker party to the question, etc., whereby in a few strokes of the pen *the tendency* could certainly be delineated or intimated." This would make confiscation difficult for the government, he said.[24]

On 9 February, Engels sent Marx the manuscript, which—as he said —had grown to full brochure size and so was no longer suitable for the newspaper. He commented that the revision he had been able to do was "very hasty" and had to be redone. But he awaited Marx's comments on the document and on where to submit it for publication.[25]

The brochure was a fairly hefty one that takes up thirty-seven pages of small print in the *Werke*.[26] Marx commented on 10 February that it was good. The style here and there was careless, but to polish and perfect it now would be "nonsense," since the point was to get it published before the issue it dealt with was resolved. He therefore urged Engels to sent it immediately to Otto Meissner in Hamburg, the later publisher of *Capital*, and to press for quick publication.[27]

The next day, Marx dispatched another letter. He said that since it was Saturday, he surmised that Engels would not yet have sent off the manuscript, so there was still time for some changes. He suggested that where Engels asked what the workers wanted, he should not answer for workers in Germany, France, and England because "the answer makes it sound like we accept Itzig's [Lassalle's] catchwords (it will at least be so interpreted)."[28] Marx advised instead that Engels formulate the answer in terms of what the most advanced workers in Germany demanded.

Marx also advised Engels not to say that the movement of 1848–1849 failed because the middle class opposed direct, general suffrage. He suggested instead saying something like "the middle class preferred peace with servitude to the mere prospect of battle with freedom." He also pointed to a place where Engels had said the opposite of what he meant to say.[29]

Engels made the changes Marx suggested, and the brochure appeared in February 1865.[30] It may seem that such collaboration on this long-since-forgotten work is not significant enough to merit such extended commentary, but the point is that Marx obviously felt the piece was sufficiently important for their policies in Germany that Engels should take the time to write, and he to critique it. Even though he was then working to finish the first volume of *Capital*—which he had promised to deliver to Meissner by May, a deadline he failed to meet[31]—he even took the time to write a review of the brochure for the periodical *Hermann*.[32]

More importantly, Marx consulted Engels on several occasions about technical matters he was treating in *Capital* and even about some of his theoretical formulations. Unfortunately, the existing correspondence frequently does not reveal Engels' answers.[33] On 6 March 1862, for example, Marx asked Engels how to translate "gigs" into German, what "feeders on circular frames" were, and whether Engels could tell him all the kinds of workers in his factory except those in the warehouse, as well as what the proportions among them were. He wanted the last item of information to show that in mechanical concerns the division of labor did not exist in the way Adam Smith had described.[34] Engels' letter of 8 March began, "Enclosed what was promised," but what he evidently referred to was his article on the American Civil War (discussed above).[35] There is no further mention of the matter in succeeding letters on either side. Even if Engels did answer the question, it is not evident that Marx used the material in *Capital*.[36]

On 2 March 1862, Marx set forth to Engels his views on rent theory, constant and variable capital, surplus value, exploitation, and so forth at some length (four closely printed pages in the *Werke*), "so that you [can] *communicate* to me *your opinion*" (Marx's emphasis). Among other things, he spoke of Ricardo's confusing the concepts of value and cost price. "He believes, therefore, if an *absolute rent* exists (that is, a rent *independent* of the variable fertility of the types of soil), then agricultural produce, etc., would be sold continually *over* the value because *over* the cost price (the advanced capital + the average profit). . . . He therefore disavows the absolute rent and assumes only the differential rent."[37]

On 8 August, Engels said he would comment on the rent theory that day but had a terrible case of hemorrhoids and could sit no longer at that moment. He confessed, however, that the existence of absolute rent was not clear to him.[38] If he did return to the point, the letter apparently has been lost. On the 9th, however, Marx explained that Ricardo disavowed absolute rent based on the theoretically incorrect dogma of the supposed identity between cost prices and values of commodities. He would demonstrate that, assuming the existence of absolute ground rent, it did not follow that under all circumstances the worst cultivated land or worst mine paid rent. Ricardo claimed falsely that the commodity produced under the most unfavorable circumstances determined the market value. Marx added that Engels had made the correct rejoinder to that view in his "Outlines of a Critique of Political Economy."[39]

The surviving letters do not return substantively to this point, but on 20 August, Marx asked if Engels could not pay him a visit. "I have overthrown so many old views in my critique [meaning *Capital*]," he wrote, "that I would at least like to consult with you over a few points. Writing about the rubbish is tedious for you and me." This suggests at least the possibility that Engels may, in fact, have replied to some of Marx's questions in letters that do not survive. However that may be, Marx then asked Engels for a short reply—despite his hemorrhoids—on a practical matter regarding money put aside to pay for the costs of replacing machinery that gave out in twelve years and asked several questions about it.[40]

Engels wrote on 9 September 1862 that he was frightfully busy informing customers of successive increases in prices as a result of the shortage of cotton stemming from the Yankee blockade of the South in the Civil War. In this situation, rent theory had become too abstract for him to deal with. He would have to ponder it when he had some rest. The same with the question about wear and tear on machinery, but he did say he thought Marx was on the wrong track with the latter. Not all machines wore out at the same speed. But more on that later, he said. Meanwhile, Engels indicated that he was going on a fourteen-day trip to Germany and would not have time to stop in London (to see Marx on the way through).[41]

Marx's reply the next day stated that he would not "ballast" Engels with the "economic stuff," but perhaps he could write when and where he would be in London as he passed through so maybe they could get together after all. The available evidence does not indicate whether they did meet. Engels was gone from 12 to 29 September. He traveled along the Mosel and Rhine, then through Thuringia before visiting his relatives in Engelskirchen and Barmen along the lower Rhine.[42]

Upon his return, his hands were full with business matters, so apparently he did not write to Marx until 16 October. In that letter he failed to mention the matters Marx had asked him about. The remaining correspondence for the balance of the year 1862 is also silent on the material Marx was working on for *Capital*. In early December, Marx did spend about a week with Engels in Manchester,[43] and it is probable that they discussed the "economic stuff" then if they had not had occasion to do so when Engels passed through London on the way to Germany.

On 24 January 1863 Marx again sought Engels' counsel. "For the section about machinery in my book, I am in a great quandary," he wrote. "It was never clear to me how selfactors [sic, English in the letter] changed the spinneries or, still more, since steam power came into use before that, how the spinner began with its motive force in spite of the steam power [?]. I would be glad to have you explain that to me."[44]

Engels apparently did not respond, perhaps because Mary Burns had died that month and he had been upset at Marx's brief and rather cool response to the news. The persistent Marx, however, returned to the question on 28 January. "I asked you in my last letter about the selfactor," he wrote. Specifically, he wanted to know how the spinner operated before the self-actor was invented. He said that mechanics were like languages for him. He understood mathematical laws, but "the simplest technical reality" presented a real problem for him to grapple with.[45]

There followed a long silence on Engels' part, which disturbed his friend. On 17 February, Marx wrote that he hoped Engels was not sick or, on the other hand, that he had not again unintentionally vexed his bereaved comrade. When he had written about machinery, he had done so, he said, in order to provide a diversion from Engels' (emotional) pain. Engels replied that Marx had to pardon his long silence. He was in a very desolate state of affairs and had to work himself out of it. He was studying Slavic languages, but his loneliness was still unbearable. He had to divert himself forcibly. That had helped, and he was again his old self. Two days after this, he said that he would write about machinery that day,[46] but if he did, the letter apparently does not survive.[47]

Thus, on several occasions Marx did ask Engels for assistance on matters he was pondering in the writing of *Capital*, but there is little concrete evidence that Engels contributed in a significant way to Marx's magnum opus, at least in its first draft. There was at least one instance when Marx did use some material Engels had sent him. On 19 January 1867, Marx asked for material on a dispute of the weavers in Manchester. Engels replied on the 29th that calicos had been almost impossible to sell in the last six months, so manufacturers had sought in some places to put the workers on "short time." Meanwhile, they consigned the commodities that no one would buy in England to India and China, increasing the glut. They then proposed to the factory hands a 5 percent reduction in wages. The workers proposed instead to shorten the working week to four days. The masters refused at first but finally did reduce the work week, sometimes with, sometimes without a 5 percent reduction in wages. Marx reworded the material somewhat but used almost all of it in a footnote in *Capital*. Since this was only a footnote, it is perhaps more significant that Marx cited Engels' writings fifteen times in volume 1 of *Capital*, making him a major source.[48]

Even more significantly, without Engels' urging Marx might never have published volume 1 of *Capital* in his lifetime. On 15 July 1865—two months after Marx's initial deadline with Meissner—Engels asked how things stood with the book. Marx replied on the 31st that there were still three chapters of the theoretical part of the work (the first of three books) to write. Then there was the fourth book, dealing with historical materials (the later *Theories of Surplus Value*). That would be the easiest part to write because he had already answered all the questions in the first three books. "I cannot make up my mind, though, to send off anything before the whole lies in front of me. Whatever shortcomings they may have, it is the merit of my writings that they constitute an artistic whole," he said, "and that is only achievable with my method never to let them be printed before the *whole* lies in from of me." He added that he had been living off the pawn shop for the past two months.[49]

Engels' reply has not been preserved, but from Marx's response of 5 August 1865, it is clear that Engels complained about overmuch concern with artistry. Marx said he was going forward as fast as possible, regardless of artistic considerations. Besides, he had a maximum limit of sixty proof sheets. Thus, it was absolutely necessary for him, he felt, to have the whole work before him so he could know how much to condense and delete without destroying the symmetry of the whole. Engels expressed delight that the work progressed. He had feared from his friend's previous comments that there would be indeterminate delays. In the meantime, as he done so often in the past, Engels sent him monetary help—this time fifty pounds.[50]

On 10 February 1866, Marx wrote that his work had progressed famously since the first of the year, when problems with his liver had disappeared, but now carbuncles prevented him from going forward with the theoretical part of the work, his intellect being affected. At this point, Engels asked him if he couldn't publish the first volume right away and the second a few months later. Marx agreed to this proposal on 13 February, and in April 1867 he delivered volume 1 to Meissner in Germany.[51]

On 7 May 1867 he wrote to Engels from Hannover with reference to the many financial contributions the latter had made over the years to the Marx household:[52] "Without you, I would never have been able to bring the work to completion, and I assure you, it has always weighed on my conscience like an Alp that you have dissipated your splended energy and let it rust on commercial matters, principally on my account, and into the bargain, still had to participate vicariously in all my minor troubles."[53]

On his return from Germany, Marx spent over a week in Manchester with Engels. Upon his arrival back in London on 3 June, he sent his friend the first five proof sheets for *Capital*, saying he could keep them eight to ten days but then must give his opinion on what points in the discussion of the form of value needed to be popularized for the philistines.[54] Engels apologized on 16 June for not sending the proofs back with his comments sooner. He had been involved for eight days in a squabble with his partner, Gottfried Ermen, and had enjoyed little peace for studying the form of value. Proof sheet 2 clearly showed the impression of Marx's carbuncles, he said, but that could not now be changed. And he was of the opinion that Marx should add nothing because the philistines were not accustomed to this kind of abstract thinking anyway and would not trouble much with it. Perhaps the dialectical points might be demonstrated more historically, Engels felt, but the most necessary points were already made. On the other hand, Marx had so much material on the subject that he could certainly provide an appendix that would demonstrate historically to the philistines the necessity of capital formation.

Marx had also made a great error in not including more subdivisions and subheadings to make this abstract discussion clearer to the reader. He should have followed the pattern of Hegel's *Encyclopedia* and used short paragraphs, provided each dialectical transition with a special heading, and, where possible, used a special print for all digressions and illustrations. Doing so would make the section a bit pedantic, but it would also make it easier sledding for a large class of readers.

By comparison with *A Contribution to the Critique of Political Economy*, Engels said, the acuteness of the dialectical development was significantly improved, but much of the description in the earlier book had pleased him better. "It is very unfortunate," he wrote, returning to the point made above, "that the important second sheet" had been the one to suffer from the effects of the carbuncles. But he reiterated that there was nothing to change further; anyone capable of thinking dialectically would still understand it. (As already seen in the case of Marx, neither man was at all squeamish about criticizing the other's work.)

"The remaining sheets," Engels added, "are very good and have given me great joy." Engels also noted some printer's errors and said he would list the important ones.[55]

Marx dispatched four more sheets on 22 June that he said had arrived the day before. (Apparently, at this point he was going over them only perfunctorily and relying on Engels for the major proofreading effort.) He hoped that Engels would be satisfied with them. "Your previous satisfaction," he said, ignoring for the moment Engels' critical comments, "is more important to me than anything the rest of the world may say of it. In any case, I hope that the bourgeoisie will think its whole life long about my carbuncles."[56]

He added that concerning the development of the form of value, he had both followed Engels' advice and not followed it, ''to proceed dialectically in this regard also." He had written an appendix where he covered the same material as simply and as pedantically as possible. He had also added subheadings as Engels had advised and told the nondialectical reader to skip the text and go to the appendix. (In the second edition, Marx worked the appendix into the text—on pages 62–85 of the *Werke*, volume 23.)[57]

On 24 June 1867, Engels thanked Marx for the first twelve proof sheets. He had only read through number 8, however. He thought that the chapter on the transformation of money into capital and the production of surplus value constituted the climax of the work as far as presentation and content were concerned. At this point, however, Engels wrote Marx that he needed a commercial address, if possible, to which he could send one hundred pounds for Marx, as he contemplated a four-week trip to the Continent with Lizzie. He would visit Meissner on the trip (which obviously would limit his help on the proofs, though he did not say so). In reply, Marx thanked him for a five-pound note and said to send the hundred pounds to Sigismund Borkheim, a friend and fellow revolutionary of 1848 who had become a merchant in London. Marx spoke of sending Engels more proof sheets before he left, but whether that happened is not clear.[58]

Upon his return from the trip, Engels wrote Marx on 11 August that he had hastily read through the sheets up to number 32. He would report on them later. He did comment that the many illustrations in this part interfered with grasping the larger context, at least on first reading. There were, nevertheless, some fine things therein. Capital and its sycophants would be eternally thankful to Marx for them, he remarked sarcastically. (Engels, incidentally, also dispatched another five-pound note in this letter.)[59]

On 14 August Marx reported receipt of the forty-eighth proof sheet. That week, he said, he would be finished with the "shit." He also told Engels that in view of the enormous amounts of money the younger man had sent him that year, he would not have been under such financial pressure had it not been for two hundred pounds of debts. On the 15th, Engels sent three more five-pound notes and said that he had read the proofs Marx had sent him quickly through to the end. He believed the uncompleted second volume was very necessary, so the sooner Marx finished it, the better. Nevertheless, "the chaps" would marvel when they saw how easily Marx dispatched the most difficult points, like Ricardo's profit theory.[60]

At 2 a.m. on 16 August 1867, Marx wrote Engels that he had corrected the last proof sheet. Once again, he expressed his appreciation to Engels for enabling him to finish. "I embrace you, full of thanks," he wrote in English. Then, in German: "Salutations, my dear, cherished friend."[61]

Engels' advice nevertheless did not stop. His trip to the Continent had evidently delayed his suggestions beyond the point when they would be usable in correcting the first edition of *Capital*, but on 23 August 1867 he returned to the chore. He congratulated Marx on his handling of the most intricate economic problems, of the relations between work and capital, and of technological terminology. He said he had corrected a few slips of the pen and risked a few conjectures. More importantly, perhaps, he pointed out that the fourth chapter was almost two hundred pages long and had only four divisions. Moreover, the train of thought was constantly interrupted by illustrations, whose major points were never summarized at the end. Consequently, the reader had always to jump from the illustration of one point to the development of another. This was extremely tiring and, without sharp vigilance, confusing. Engels recommended subdivisions and more prominent main divisions.[62]

Marx heeded this criticism in the second edition through the "clearer division of the book" that he pointed to in his afterword.[63] Meanwhile, on 24 August 1867 Marx asked Engels' advice again. He said he was working on the conclusion to the second book dealing with the process of circulation and needed to ask once again about a point he had raised several years before (20 August 1862; see above). Fixed capital had to be replaced in kind after, say, ten years, he wrote. In the interim, its value came back to the capitalist partially and gradually with the sale of the commodities it helped produce. This "progressive return" on the fixed capital had only to be expended (apart from repairs) when a machine wore out.

Marx said that when he had written Engels about the matter before, asking about an accumulation fund and the capitalist's employment of the money in the interim before he had to replace the fixed capital, Engels had dismissed the matter "somewhat superficially." Marx had found later that "MacCulloch" [sic] described this "sinking fund" as accumulation funds. In the conviction that M'Culloch was never right, Marx said he had let the matter drop. The Malthusians, however, also accepted the fact of a sinking fund. As a manufacturer, Engels must have known what he did with returns on capital before the time when he used them to replace that capital. Marx wanted an answer on this point, therefore, "without theory, *purely in a practical sense.*"[64]

Engels replied on 26 August that he would provide fuller material on replacement funds the next day. He had to ask a couple of manufacturers if Ermen and Engels' practice was general or exceptional. It was a question whether with £1,000 original cost for the machinery, where in the first year £100 was held back, if in the second year the amount kept in reserve was 10 percent of £1,000 or of £900. Ermen and Engels did the latter. Otherwise, there was no doubt that the manufacturer used the replacement funds on average four and a half years before the machinery wore out—or at least had it at his disposal. As a rule, the rate for holding back the funds was 7.5 percent, so the length of time it took for the machinery to wear out could be figured at about thirteen years. Engels said it was not entirely clear to him what the economic importance of this was. He did not see how the manufacturer would be in a position through a misrepresentation to swindle the other part-owners out of surplus value or to cheat the customers—at least in the long run.[65]

On the 27th, Engels returned to the question as promised. He confirmed that the rule was to hold back 7.5 percent of the cost each year. Then he provided two extensive examples using a rate of 10 percent to simplify the calculations. In one, he showed the manufacturer putting the replacement funds aside with interest; in the other, the manufacturer used it to purchase new machinery every year. Marx thanked him for the information, but he appears not to have used it directly in the section dealing with replacement costs in what became, under Engels' editing, volume 2 of *Capital.*[66]

As late as 1 September 1867 Engels was still writing Marx about the proof sheets for the first volume of *Capital*, of which Marx had somehow sent him eight more. Engels said the theoretical treatment was splendid, as was the development of the history of expropriation. But he faulted material in a section on Ireland as hurriedly written and poorly developed. Indeed, much of it was unintelligible on first reading. Here, again, Marx apparently took advantage of Engels' criticism in the second edition, where he expanded the treatment of Ireland significantly and added a series of notes.[67]

The book appeared in the third week of September 1867.[68] On 10 October, Marx sent Engels a letter from Dr. Kugelmann asking if he wanted a short review in a political newspaper. A liberal Hannoverian lawyer named Ernst Warnebold had offered to help get such reviews published in middle-class journals. Kugelmann requested "guiding viewpoints with which to compose an appropriate article for bourgeois feelings." Marx said that Engels could write to Kugelmann about the book better than he could himself.[69] Engels replied on the 13th that he had written two reviews from different points of view and sent them to Kugelmann. He believed they were composed in such a way that almost any newspaper could publish them. Thereafter, Kugelmann could write others himself. In fact, however, Engels ended up writing reviews for nine different journals, not all of which published them.[70]

In short, Engels' contributions to the first volume of *Capital* appear to have been more monetary and critical than substantive—if the initial impetus from his article "Outlines of a Critique of Political Economy" is left out of account—and much of the criticism came too late to produce changes until the second edition. There was, nevertheless, a significant amount of collaboration at various stages in the work's progress. As already seen in chapters 2 and 3, Engels' contributions to volumes 2 and 3 of *Capital* were more extensive. Because of the undigested and fragmentary nature of Marx's manuscripts, Engels had to make choices among different manuscripts Marx left behind and even to add material in places. While it is true that he did not acknowledge all the additions, there is no proof of any intent to deceive in this lapse. The editorial work was obviously demanding in the extreme and was far from being his only project in his declining years. As also shown already, not all of Engels' changes were in a positivistic direction, and those that were agreed in this respect with other statements Marx had made elsewhere in his writings, including the first volume of *Capital*.

The examples discussed above in this chapter were, as I have already suggested, by no means the only ones that could be provided of Marx and Engels' collaboration. This chapter would have to be expanded many times over to include them all. The ones adduced here, however, demonstrate clearly a pattern of joint work extending from *The Holy Family* in 1844 to Marx's principal work, *Capital*, which Engels did not finish editing until nearly the time of his own death in 1895. In many cases, Engels' contributions were only factual or editorial in nature, but in others —like the *Eighteenth Brumaire* and the Asiatic mode of production— the younger man made important, if unacknowledged, interpretive suggestions.

The pattern of collaboration between them also shows a mutual respect for each other's views and a resultant lack of squeamishness about offering criticism. One final example, this time of a collaboration that failed to materialize, will underline the extent of Marx's respect for Engels in an area where many scholars have disputed the latter's competence —philosophy. On 25 January 1854 Marx wrote to Engels of American journalist and editor Charles A. Dana's proposal to write an article on the history of German philosophy since Kant. Marx said that if he and Engels were together, they could quickly earn fifty to sixty pounds. Despite his poverty at the time, however, Marx said he would not risk doing the work by himself.[71]

Even without this article that, given Marx's prolixity, might easily have turned into a book, the two friends' collaboration was far too extensive for any researcher not absolutely blinded by presupposition to overlook. To say this is not to support the "general theory of joint authorship" that Carver derides.[72] Despite Engels' contributions, *Capital*, especially the first volume, was principally Marx's work. Likewise, despite Marx's contribution, *Anti-Dühring* was primarily Engels'. The same is true to an even greater extent of works like *A Contribution to the Critique of Political Economy* and *Ludwig Feuerbach*. Nevertheless, the extent of the two men's collaboration elsewhere was easily great enough to support a claim of significant intellectual partnership between them.

CHAPTER IX

Conclusion

The evidence presented in these pages supports an interpretation of Engels' life and his intellectual relationship to Marx that has not been common in recent scholarship. Engels was not only an extremely talented but also a multifaceted student of the human condition on this planet. Moreover, he and Marx were in fundamental agreement on such important matters as humanism, revisionism, determinism, and positivism. In all of these areas, both Marx and Engels were much more ambiguous and even inconsistent than most students of their thought have been willing to admit. But the two men agreed even in their inconsistencies. They collaborated together on a great variety of works—both important and not so important—over a period that extended even beyond Marx's death. In view of Marx's heated and repeated ruptures with such former friends and allies as Bruno and Edgar Bauer, Wilhelm Weitling, August Willich, Pierre Proudhon, Arnold Ruge, and Michael Bakunin, his working together so harmoniously over such an extended period with Engels is itself significant testimony to their fundamental intellectual agreement. Marx was not a man who easily tolerated views even slightly discordant with his own. In this connection, it is significant that not just Lafargue and Liebknecht but Marx himself referred to Engels as his alter ego. In fact, Marx even told Engels in 1864 that everything came late to him and that he always followed in his younger friend's footsteps.[1]

Why, then, have so many scholars refused to accept this view? It is perhaps understandable that avowed Marxists should be reluctant to admit inconsistencies in Marx's thinking. According to the late Alvin Gouldner, the critique of Engels by what he called critical Marxists like Lukács sought to resolve the contradiction within Marxism between them and the scientific Marxists like Louis Althusser by blaming Engels for the positivistic elements in Marxism.[2] Similarly, Gareth Stedman Jones has suggested that dissident Communists and others seeking to create a Marx different from the one presented in the orthodox interpretation have blamed Engels for "all the unwanted components of Soviet Marxism, from which they were so anxious to distance themselves."[3]

Stedman Jones' comment, in particular, gets into the always tricky area of motivation, but to the extent that scholars have sought to distance themselves and Marx from Soviet Marxism, they have been right about Marx but wrong about Engels. Surely, the nature of the Soviet Union under Stalin is sufficiently explained by Lenin's Blanquist adaptations of Marxism to a partly underdeveloped country, as well as the Russian political tradition and Stalin's peculiar and devious personality.[4] Marx and Engels both were too committed to majoritarian revolution and to a humanist liberation of the working classes—and thereby of mankind, they believed—to be fairly blamed for events in the Soviet Union so long after their deaths.

But if the dichotomists have been misled by their dislike of Soviet Marxism into unfairly blaming Engels for it, that does not necessarily explain the widespread acceptance of the dichotomist argument by scholars who presumably are not so freighted with ideological ballast. Here, the extensive nature of the Marx/Engels corpus of writings, its complexity, and its many nuances are perhaps to blame. The enormous literature on Marx and Engels' thought bears eloquent testimony to the fact that even the experts have been unable to reach anything approaching a consensus on the subject.

It seems clear that in the search for a coherent explanation of Marx and Engels' ideas, Engels' writings, while certainly not altogether ignored, have not been so thoroughly studied as those of Marx. The result has been to seize upon some of the things he wrote to the neglect of others. But for reasons that are not readily apparent, scholars have also overlooked many comments of Marx that are in line with some of the more noticed of Engels' statements. Perhaps these oversights are attributable to a natural disinclination on the part of intellectual historians to accept contradictions in the utterances of great thinkers.

Whatever the explanation for the existing interpretations, however, the evidence presented above should demonstrate to anyone not utterly blinded by ideology that Marx and Engels basically agreed with each other. Perhaps, to return to Nicolaievsky and Maenchen-Helfen's metaphor, Marx and Engels did not follow quite "the same path towards the same goal." But here again, Marx himself supplies us with the correct metaphor. In the foreword to *A Contribution to the Critique of Political Economy*, he wrote: "Friedrich Engels, with whom I have maintained a continuous epistolary exchange of ideas since the appearance of his brilliant sketch on the critique of economic categories (in the 'Deutsch-Französischen Jahrbüchern'), has arrived by a different path (compare his 'Condition of the Working Class in England') at the same result as I have."[5]

Marx penned these lines in 1859, but nothing in the available record suggests that he would have changed his view had he written them in 1883 or even—had he lived that long—1895. The later comments of his son-in-law and youngest daughter in fact strongly indicate the contrary.[6] Marx and Engels were not, by any stretch of the imagination, intellectual clones. They did, on occasion, disagree. But none of their disagreements were fundamental. As Marx said, they marched along slightly different paths, but they clearly were headed for the same goal, which was *not* Soviet Marxism, at least as it manifested itself down to the time of Mikhail Gorbachev.

Notes

Preface

1   I call the writings of many authors from George Lichtheim to Terrell Carver and Norman Levine "dichotomist" because they split what once had been considered the basically compatible ideas of Marx and Engels into two opposing systems of thought.

2   Sir Edward Grey, *Twenty-Five Years, 1892–1916*, 2 vols. (New York: Frederick A. Stokes, 1925), 1:xv.

Chapter 1   Engels' Early Years

1   Hans Magnus Enzensberger, ed., *Gespräche mit Marx und Engels*, 2 vols. (Frankfurt a. M.: Insel Verlag, 1973), 2:353. The phrase "last not least" is English in the original, the rest in German.

2   Ibid., 415.

3   Ibid., 553–554.

4   *Reminiscences of Marx and Engels* (Moscow: Foreign Languages Publishing House, n.d.), 306.

5   See, for example, his comment that Engels could not bear for someone else to be close to Marx. Consequently, he used H. M. Hyndman's failure to state in his *England for All* his intellectual debt to Marx to widen the distance between Hyndman and Marx. *Gespräche mit Marx und Engels*, 2:587–588. Hyndman's own account of the matter appears in his *The Record of an Adventurous Life* (1911; repr., New York: Garland, 1984), 251–252.

6   *Reminiscences of Marx and Engels*, 306.

7   Ibid., 309, 314.

8   Karl Marx and Friedrich Engels, *Werke*, 41 vols. (Berlin: Dietz Verlag, 1956–1979), 1:413 (hereafter cited as *MEW*). A rather wooden and not always accurate translation of these letters is available in Marx and Engels, *Collected Works*, vol. 2 (New York: International Publishers, 1975), 7–28. The Turkey red dye-works had arisen in the twin cities beginning in 1785, according to the unpublished manuscript of Herbert Kisch, "From Monopoly to Progress: The Early Growth of the Wupper Valley Textile Trades," a copy of which he was kind enough to furnish me in the early 1970s. Turkey red was a kind of dye.

9   *MEW*, 1:417. At this time, factories had begun to assemble workers under one roof in the spinneries and Turkey red dye-works. Weaving remained predominately a cottage industry until much later in the century, making the Wuppertal

much less an industrial center in the modern sense of the word than many commentators have suggested. See my *Boom and Bust: Society and Electoral Politics in the Düsseldorf Area, 1867–1878* (New York: Garland, 1987), 49ff.

10 *MEW*, 1:417–418.
11 Ibid., 419–420.
12 Ibid., 422.
13 Ibid., 422–423.
14 Ibid., 425.
15 Ibid., 425–426.
16 Ibid., 426–428.
17 *Sozialgeschichte der Stadt Barmen im 19. Jahrhundert* (Tübingen: J. D. B. Mohr, 1960), 109, 144–145.
18 Gustav Mayer, *Friedrich Engels: Eine Biographie*, 2 vols., rev. ed. (Haag: Martinius Nijhoff, 1934), 1:5.
19 Ibid., 6–8; W. O. Henderson, *The Life of Friedrich Engels*, 2 vols. (London: Frank Cass, 1978), 1:2–3; idem, *Marx and Engels and the English Workers and Other Essays* (London: Frank Cass, 1989), 34–35. In the last-cited work, Henderson states that the firm was founded in 1838, but other sources give the earlier date.
20 Marx and Engels, *Collected Works*, 2:582.
21 L. F. Ilychov et al., *Friedrich Engels: A Biography*, trans. Victor Schneierson (Moscow: Progress Publishers, 1974), 17.
22 Marx and Engels, *Collected Works*, 2:584–585.
23 Henderson, *Engels*, 1:6–7; Hans Peter Bleuel, *Friedrich Engels, Bürger und Revolutionär: Die Zeitgerechte Biographie eines grossen Deutschen* (Bein and Munich: Scherz Verlag, 1981), 32. Henderson says Engels left Barmen in the fall of 1838, but on 28 August he wrote a letter to his sister Marie from Bremen, and the editors of *MEW* state that he left Barmen for Bremen in the middle of July. See *MEW*, Ergänzungsband (hereafter, Eb.) II:325 and *MEW*, 1:631.
24 See *MEW*, Eb. II: passim, esp. 454–461, letters to Marie dated 20–25 Aug. 1840 and 18–19 Sept. 1840.
25 Peter Demetz, *Marx, Engels und die Dichter* (Stuttgart: Deutsche Verlags-Anstalt, 1959), 78.
26 Věra Macháčková, *Der Junge Engels und die Literatur (1838–1844)* (Berlin: Dietz Verlag, 1961), 54.
27 *MEW*, 1:413–432; Eb. II: 7–140. This tally includes one article published in five succeeding numbers of the *Morgenblatt für gebildete Leser* in August 1841 after Engels had left Bremen, but he had written the piece in July 1840 before he departed.
28 Macháčková, *Engels und die Literatur*, 279.
29 Ibid.; Demetz, *Marx, Engels*, 26, 28, 31, 40. Young Germany was a literary movement of a group of radical writers active in the 1830s. They wrote political dramas and stories directed against the reactionary governments in their country. Börne greatly influenced them from exile in Paris.
39 See *MEW*, Eb. II:325–483; cf. Macháčková, *Engels und die Literatur*, 25–26, and Ilychov et al., *Engels*, 19.
31 *MEW*, Eb. II:444, 540, 433, 403, 397; on Leo, see Sidney Hook, *From Hegel to Marx: Studies in the Intellectual Development of Karl Marx* (Ann Arbor: University of Michigan Press, 1962), 139–141, and John Edward Toews, *Hegelianism:*

The Path toward Dialectical Humanism, 1805–1841 (Cambridge: Cambridge University Press, 1980), 124ff. Schleiermacher (1768–1834) was a German Protestant theologian and philosopher who, among other things, saw feelings as mirroring the divine unity and developed a conception of Christianity that reconciled the conflicting one-sidednesses of rationalism and supernaturalism, at least in his view. He excluded from his theology all historical events, the entire Old Testament, and the doctrine of the Trinity. Leo (1799–1878), on the other hand, had a much more conservative bent, although he had been a radical as a student. He favored an organic society and opposed centralization and rationalization. He explained the presence of God's hand in events he opposed with the biblical notion of the sins of one generation being visited upon another, a view Engels saw as absurd.

32 *MEW*, Eb. II:435–440.
33 Ibid., 368.
34 Ibid., 371.
35 Preceding five paragraphs, including quotations, based on ibid., 403–409.
36 Ibid., 419, 435.
37 "Engels and the Genesis of Marxism," *New Left Review* 106 (Nov.–Dec. 1977): 88–89.
38 "Engels and the History of Marxism," in *The History of Marxism*, vol. 1: *Marxism in Marx's Day*, Eric J. Hobsbawm, ed. (Brighton: Harvester Press, 1982), 321.
39 On this, see esp. Macháčková, *Engels und die Literatur*, 157–162.
40 Demetz, *Marx, Engels*, 50.
41 *MEW*, 1:567. Incidentally, Engels had written this article in February and March 1844, before his famous Paris meeting with Marx in August and September of that year.
42 Letter to Marx, 19 Nov. 1844, ibid., 27:12.
43 Again, the evidence comes from his letters to his sister Marie, which are perhaps exaggerated. See especially the one dated 2–8 Aug. 1842, *MEW*, Eb. II:500, where he noted that he had missed a night march and a two-hour drill by complaining of a toothache.
44 Auguste Cornu, *Karl Marx et Friedrich Engels: Leur vie et leur oeuvre*, 4 vols. (Paris: Presses Universitaires de France, 1955–1970), 1:261. Cornu explained that as a volunteer Engels could choose his garrison.
45 Ibid., 2:55; Horst Ullrich, *Der Junge Engels: Eine historisch-biographische Studie seiner weltanschaulichen Entwicklung in den Jahren 1834–1845*, 2 vols. (Berlin: VEB Deutscher Verlag der Wissenschaften, 1961–1966), 1:247.
46 Martin Berger, *Engels, Armies, and Revolution: The Revolutionary Tactics of Classical Marxism* (Hamden, Conn.: Archon Books, 1977), 24, counted ten articles and two poems for the *Rheinische Zeitung*; a book review; a long, satirical, antireligious poem; plus articles and pamphlets on Schelling's anti-Hegelian lectures, on which see below. Cf. *MEW*, 1:433–453, and Eb. II:150–316.
47 Cornu, *Marx et Engels*, 2:60.
48 Ullrich, *Der Junge Engels*, 1:247; Henderson, *Engels*, 1:14; *MEW*, 1:626–627, 631–632; David McLellan, *Marx before Marxism* (New York: Harper and Row, 1970), esp. 46–52.
49 Ullrich, *Der Junge Engels*, 1:273–278. As Ullrich pointed out, Engels later espoused this view in his article "North and South German Liberalism," pub-

lished in the *Rheinische Zeitung* on 12 April 1842. See *MEW*, Eb. II:248, where he said that north German liberals would move from theory to practice, not the reverse.

50 Robert Anchor, "Schelling, Friedrich Wilhelm Joseph von," *Encyclopedia of Philosophy*, 8 vols. (New York: Macmillan, 1967), 7:306; Cornu, *Marx et Engels*, 1:253. Schelling was, of course, an idealist and romantic who criticized Hegel's philosophy as negative and attempted to develop what he called a "positive philosophy" with emphasis on revelation.

51 *MEW*, Eb. II:163–170.

52 Ibid., 173–221.

53 See, e.g., Susan Thornton Frey, "Friedrich Engels' *Dialectics of Nature* and Nineteenth-Century Science" (Ph.D. diss., University of Washington, 1978), 97–99, but note also her pointing out his understanding of Hegelianism (p. 96) and the soundness of his explanation of the break between Schelling and Hegel (p. 102).

54 Ilychov *et al.*, *Engels*, 31.

55 Franz Mehring, *Karl Marx: The Story of His Life*, trans. Edward Fitzgerald (Ann Arbor: University of Michigan Press, 1973), 92.

56 Henderson, *Engels*, 1:18–19; *MEW*, 1:628, 632.

57 Henderson, *Engels*, 1:20–21.

58 *MEW*, 1:454–568.

59 Ibid., 499–524, esp. 502–503, 505, 508, 512.

60 *Marx and Engels: The Intellectual Relationship* (Bloomington: Indiana University Press, 1983), 36–37.

61 David McLellan, *Karl Marx: His Life and Thought* (New York: Harper and Row, 1973), 106.

62 Cf. Ilychov et al., *Engels*, 37; Mayer, *Engels*, 1:128; Bleuel, *Engels*, 101; and see esp. Roy Whitfield, *Frederick Engels in Manchester: The Search for a Shadow* (Manchester: Manchester Free Press, 1988), 69–75, 81–88. The quotations from Eleanor Marx appear in Whitfield and are taken from a letter to Karl Kautsky, 15 March 1898, Kautsky Papers DXVI489, in the International Institute for Social History in Amsterdam.

63 Peter Cadogan, "Harney and Engels," *International Review of Social History* 10 (1965):67 and passim; *Reminiscences of Marx and Engels*, 192.

64 Henderson, *Engels*, 1:26–27, 43.

65 *Friedrich Engels* (New York: Viking, 1978), 42.

66 John M. Sherwood, "Engels, Marx, Malthus, and the Machine," *American Historical Review* 90 (1985): 837–839, provides a recent examination of the literature on the subject.

67 See ibid., 845–848 and the literature cited there.

68 Ibid., 848, 851, for example.

69 Sherwood notes (ibid., 847–848) that some of Engels' contemporaries like Peter Gaskell and William Cooke Taylor shared his misconceptions about the impacts of factories and machinery.

70 *MEW*, 2:281–284.

71 Ibid., 9–20, 97–99, 690–694.

72 See chapter 4 for details.

73 Oscar J. Hammen, *The Red '48ers: Karl Marx and Friedrich Engels* (New York: Scribner's, 1969), 222–227.

74 *MEW*, 5:14–17, 19–21, 34–35, 55–56, 64–77, 256–259, 366–368, 410–413; 6:15–18, 64–68, 381–384.

75 *MEW*, 6:503–515; Hammen, *Red '48ers*, 397.

76 Engels to Jenny Marx, 25 July 1849, *MEW*, 27:501. For Marx's travels to Paris, *MEW*, 6:694.

77 The surviving Marx-Engels correspondence, disregarding letters lost and moneys Engels may have given to Marx in person, shows that Engels sent Marx a total of about £4,000—£31 in 1851, £41 in 1852, and so forth up to £159 in 1860, at least £482 in 1868, and apparently about £350 a year after 1869. Henderson, *Engels*, 1:205, 224–225.

78 Ibid., 1:175. For Freiligrath's salary, Saul K. Padover, *Karl Marx: An Intimate Biography* (New York: New American Library, 1980), 194.

79 Mayer, *Engels*, 2:12, 29, 61.

80 *Reminiscences of Marx and Engels*, 88.

81 *MEW*, 28:85.

82 See chapter 8 for a discussion of Marx's work for that newspaper.

83 Engels to Marx, 17 Feb. 1852, 6 June 1853, and 21 April 1854, *MEW*, 28:23, 255, 344–345. For a further instance of long working hours, see Engels to Marx, 20 Feb. 1868, ibid., 32:35.

84 Engels to Ludwig Kugelmann, 13 Dec. 1867, ibid., 31:580.

85 *MEW*, 28:596 for Marx's comments to Cluss; pp. 694n254 and 778 for the information on Cluss and *Die Reform*.

86 Berger, *Engels, Armies, and Revolution*, 46–47.

87 Marx to Engels, 15 June 1855, *MEW*, 28:448.

88 Marx and Engels, *Collected Works*, 14:401–469.

89 On the scrofula, see Marx and Engels' correspondence from 12 June 1857 to 8 February 1858, *MEW*, 29:143–276. From 28 July to 6 November 1857, Engels had to remove himself from the office for rest at Waterloo and on the isles of Wight and Jersey while he recovered from this chronic illness. During his cure, he nevertheless wrote many of the articles for the *Cyclopaedia*.

90 See Marx and Engels, *Collected Works*, 18:3–375, 545; 14:742–743n295.

91 *Engels, Armies, and Revolution*, 50.

92 Scattered throughout Marx and Engels, *Collected Works*, vols. 12–14.

93 *MEW*, 13:225-268 and 571–612, respectively.

94 Ibid., vols. 15–16 passim; 17:9–264.

95 Berger, *Engels, Armies, and Revolution*, 62. Berger did attest to its high quality, however.

96 *Die Kriegslehre von Friedrich Engels* (Frankfurt a.M.: Europäische Verlagsanstalt, 1968), 21.

97 "Engels and Marx: Military Concepts of the Social Revolutionaries," *Makers of Modern Strategy: Military Thought from Machiavelli to Hitler*, ed. Edward Meade Earl (Princeton: Princeton University Press, 1943), 165–166. Cf. Mark von Hagen's revision of this article in Peter Paret, ed., *Makers of Modern Strategy from Machiavelli to the Nuclear Age* (Princeton: Princeton University Press, 1986), esp. 272–275.

98 Engels to Marx, 31 July 1870, *MEW*, 33:15.

99 Engels, "Über den Krieg—III," *MEW*, 17:19–21.

100 Recollections of Charles Longuet in *Gespräche mit Marx und Engels*, 2:358. Marx's daughter Jenny, Longuet's wife, reported the same thing (ibid., 373) in a letter of 19 November 1870 but added that he began by being called "General Staff" because *Figaro* had used the term to apply to a single person.

101 Neumann, "Engels and Marx," 166.

102 Henderson, *Engels*, 2:435. Marx was more prescient on this matter, telling Engels he was too much influenced "by the military aspect of things."

103 Engels, "Betrachtungen über den Krieg in Deutschland" (from the *Manchester Guardian*, 20 June 1866), *MEW*, 16:170–173.

104 Cf. Henderson, *Engels*, 2:425.

105 Mayer, *Engels*, 2:50.

106 Henderson, *Engels*, 2:442–443; *MEW*, 39:27–28, 35, 262, 585n296, and 682. Henderson quoted Gerlach as saying in his memoirs that Engels did not speak quite so enthusiastically about Wachs (whom Gerlach had called "the military authority for the entire right wing press" and "the recognized expert on the strategic importance of Bizerta harbour") as Wachs had spoken about Engels. But Engels wrote August Bebel in 1893 that Wachs's General Staff work had been laudably mentioned and that he had read some of Wachs's strategic/political writings, which were quite good, although Engels, again, disagreed with their politics.

107 Hellmut von Gerlach, *Von Rechts nach Links* (Hildesheim: Gerstenberg Verlag, 1978), 138–139.

Chapter 2 Engels' Later Life

1 Including, in this period, articles on the French proletariat for the Chartist *Notes to the People*, on the Cologne Communist trial for the *New-York Daily Tribune*, on Poland for the *Commonwealth* (a publication of the First International), and reviews for a number of papers on Marx's first volume of *Capital* (see also chapter 8). See Marx and Engels, *Collected Works*, 11:212–222 and 388–393; *MEW*, 16:159–163, 207–218 and 226–242.

2 Moses Baritz, "Friedrich Engels in Manchester: His Relations with Marx," *Manchester Guardian*, 14 March 1933: 18; Henderson, *Engels*, 1:195, 211, 220; *MEW*, 29:245 and 32:149; Bleuel, *Engels*, 296; Whitfield, *Engels in Manchester*, 19–45; Edmund and Ruth Frow, *Frederick Engels in Manchester: Two Tours with Maps* (Manchester: Working Class Movement Library, n.d.), 29.

3 *MEW*, 32:695.

4 *Reminiscences of Marx and Engels*, 183; *Gespräche mit Marx und Engels*, 2:631.

5 Mayer, *Engels*, 2:108–109; Henderson, *Engels*, 1:212–213.

6 Cf. Henderson, *Engels*, 1:213, 216; "Agreement, 25 Dec. 1862 between Godfrey Ermen, Cotton Spinner, Thread Manufacturer and Bleacher, and Friedrich Engels" and "Articles of Partnership, Ermen and Engels, 30 Jun. 1864," the latter two sources from the Lancashire Record Office, DDX 358/1 and 358/2, respectively. Quotation from the articles of partnership. Henderson states that from 1860 to 1864 Engels got 10% of the profits plus 5% on his capital, but the "agreement" says he would receive £100. I found no mention of 5% therein, but I admit that I had to look through the documents hurriedly.

7   *MEW*, 31:69.
8   Engels to Marx, 4 Oct. 1865, ibid., 149.
9   Engels to Marx, 13 Nov. 1865, ibid., 153. It is interesting to note, on the other hand, that according to Bleuel (*Engels*, 315), Ermen and Engels employed no children and conditions of work there were more favorable than elsewhere. The firm also, according to him, helped finance workers' dwellings and schools.
10 Engels to Elisabeth Engels, 1 July 1869, and to Ludwig Kugelmann, 10 July 1869, *MEW*, 32:615–617, 619–620. Before July 1869, Engels had withdrawn £7,500 of his capital, according to Mike Jenkins, *Frederick Engels in Manchester* (Manchester: Lancashire and Cheshire Communist Party, [1951]), 10. The final dissolution of the partnership, the agreement for which is in the Lancashire Record Office (DDX 358/3), dated 18 Aug. 1869, stipulated he would receive £1,750 for "goodwill and benefits" and an additional £4,964, 16 s., 4 p. to be paid in installments by the next February at 5% interest on the unpaid balance.
11 On this lengthy visit, lasting from May to October, see Yvonne Kapp, *Eleanor Marx*, 2 vols. (New York: Pantheon, 1972–1976), 1:112–117.
12 *Reminiscences of Marx and Engels*, 185–186.
13 Also one of the names of all three of the Marx girls, though of course only the eldest daughter was called Jenny. See Kapp, *Eleanor Marx*, 1:21.
14 On Frau Marx's help with the renting, her letters to Engels, 12 July 1870, *MEW*, 32:714–715, and 10 Aug. 1870, *MEW*, 33:675–676, plus Engels' letter to her, 15 Aug. 1870, *MEW*, 33:137–138. For the date of Engels' move, *MEW*, 17:770.
15 Engels to Ludwig Kugelmann, 28 April 1871, *MEW*, 33:218–219.
16 *Reminiscences of Marx and Engels*, 90, 73, 89, 93; *Gespräche mit Marx und Engels*, 2:354.
17 Marx to Engels, 23 Aug. 1866, *MEW*, 31:253.
18 See, e.g., the letters cited in note 14.
19 Bleuel, *Engels*, 301, for example, stated that Frau Marx did not like Mary or Lizzie Burns and made fun of them. Jerrold Seigel, *Marx's Fate: The Shape of a Life* (Princeton: Princeton University Press, 1978), 266, referred to "a history of coolness between the Marx family and Engels' unconventional household."
20 Stephan Born, *Erinnerungen eines Achtundvierzigers*, edited and introduced by Hans J. Schütz (Berlin and Bonn: Verlag J. H. W. Dietz Nachf., 1978), 41.
21 Kapp, *Eleanor Marx*, 1:183–184; Engels to Wilhelm Liebknecht, 11 Sept. 1871, *MEW*, 33:281.
22 On this famous episode, see *MEW*, 30:309–319.
23 Bleuel, *Engels*, 335, 340–346.
24 See *MEW*, vols. 17 and 18.
25 *MEW*, 18:735n214.
26 "Zur Wohnungsfrage," ibid., 213.
27 Ibid., 219–221.
28 Ibid., 238–241.
29 Ibid., 238–241, 246, 261–263.
30 *MEW*, 7:327–413, 531–542.
31 See, e.g., the review by Thomas A. Brady, Jr., of Horst Buszello et al., eds., *Der deutsche Bauernkrieg*, *The American Historical Review* 91 (Oct. 1986):942–943.
32 *MEW*, 7:337–339, 345, 354, 373–374, 400–402, 413. Cf. the more detailed and critical discussion of Engels' book in Gerhard Kluchert, *Geschichtsschreibung*

und Revolution: Die historischen Schriften von Karl Marx und Friedrich Engels, 1846 bis 1852 (Stuttgart: Fromann Holzboog, 1985), 280–304. In general, Kluchert sees differences between Marx and Engels as historians that I do not find altogether persuasive, but he also emphasizes their collaboration and notices many points on which they agreed.

33 Preface to first edition, *MEW*, 20:7.

34 Ibid., 69, 83.

35 Ibid., 568.

36 Frey, "Engels' 'Dialectics of Nature,'" 20, 319, 441, 468, 507, 509–514, 528, 544, 576–577.

37 Ibid., 466.

38 Ibid., 468.

39 Ibid., 565. Frey pointed to Engels' "uncanny ability to ferret out from the history of science those debates that were not resolved by the science of one period despite the contemporaries' declarations of success" and noted that recently, only two physicists—Leon H. Fisher and Robert N. Varney—had recognized the confusion underlying the debate over contact theory and chemical theory with respect to electrolysis. These were issues that Engels had been concerned with in "Dialectics of Nature" and the two physicists "called, as Engels did, for clarification of the issues." Thus, some of Engels' points are still relevant today, despite the enormous progress in physics since his death.

40 Ibid., 604. Frey qualified this statement by saying that Engels did not discuss the "specific lines of research leading to these discoveries." But in a note on p. 627 she said he "did obliquely recognize the relevant research." She then went on to point to specific research efforts—not those of Arrhenius and Nernst, however—that he discussed.

41 Ibid., 615, 621. It would be both foolish and presumptuous for a nonstudent of the history of science to make such judgments about Engels' scientific arguments. Hence the reliance on Frey's conclusions and even her wording.

42 See also on this ibid., 313, 495, 502, 506–507, 509–514, 516–517, and 522–535, among other places.

43 This is not, however, to accept the exaggerated claims some Soviet writers have made for *Dialectics of Nature*, on which see ibid., chapter 2 and 588, 631. The judgment does seem to run counter to Einstein's well-known comment on the work: "Its content is not of any special interest either from the standpoint of contemporary physics or of the history of physics" (quoted in Sydney Hook, *Reason, Social Myths and Democracy* [New York: Humanities Press, 1940], 222; see also 225–226). But that is not the same thing as saying it was of no interest to the history of *science*. Engels' insights were more in the realm of chemistry than physics, although he was particularly interested in the areas where these two and other sciences overlapped. In any event, Frey is not the only noncommunist historian of science who has found Engels' comments significant, though as far as I know she is the only one to have done so in print.

44 *MEW*, 21:25–28.

45 Cf. ibid., 28–29, and Lawrence Krader, "The Works of Marx and Engels in Ethnology Compared," *International Review of Social History* 18 (1973):241–243.

46 Letter of 13 June 1891, *MEW*, 38:117.

47 *MEW*, 21:553.

48 See ibid., 39, 40, 49–50, 60, 63, for some of Engels' references to studies he had consulted. See also *MEW*, 38:596n129, 107–108 and 117 for his discussion of other sources; and cf. Krader, "Works," 257.

49 For example, *MEW*, 21:48–49.

50 *Ursprung der Familie, des Privateigenthums und des Staats*, ibid., esp. 30, 38, 47–48, 57–58, 60–62, 85, 96–97, 107, 109, 149, 157, 164, 170–173; the foreword to the fourth edition thereof, *MEW*, 22:211–222. On Morgan, see Leslie A. White, "Morgan, Lewis Henry," *International Encyclopedia of the Social Sciences*, 17 vols. (New York: Macmillan, 1968), 10:496-498.

51 *Ursprung der Familie, MEW*, 21:40, 60, 101, 105, 130–131, 133, 142, 145.

52 See, e.g., Eleanor Burke Leacock, "Primitive Communism," in Tom Bottomore, ed., *A Dictionary of Marxist Thought* (Cambridge, Mass.: Harvard University Press, 1983), 395.

53 Cf. Henderson's dismissal of the work (*Engels*, 2:606), based on the quoted comments of Grace Carlton in her popular *Friedrich Engels: The Shadow Prophet* (London: Pall Mall Press, 1965), 218, that *The Origin of the Family* was "not one of Engels's most important books" but was of some significance as a political tract.

54 E.g., *Ursprung der Familie, MEW*, 21:49–51.

55 *Ludwig Feuerbach und der Ausgang der klassischen deutschen Philosophie*, ibid., 263–264, 267, 272.

56 Ibid., 286.

57 David Lamb, "Hegelian Marxist Millenarism," *History of European Ideas* 8 (1987):271-281, noted, in this connection Engels' clear awareness of "the richness of Hegel's theory of truth" (p. 277) and pointed, incidentally, to the importance of Hegel for Marx and, at least implicitly, to the fundamental agreement of Engels' and Marx's views about Hegel, with particular regard to Hegel's concept of truth. See chapter 5 below for further discussion and some qualification about Engels' understanding of Hegel.

58 See below, chapter 8, for further discussion of this effort.

59 *MEW, Verzeichnis*, I:174–201; II:410–578 for a list of only the letters that have survived. Engels had actually taken over full responsibility for this correspondence before Marx died, during the latter's illness and absences from home. See, e.g., Engels' letter to Karl Kautsky, 15 Nov. 1882, *MEW*, 35:399.

60 Cadogan, "Harney," 100, 104. Quotation from letter, Harney to Engels, 3 Jan. 1895.

61 *Gespräche mit Marx und Engels*, 2:597. Engels wrote to Laura Lafargue on 17 December 1894 (*MEW*, 39:346) that he subscribed to three daily and two weekly German newspapers, two English dailies, one daily and two weekly Italian journals, one daily Austrian paper and seven weeklies, one French weekly, three weekly papers from America (one in German), plus weeklies in Polish, Bulgarian, Spanish, and Czechoslovakian. Three of these—Polish, Bulgarian, and Czech, presumably—were in languages he was only slowly learning (but he inclined to exaggerating his ignorance in such matters). He complained that he was constantly getting visitors and had an always growing number of correspondents who took away his time. These things, plus correcting the proofs of the third volume of *Capital*, had limited him to reading only one book in 1894.

62 Reported by Paul Lafargue in *Reminiscences of Marx and Engels*, 92.

63 *MEW*, 36:320; 37:168; 38:107–109; 39:228. At a meeting of the Second Interna-

tional on 12 August 1893, he gave a speech in all three languages. *MEW*, 22:408–409; 39: 560.

64 *MEW*, Eb. II:389, contains a letter to Wilhelm Graeber dated 28–30 April 1839 with long passages in Latin and Greek and shorter ones in English, Italian, Spanish, Portuguese, and French, none of which appear to have been simply lifted from some other source.

65 See, for instance, *MEW*, 33:373–375 for a long letter he had written in Italian, although he later did write to Filippo Turati in French despite the fact that he could still write as well as read Italian, a fact evidenced by a letter of 7 June 1893 to Giovanni Domenico in that language. See *MEW*, 36:52; 38:274, 622–623; 39:62. For a letter in Spanish, see *MEW*, 33:394. The same volume (p. 357) contains his complaint to Paul Lafargue about having to write in Spanish and Italian. The evidence for his knowledge of Portuguese is Paul Lafargue's letter to Nikolai F. Danilson, 14 Dec. 1889, in *MEW*, 37:537–538. See also below in the narrative.

66 *Reminiscences of Marx and Engels*, 92.

67 See *MEW*, 36:334, where in a letter to Hermann Schlüter of 6 June 1885 he spoke of revising Danish as well as French, Italian, and English translations. See also ibid., 400, where in a letter to Johann Philipp Becker he stated that his knowledge of Russian and Polish fortunately was not adequate for revising works in those languages. On the Danish, see also *MEW*, 30:625 and 33:428–429. On his knowledge of Russian, see *MEW*, 35:254 for a short letter in that language to Lev Nikolayevich Hartmann and 33:437, where in a letter to Nikolai F. Danielson of 8 Feb. 1886, written in English, he noted that a word was missing from a Russian translation of *Capital*, vol. 2.

68 *MEW*, 22:407; 28:260–261, 515, 667n45; 30:348; 31:129; 32:471, 776n415; 36:8, 434, 615; 37:537; 38:109, 273; 39:222, 310, 346. He subscribed at times to newspapers in Rumanian as well as the languages listed in note 61 above. The list of languages may not be exhaustive. I cannot now find references to the fact, but I believe he was also acquainted with modern Swedish and Norwegian as well as Danish. Also not counted but among his accomplishments were modern Irish and the Milanese dialect. See, for example, *MEW*, 32:506, 510; 36:321.

69 *MEW*, 6:48. For the translation, Smith Palmer Bovie, trans., *Satires and Epistles of Horace* (Chicago: University of Chicago Press, 1959), 170.

70 "Die Persönlichkeiten des Bundesrats" (29 Nov. 1848), *MEW*, 6:64.

71 "Der preussische Fusstritt für die Frankfurter," *Neue Rheinische Zeitung*, 2 May 1849, ibid., 459.

72 Ibid., 18:530.

73 Ibid., 19:202–206.

74 Ibid., 21:9–11. These conclusions are undoubtedly debatable, but they show Engels' wide-ranging learning as well, perhaps, as his prejudices.

75 "Was nun?" from *Der Sozialdemokrat*, 8 March 1890, *MEW*, 22:9.

76 Letter to Marx, 6 June 1863, *MEW*, 28:256, 259.

77 E.g., letter to Marx, 23 May 1862, *MEW*, 30:241.

78 Letter of 10 April 1888, *MEW*, 37:45. Engels took the punning one step further and said that in the French word for mustard (*moutard*) there was no doubt that the *m* had originally been a *b*, derived from *bous*, which fact shed dazzling light on the practice of using mustard only on beef, never on lamb. Since Engels was

himself fond of etymology and knowledgeable about it, he obviously was poking fun at himself here at least as much as at Paul Lafargue.

79   *MEW*, 31:240–241.

80   Letter to Nikolai F. Danielson, 12 Sept. 1880, *MEW*, 34:464.

81   See, e.g., Oran J. Hale, *The Great Illusion, 1900–1914* (New York: Harper and Row, 1971), esp. 21–27, 285–314.

82   *MEW*, 36:390–391.

83   Ibid., 401. Here, Engels grossly underestimated the death toll, which may have been as high as twelve million without counting civilian casualties, although R. Ernst and Trevor N. Dupuy put the deaths at only 8,020,780—still a much higher figure than Engels'—and the economic cost of the war at $281,887,000,000. According to their figures, the total forces mobilized were 65,038,810 people. (*The Encyclopedia of Military History from 3500 B.C. to the Present*, 2d rev. ed. [New York: Harper and Row, 1986], 990.) Despite such underestimation, Engels still hit upon a major element of war in 1914—its great destructiveness. In this, he was not alone, of course. (See, e.g., Michael Howard, "Men against Fire: The Doctrine of the Offensive in 1914," in *Makers of Modern Strategy*, 510–526.) Where he was prescient was in anticipating the effects of such destruction upon the national will of the countries involved, especially, of course, Russia.

84   *MEW*, 36:524–526.

85   *MEW*, 37:11.

86   Ibid., 199.

87   Ibid., 39–40.

88   Ibid., 52.

89   Engels gave credit to a Mr. Inglis Palgrave for first calling attention to this problem in 1883.

90   As quoted in the preface to the 1892 edition of *The Condition of the Working Class in England*, edited and translated by W. O. Henderson and W. H. Chaloner (Stanford: Stanford University Press, 1958), 369–370.

91   *MEW*, 22:198. See Mark Twain and Charles Dudley Warner's *The Gilded Age* for a similar depiction of American politics in this period.

92   *MEW*, 36:392–393.

93   Written in Italian.

94   *MEW*, 37:260.

95   Kapp, *Eleanor Marx*, 1:184–186, 191–192. As in many other particulars, here too, Kapp's study provides many details about Engels' life that have eluded his own biographers.

96   *MEW*, 34:341–342.

97   *MEW*, 37:498. On Freddy's parenthood, see especially Kapp, *Eleanor Marx*, 1:289–297 and 2:435–439, plus the literature she cites. See also McLellan, *Karl Marx*, 271–272.

98   Kapp, *Eleanor Marx*, 1:285n; 2:444n.

99   *MEW*, 37:106–107. As Engels explained the situation to Laura Lafargue (ibid., 108–109), Kautsky's mother and sister both hated Louise, and, encouraged by the sister, Karl had fallen in love with a young lady named Bella, who later ran off with Karl's brother, Hans. To make matters more confusing for biographers, Karl later married a woman named Luise.

100   Letter of 17 Oct. 1888, ibid., 114–115.

101 Ibid., 500.
102 Letter of 26 Nov. 1890., ibid., 505.
103 Ibid., 113, 132, 519–520.
104 *Reminiscences of Marx and Engels*, 187.
105 *MEW*, 38:257–258.
106 Ibid., 421.
107 Letters to Laura Lafargue and Victor Adler, ibid., 436, 501.
108 *MEW*, 33:19.
109 Letters to Sorge, 23 Feb. and 10 Nov. 1894, ibid., 212, 307.
110 Letters to Richard Fischer, 9 May 1895, and Laura Lafargue, 14 May 1895, ibid., 475, 477; Henderson, *Engels*, 2:726.
111 Letter of 18 June 1895, *MEW*, 39:489.
112 Ibid., 493.
113 Letter to Isaac A. Gurwitsch, ibid., 542.
114 Letter of Samuel Moore to Eleanor Marx Aveling, ibid., 543.
115 Kapp, *Eleanor Marx*, 2:544–545, 597–598, 651–653, 656. On 12 May 1894 Engels had written to F. A. Sorge: "The Social Democratic Federation here shares with your German-American socialists the distinction of being the only party to have reduced the Marxist theory of development to a rigid orthodoxy that the workers should not develop out of their own class consciousness but that they have to swallow as articles of faith instantly and without development. For that reason, both remain mere sects and come, as Hegel said, from nothing through nothing to nothing." *MEW*, 39:245. Note here, incidentally, Engels' opposition to narrow orthodoxy and his emphasis on the workers' developing their own theory rather than having it imposed on them from above, à la Lenin.
116 Ibid., 599.
117 Henderson, *Engels*, 2:727–728.

Chapter 3   Engels in the Dichotomist Portrait

1 *Karl Marx: Man and Fighter*, trans. Gwenda David and Erich Mosbacher (1936; rev. ed., 1970; repr. Bungay, Suffolk: Penguin Books, 1976), 92.
2 *Reminiscences of Marx and Engels*, 83, 148, 182.
3 George Lukács, *Geschichte und Klassenbewusstsein: Studien über Marxistische Dialektik* (Berlin: Der Malik Verlag, 1923), 17n. David MacGregor has communicated to me privately his view that "'our knowledge of nature' is in itself a form of consciousness, and therefore dialectical, and not fast frozen as Lukács thinks." My thanks to him for the comment.
4 See ibid., 16, 32, 240, 250, and 254 for mentions of Marx and Engels together, and 16, 28, 238, 243, and 259 for favorable references to or approving quotations of Engels.
5 Karl Korsch, *Marxism and Philosophy*, trans. Fred Halleday (London: NLB, 1970), 14, 51, 67, 69–70, 79. On Lukács's life, see George Lichtheim, *George Lukács* (New York: Viking, 1970). Patrick Goode provides a critical account of Korsch's life in *Karl Korsch: A Study in Western Marxism* (London: Macmillan, 1979).
6 *Marxism and Philosophy*, 18, 80, 108n.
7 *From Hegel to Marx: Studies in the Intellectual Development of Karl Marx* (Ann Arbor: University of Michigan Press, 1971), 75.

8   *Marxism: A Historical and Critical Study* (New York: Praeger, 1961), 58–59.

9   Ibid., 59–60. This is not to deny, of course, that there were also *some* similarities between social democracy and Leninism.

10 Ibid., 60–61.

11 Ibid., 236–243.

12 Ibid., 234–235, 246.

13 Ibid., 247.

14 Ibid., 249–250.

15 Ibid., 251.

16 Ibid., 254. Elsewhere, Lichtheim defined the dialect as "self-transcendence by way of internal conflict to higher levels of development." "Historical and Dialectical Materialism," *Dictionary of the History of Ideas*, 5 vols. (New York: Scribner's, 1973), 2:454.

17 Ibid., 254–255.

18 Ibid., 256. The *Grundrisse* was an uncompleted work never published in Marx's lifetime. Most scholars treat it as a draft for *Capital*. Its full title was *Grundrisse der Kritik der politischen Ökonomie* (Outlines of a critique of political economy).

19 Ibid., 256–258.

20 Robert C. Tucker, *Philosophy and Myth in Karl Marx*, 2d ed. (Cambridge: Cambridge University Press, 1972), 23.

21 Ibid., 184, 199; Tucker, *The Marxian Revolutionary Idea* (New York: Norton, 1970), 91. Interestingly, especially throughout the latter work, Tucker continued to treat Marx and Engels as a team despite the differences between them that he noted. Unlike Lichtheim, therefore, he remained to some degree a part of the old school of interpretation even though he added ammunition to the dichotomist interpretation.

22 Alfred Schmidt, *Der Begriff der Natur in der Lehre von Marx* (Frankfurt: Europäische Verlagsanstalt, 1962), 41, 43–45.

23 Ibid., 46, 81–82, 93.

24 Ibid., 109, 115–116.

25 Shlomo Avineri, *The Social and Political Thought of Karl Marx* (Cambridge: Cambridge University Press, 1968), 153, 143–144.

26 Norman Levine, *The Tragic Deception: Marx contra Engels* (Oxford and Santa Barbara: Clio Books, 1975), xiii-xv. Incidentally, this was the first full-length book devoted to the theme of the dichotomy between Engels' and Marx's ideas.

27 Z. A. Jordan, *The Evolution of Dialectical Materialism: A Philosophical and Sociological Analysis* (New York: St. Martin's Press, 1967), 26–27.

28 Avineri, *Social and Political Thought*, 65–72.

29 *Marx and Engels: The Intellectual Relationship* (Bloomington: Indiana University Press, 1983), 116–117.

30 Ibid., 133.

31 Norman Levine, *Dialogue within the Dialectic* (London: Allen and Unwin, 1984), 169.

32 Ibid., 170.

33 Ibid., 202.

34 *MEW*, 31:312–313.

35 For example, he claimed that Engels did not "account properly" for pp. 472–476

of *Capital*, vol. 2, when Levine's own table shows that Engels in fact accounted correctly for them. Levine, *Dialogue*, 207–208.

36 See esp. ibid., 195–254.

37 In his foreword to vol. 2, for instance, Engels had complained that the manuscripts' "logical sequence is frequently interrupted, the treatment is in places full of gaps and especially at the end, completely fragmentary." He said, however, that he had attempted to resolve these hardly trifling difficulties exclusively in the spirit of Marx. *MEW*, 24:12.

38 Seigel, *Marx's Fate*, 339–344.

39 Levine, *Dialogue*, 171.

40 Seigel, *Marx's Fate*, 339–340.

41 Frederick L. Bender, ed., *The Betrayal of Marx* (New York: Harper and Row, 1976), 29.

42 *Evolution*, 3, 9.

43 *Social and Political thought*, 65.

44 See esp. Bender, *Betrayal*, 2, 22, 24; Cecil L. Eubanks, *Karl Marx and Friedrich Engels: An Analytical Bibliography*, 2d ed. (New York and London: Garland, 1984), xxxiv-xxxv; Carver, *Marx and Engels*, 126. But cf. the comment of Stanley Moore in "Marx and the Origin of Dialectical Materialism," *Inquiry* 14 (1972):427: "Marx, not Engels, is the founder of dialectical materialism and in his version, even more than in that of Engels, the dialectic is incompatible with materialism."

45 Although seldom defined by scholars, these two terms served roughly as synonyms in the writings of the dichotomists as well as those of the early Marx; the terms referred to the emphasis these scholars saw in Marx's writings upon man's transformation of nature and society.

46 Jordan, *Evolution*, 26–27.

47 Levine, *Marx contra Engels*, 108, 137. These assertions about Engels' views, incidentally, were unaccompanied by any reference to where in his writings they allegedly appeared.

48 *Betrayal of Marx*, 28–29.

49 *Evolution*, 9. As Jordan explained on p. 33, Engels' theory of knowledge involved conceiving perception as consisting of images produced by external stimuli. What the cognizing subject contributed to the process was allegedly lost on him. Here, however, Jordan called Engels' view "naive realism," which he distinguished from Lenin's copy theory of perception, although as noted above, on p. 9 he had called Engels' view a copy theory.

50 *Betrayal*, 67.

51 *Marx and Engels*, 76–77, 96–100.

52 "Marx's Dialectic Method," *History and Theory* 19 (1980):294–298, 300, 309; "Marx's Theory of Ideas," *Studies in Marxist Historical Theory, History and Theory* 20 (1981):367; "Marx, Engels, and the Dialectics," *Studies in Soviet Thought* 23 (1982):275, 279n5. See also Kain's *Marx' Method, Epistemology, and Humanism: A Study in the Development of His Thought* (Dordrecht: D. Reidel, 1986), esp. 7–10, 34–36, 58, 62–63, 73, 88, 94, 108, 167–168; my thanks to him for providing me a copy.

53 Kain, "Marx, Engels, and the Dialectics," 275, 282n35; "Marx's Dialectic Method," 296.

54 "Marx's Dialectic Method," 305, 296.
55 *MEW*, 13:474.
56 Entire paragraph except parenthetical sentence from Carver, *Marx and Engels*, 110–111; *MEW*, 13:7, 475. My translation of the second quotation, which Carver quoted only in part.
57 My translation of the passage quoted in Carver, *Marx and Engels*, 111; translation from *MEW*, 13:638.
58 "Marx, Engels, and Dialectics," 275–276.
59 *Marx and Engels*, 116–117.
60 *Dialogue*, 10–12, 96–98.
61 *Betrayal of Marx*, 2, 53.
62 *Social and Political Thought*, 3.
63 *Marx and Engels*, 37, 50, 52.
64 Ibid., 154–157, 151.
65 Jordan, *Evolution*, 26–27, 48.
66 Ibid., 125.
67 Ibid., 125, 307–308, 324, 392, 299.
68 Ibid., 65–66, 78–79, 82, 86.
69 Ibid., 322–323.
70 *Marx and Engels*, 116–117.
71 Ibid., 96–109, 154–157.
72 *Marx contra Engels*, 108. Quite apart from the fact that Levine failed to document where Engels expressed this grim view of communist society, one can hardly imagine the man whom Eleanor Marx portrayed as so joyously celebrating the end of his years at Ermen and Engels desiring this sort of future for mankind. Work at the office had been "highly productive of the necessities and luxuries of life" for him, but he had despised it nonetheless. Surely he did not work so hard during the years of his "retirement" merely to impose that kind of drudgery on his fellow creatures. Yet Bender (*Betrayal*, 28–29) made essentially the same point as Levine in this regard.
73 *Betrayal*, 8, 38.
74 "Marx, Engels, and Dialectics," 278, 282n35.
75 *Dialogue*, 8, 94–96.

Chapter 4 The *Communist Manifesto*

1 Avineri, *Social and Political Thought*, 153; Lichtheim, *Marxism*, 59.
2 Carver, *Marx and Engels*, 86, 94.
3 Oscar J. Hammen, *The Red '48ers, Karl Marx and Friedrich Engels* (New York: Scribner's, 1969), 159.
4 Henderson, *Engels*, 1:111, 114.
5 Ibid., 116; Dirk J. Struik, ed., *Birth of the Communist Manifesto* (New York: International Publishers, 1971), 58; Engels to Marx, 25–26 Oct. 1847, *MEW*, 27:98. Hess was close to the "true socialists," so both Marx and Engels had distanced themselves from him.
6 Engels to Marx, 23–24 Nov. 1847, *MEW*, 27:107.
7 According to Hammen (*Red '48ers*, 169), however, both men completed a draft of the *Manifesto*; "then the final draft was made," with Marx having responsibil-

ity for the final copy after Engels returned from Brussels to Paris.

8 Engels, "Grundsätze des Kommunismus," *MEW*, 4:363–364 (henceforth cited as "Grundsätze").

9 I say Marx as a piece of convenient stylistic shorthand. As noted above, both men seem to have had a direct hand in the *Manifesto*'s composition (that is, as distinguished from what Marx took over from the "Principles"), and conventional practice correctly lists both as its authors.

10 Marx and Engels, "Manifest der Kommunistischen Partei," *MEW*, 4:463–464, 468–469 (henceforth cited as "Manifest").

11 "Grundsätze," 365.

12 "Manifest," 476, 473–474, respectively.

13 "Grundsätze," 370.

14 "Manifest," 467–468, 482.

15 "Grundsätze," 371–372.

16 "Manifest," 467, 469, 471–477.

17 "Grundsätze," 372.

18 "Manifest," 493.

19 "Grundsätze," 372–373.

20 "Manifest," 481–482.

21 "Grundsätze," 373–374; "Manifest," 481–482.

22 "Grundsätze," 377.

23 "Manifest," 478–479.

24 Struik, *Birth*, 162; Marx and Engels, *Collected Works*, 6:354na and 672n69.

25 Cf. the slightly different renditions in Struik, *Birth*, 168–169, and Marx and Engels, *Collected Works*, 6:103.

26 "Manifest," 479–481.

27 "Grundsätze," 377–379.

28 "Manifest," 482–492.

29 "Grundsätze," 379–380.

30 "Manifest," 492–493.

31 See note 7 above.

Chapter 5 Epistemology and Method

1 Seigel, *Marx's Fate*, 316–320, 331, 360–362. Cf. the similar thesis of Stanley Moore in "Marx and the Origin of Dialectical Materialism," *Inquiry* 14 (1971):420–422, 426.

2 Seigel, *Marx's Fate*, 361.

3 Ibid., 323–326. Cf. the in some respects simpler, in other respects more complicated views of Kain discussed in chapter 3 above. See also Walter L. Adamson, *Marx and the Disillusionment of Marxism* (Berkeley: University of California Press, 1985), 1–154.

4 *MEW*, 23:27.

5 Kain, "Marx's Dialectic Method," 305; John Maguire, *Marx's Paris Writings: An Analysis* (Dublin and London: Gill and Macmillan, 1972), 107.

6 Quoted by Bender in *Betrayal of Marx*, 77.

7 *MEW*, 31:313.

8 *Humanist Marxism and Wittgenstein in Social Philosophy* (Manchester: Man-

chester University Press, 1983), 22, 31, 34. Easton agreed, for example (p. 33), that Marx did make use of the distinction between essence and appearance in his treatment of the labor theory of value, discussed below.

9 *Das Kapital*, vol. 1, in *MEW*, 23:86.

10 Ibid., 88–89. Note, again, the Hegelian language here.

11 Ibid., 89–90.

12 Ibid., 335.

13 Ibid., 669, 687.

14 Ibid., 254n48. For evidence of the reliance on these kinds of reports in *Capital*, vol. 1, and *Condition of the Working Class*, one has merely to page through any edition of both.

15 The letter itself is printed in *MEW*, 31:327.

16 *MEW*, 25:34, 37, 41.

17 Ibid., 43–44.

18 Ibid., 46.

19 Marx inserted the French expression parenthetically after the German *"eigentlicher Wert."*

20 *MEW*, 25:53–54.

21 Ibid., 55.

22 Ibid., 58.

23 Another extended application of the distinction appears in chapter 12, p. 219, of *Capital*, vol. 3, in ibid.

24 *MEW*, 21:292–293.

25 Ibid., 183.

26 *MEW*, 20:20–22.

27 Ibid., 26.

28 Seigel, *Marx's Fate*, 320; Marx and Engels, *Gesamtausgabe* (Berlin: Marx-Engels Verlag, 1927–1934), series 1, vol. 6:473 (Marx's original version printed in the *Neue Rheinische Zeitung*, 5 April 1849); *MEW*, 6:399 (showing, in footnotes, the changes Engels introduced in 1891). I have revised the translations that appear in Seigel to make them conform more closely with the German, but he correctly and perceptively made the substantive point.

29 *MEW*, 20:33, 36.

30 Ibid., 39.

31 *MEW*, 39:430–431.

32 Kain, "Marx, Engels and Dialectics," 275. See above, chapter 3, for a summary of Carver's virtually identical position.

33 *MEW*, 13:475.

34 As discussed above in chapter 3, these points come from Kain, "Marx, Engels and Dialectic," 276–278, and "Marx's Dialectical Method," 305–309.

35 *MEW*, 13:475.

36 *MEW*, 21:298–299.

37 *MEW*, 3:7.

38 *MEW*, 3:547n1; 21:264.

39 Seigel, *Marx's Fate*, 324.

40 *MEW*, 29:260.

41 *MEW*, 21:293.

42 *MEW*, 18:516.

43 Jean Hyppolite, *Etudes sur Marx et Hegel* (Paris: Editions Marcel Rivière, 1965), esp. 121–141; Iring Fetscher, *Marx and Marxism* (New York: Herder and Herder, 1971), esp. 40–147; Michel Henry, *Marx: A Philosophy of Human Reality*, trans. Kathleen McLaughlin (Bloomington: Indiana University Press, 1976), esp. 54, 59–61, 83–84, 127–156.

44 *MEW*, 25:456; Avineri, *Social and Political Thought*, 177–181, where he quotes more extensively from *Capital*.

45 *MEW*, 19:223. Cf. Avineri, *Social and Political Thought*, 202–203, where he makes a big issue of Marx's use of the term *Aufhebung* with respect to the state *as contrasted with* Engels' use of a different term, *Absterben* (withering away). As seen above, however, Engels also used the Hegelian term (in its verb form) with all its dialectical overtones.

46 *The Philosophy of Hegel: An Introduction and Re-Examination* (New York: Collier Books, 1966), 19, 212.

47 David MacGregor, *The Communist Ideal in Hegel and Marx* (Toronto and Buffalo: University of Toronto Press, 1984), 18–20. For further criticism of Marx's understanding of Hegel in this regard, see also his "Marxism's Hegelian Blind Spot: The Theory of State in Hegel and Marx," *Current Perspectives in Social Theory* 9 (1989):143–175, and the sources cited there as well as his "The State at Dusk," *The Owl of Minerva* 21 (1989):51–64.

48 Maguire, *Marx's Paris Writings*, 97–98.

Chapter 6 Engels' Alleged Reformism

1 For a good, brief treatment of Bernstein's ideas and life, see Monty Johnstone, "Bernstein, Eduard," in Tom Bottomore, ed., *A Dictionary of Marxist Thought* (Cambridge, Mass.: Harvard University Press, 1983), 48–49. For a more extended account, see Peter Gay, *The Dilemma of Democratic Socialism: Eduard Bernstein's Challenge to Marx* (New York: Columbia University Press, 1952).

2 Lichtheim, *Marxism*, 265.

3 Charles F. Elliott, "*Quis Custodiat Sacra*? Problems of Marxist Revisionism," *Journal of the History of Ideas* 28 (1967):74–75.

4 Ibid., 73–74.

5 Ibid., 72–73.

6 The claim about Engels is in ibid., 84. Lenin, Elliott said, ignored this trend of Engels'.

7 Quoted in David McLellan, *The Thought of Karl Marx: An Introduction* (New York: Harper and Row, 1971), 204.

8 Friedrich Engels, "Revolution and Counter-Revolution in Germany," in Marx and Engels, *Collected Works*, II:85–86. Danton's famous words, as reported in *Le Moniteur*, 4 Sept. 1792, were actually "De l'audace, et encore de l'audace, et toujours de l'audace!," which can be rendered "Audacity, and again audacity, and always audacity!"

9 *MEW*, 17:416–417.

10 Ibid., 651.

11 Ibid., 652.

12 *MEW*, 18:160.

13 Karl Marx, *Capital*, trans. Eden and Cedar Paul, 2 vols. (New York: E. P.

Dutton, 1962), 2:887, where Engels' preface is reproduced in part in the original English.

14 *MEW*, 37:365–368.

15 *MEW*, 22:78–79.

16 See, e.g., *MEW*, 7:267 and 18:633ff., as quoted in McLellan, *Thought*, 206, 211.

17 *MEW*, 22:234–235.

18 *MEW*, 17:625.

19 Ibid., 622–624.

20 Ibid., 336–342, emphasis in the original.

21 Cf. Hal Draper, *Karl Marx's Theory of Revolution*, vol. 3, *The "Dictatorship of the Proletariat"* (New York: Monthly Review Press, 1986), esp. 269–70, but also 211–213, 264, which I read for the first time after these lines were written. In this connection, it is perhaps also relevant to introduce McLellan's view (*Thought*, 202–203) that Marx associated the term *dictatorship* with the Roman *dictatura* in which one man assumed temporary power during a period of crisis. But cf. the argument in Tucker, *Marxian Revolutionary Idea*, 75ff. On this whole question, see also Richard N. Hunt, *The Political Ideas of Marx and Engels*, vol. 1, *Marxism and Totalitarian Democracy, 1818–1850* (Pittsburgh: University of Pittsburgh Press, 1974), 229–329.

22 *MEW*, 18:633.

23 Quoted in McLellan, *Karl Marx*, 205.

24 See above, chapter 4.

25 *MEW*, 19:6–7.

26 The above is based on *MEW*, 22;644n433. The editors of *MEW* unfortunately did not publish Fischer's letter, and so far as I am aware, it has not been published elsewhere.

27 The last five paragraphs are based on a letter of Engels to Fischer, 8 March 1895, *MEW*, 39:424–426, and on Engels' introduction to *Civil War in France*, *MEW*, 22:523, 525.

28 *MEW*, 22:518.

29 Ibid., 519–521.

30 Ibid., 521.

31 Ibid., 521–522.

32 This document ended a lengthy struggle between ducal power and that of the nobility by recognizing the freedom and privileges of the latter.

33 *MEW*, 22:524.

34 Ibid.

35 Ibid., 524–525.

36 Ibid., 645n433.

37 *MEW*, 39:452, Engels' emphasis.

38 Ibid., 458, Engels' italics.

39 Quoted in Yvonne Kapp, *Eleanor Marx*, 2:591. As Kapp pointed out, after Engels' death Bernstein used his reluctantly abridged introduction to suggest that he had become a reformist in his last days. Cf. *MEW*, 39:606n455.

40 *MEW*, 39:161–163.

41 Engels to Lafargue, 12 Nov. 1892, *MEW*, 38:513–514. See also numerous comments in letters of this period criticizing the reformism of Fabianism and recognizing Bernstein's flirtation with it, e.g., ibid., 447–448, 519.

Chapter 7   Humanism, Positivism, and Determinism

1   See above, chapter 3.

2   For treatments of his humanism, see, e.g., Loyd D. Easton and Kurt H. Guddat, *Writings of the Young Marx on Philosophy and Society* (Garden City, N.Y.: Doubleday, 1967), 17ff.; Levine, *Marx contra Engels*, esp. 43, 84ff.; and Michel Henry, *Marx: A Philosophy of Human Reality*, trans. Kathleen McLaughlin (Bloomington: Indiana University Press, 1983), 55, 58–63, 86, 106, 121–136.

3   Quotations from Easton and Guddat, *Writings*, 17. In what follows, I will use the term *humanism* primarily in the last sense mentioned in the narrative—as referring to the view that man plays a role in the shaping of his history. This distinguishes it from *determinism*, which emphasizes the role of impersonal forces, although some of those forces (like relations of production) *were* shaped by earlier men. I use the term *positivism* to refer to the belief that the laws of nature or something like them can be applied to social relations and developments. Obviously, according to these definitions it would be possible for someone to be a determinist without being a positivist, but to the extent that a person believed natural laws applied to social relations, he would have to be a determinist. (I.e., a positivist would be ipso facto a determinist, but not vice versa.) Equally obviously, humanism and determinism are to a degree logically incompatible, but as I argue below, both Marx and Engels sometimes expressed humanist, sometimes determinist views, seemingly without being aware of any contradiction in those views, even as they applied to the capitalist era alone.

4   *MEW*, 1:505.

5   Ibid., 514–515.

6   *Writings*, 17.

7   *MEW*, 1:544–545.

8   Ibid., 545–546.

9   *MEW*, 2:98, Engels' italicization.

10   Ibid., 556.

11   *MEW*, 19:226.

12   See, e.g., his letter to P. W. Annenkow, 28 Dec. 1846, in *MEW*, 4:548.

13   *MEW*, 20:260–261.

14   Ibid., 466, Engels' italicization.

15   *MEW*, 21:296–297.

16   *MEW*, 22:83.

17   Although it was written in English, there are numerous variants of this famous letter. I have followed Kapp, *Eleanor Marx*, 2:221n., because she cites a draft of the letter in the Institute of Marxism-Leninism, Moscow. But cf. Marx and Engels, *Selected Correspondence* (Moscow: Foreign Language Publishing House, n.d.), 478–479, and *Marxism and Art: Writings in Aesthetics and Criticism*, ed. Berel Lang and Forrest Williams (New York: David McKay, 1972), 48–50, which confuses the titles of this and a letter to Lassalle on pp. 52ff. Engels went on to say that the realism of which he spoke could appear despite the views of the author. He discussed at length the example of Balzac, "a far greater master of realism than all the Zolas *passés, présents et à venir.*"

18   *MEW*, 37:463–464. Cf. the similar lines of argument in Engels' letter to W. Borgius of 15 January 1894, *MEW*, 39:205–207.

19   *MEW*, 13:10.

20 *MEW*, 1:514–515.
21 Ibid., 522.
22 Ibid., 557.
23 *MEW*, 2:38, Marx's emphasis.
24 *MEW*, 4:130.
25 "The Elections in England—Tories and Whigs," Marx and Engels, *Collected Works*, 11:329. This from Engels' translation of Marx's German text, which apparently has not survived.
26 *MEW*, 13:8–9.
27 Ibid., 7. Marx's stated reasons for not including the introduction were not, as some might be inclined to speculate, that he was dissatisfied with what he had written there. Rather, after reflection he felt that "every anticipation of results yet to be proved seems intruding, and the reader who will follow me in general must make up his mind to ascend from the particular to the general."
28 Ibid., 621.
29 *MEW*, 20:11.
30 Ibid., 131–132.
31 Ibid., 260.
32 *MEW*, 21:169–170.
33 Quoted by Engels in the 1892 preface to *The Condition of the Working Class in England*, included as appendix 3 to W. O. Henderson and W. H. Chaloner's translation of that work (Stanford: Stanford University Press, 1968), 368 (cited from this source because Engels wrote in English).
34 *MEW*, 21:249.
35 *MEW*, 37:436.
36 Ibid., 463. It was at this point that Engels began the passage, "We make our history ourselves . . . ," quoted at length earlier in this chapter.
37 Ibid., 492–494.
38 *MEW*, 38:281–282.
39 E.g., ibid., 366; *MEW*, 39:37–38. Cf. Marx and Engels' preface to the 1882 edition of the *Communist Manifesto*, *MEW*, 19:295–296. Engels tended to doubt to perhaps a greater extent than Marx that Russia could avoid the path of industrial capitalism, but he did entertain the possibility.
40 Letter to Filippo Turatti, 6 June 1893, *MEW*, 39:80.
41 Letter to Friedrich Albert Lange, 29 March 1865, *MEW*, 31:466.
42 Letter to Conrad Schmidt, 12 March 1895, *MEW*, 39:431.
43 Letter to Werner Sombart, 11 March 1895, ibid., 428.
44 Letter to August Bebel, 18–28 March 1875, *MEW*, 34:127. In its Gotha Program, the party of Bebel and Liebknecht had incorporated many Lassallean ideas in conjunction with the unification of the two socialist parties in Germany.
45 Engels to P. L. Lavrov, 12–17 Nov. 1875, ibid., 169–172.
46 Letter to George William Lamplugh, 11 April 1893, *MEW*, 39:63. Retranslated from German into English, a version containing the original English not being available.
47 *MEW*, 23:15–16.
48 Ibid., 89. In this connection, Marx also quoted Engels' comments from "Outlines of a Critique of Political Economy" about a natural law resting on the unconsciousness of all concerned.

49 Ibid., 327, 335.
50 Ibid., 466, 674, Marx's italicization.
51 Carver, *Marx and Engels*, 136.
52 *MEW*, 30:131.
53 Ibid., 578.
54 Letter of 11 July 1868, *MEW*, 32:553.
55 *MEW*, 23:25–27.

Chapter 8 The Intellectual Partnership

1 Carver, *Marx and Engels*, 52.
2 *MEW*, 8:233–235, 627.
3 See *MEW*, 7:244–326 and vols. 8–14, passim.
4 Henderson, *Life*, 1:206.
5 *MEW*, 30:216, 225–226, and 725n259.
6 Cf. "The War in America," in W. O. Henderson and W. H. Chaloner, eds., *Engels as Military Critic: Articles by Friedrich Engels Reprinted from the Volunteer Journal and the Manchester Guardian of the 1860s* (Manchester: Manchester University Press, 1959), 113–117, and *MEW*, 15:486–495.
7 For the quotation alone, Henderson, *Life*, 2:415.
8 *MEW*, 15:494–495.
9 See T. Harry Williams, *Lincoln and His Generals* (New York: Alfred A. Knopf, 1952), 291–295; Shelby Foote, *The Civil War: A Narrative*, 3 vols. (New York: Random House, 1958–1974), 2:966 and 3:16–17, 126; *MEW*, 15:486–495; *Memoirs of Gen. W. T. Sherman*, 2 vols., 4th ed. rev. (New York: Charles L. Webster, 1892), 2:26, 115, 152, 164–166; *The War of the Rebellion: A Compilation of the Official Records of the Union and Confederate Armies* (Washington: Government Printing Office, 1892), series 1, vol. 39, pt. 2:411–413 and pt. 3:162, 202–203, 357–358, 394, 576, 594–595; Lloyd Lewis, *Sherman, Fighting Prophet* (New York: Harcourt, Brace, 1932), 431–432. Of course, the focus of Engels' thinking was cutting transportation lines, while Sherman's goals were to destroy the South's material resources and to deliver a political and psychological blow from which the region could not recover so as to continue fighting.
10 This commentary based on maps in E. Merton Coulter, *The Confederate States of America, 1861–1865* (Baton Rouge: Louisiana State University Press, 1960), 270, and E. B. Long with Barbara Long, *The Civil War Day by Day: An Almanac, 1861–1865* (Garden City, N.Y.: Doubleday, 1971), map facing p. 563.
11 Although even Carver had to admit that Marx had contributed to the work (*Marx and Engels*, 124–125). See also *MEW*, 34:36–37, 39–40 for the letters exchanged between Marx and Engels on the subject from 5 to 7 March. 1877. Marx also provided other materials Engels used in *Anti-Dühring*. See letter, Marx to Engels, 8 Aug. 1877, *MEW*, 34:66.
12 Carver, *Marx and Engels*, 32–41.
13 *MEW*, 27:379–381. The 18th Brumaire (9 Nov. 1799) was the day Napoleon Bonaparte overthrew the Directory and established himself as first consul in France. Marc Causidière (1808–1861) was an organizer of secret revolutionary societies during the July Monarchy; after the revolution of 1848 he became the prefect of police in Paris and a deputy to the Constituent Assembly before fleeing

to England after the suppression of the June uprising. Georges-Jacques Danton (1759–1794) was the leader of the Jacobin right wing. Louis Blanc (1811–1882) was a member of the provisional government in 1848 and chairman of the Luxembourg Commission; he emigrated to England in August 1848. Maximilien de Robespierre (1758–1794) was the preeminent leader of the Jacobins and head of the revolutionary government in 1793–1794 (during the terror); he ended up himself on the guillotine. Emmanuel Barthélemy (c. 1820–1855) was a Blanquist participant in the June uprising of 1848 in Paris. Louis Antoine Saint-Just (1767–1794) was another leading Jacobin. Ferdinand Flocon (1800–1866) was a publicist and member of the provisional government in 1848. Lazare Carnot (1753–1823) was the organizer of the French republican forces in the wars of 1792–1794; originally a Jacobin, he was elected to the Directory in 1795 and was minister of war from 1799 to 1801. By the "moon-calf," Engels of course meant Louis Napoleon, nephew of the "little corporal" (Napoleon I).

14 *MEW*, 8:115. The Mountain in the French Revolution of 1789 consisted of the Jacobin radicals, so called because they occupied the highest seats in the National Assembly. In the years 1848–1851 the Mountain consisted of democrats and republicans headed by Alexandre Ledru-Rollin (1807–1874).

15 Ibid., 561–562.

16 Cf. *MEW*, 28:259–260 and 9:129–130.

17 See Lawrence Krader, *The Asiatic Mode of Production: Sources, Development and Critique in the Writings of Karl Marx* (Assen: Van Gorcum, 1975).

18 *MEW*, 28:245–247.

19 Ibid., 252–254.

20 Ibid., 259–260.

21 Ibid., 267–268. Marx quoted the report in English. The odd punctuation is exactly as quoted in *MEW*.

22 Marx and Engels, *Collected Works*, 12:127–132. Cf. *Capital*, vol. 1, in *MEW*, 23:378–379, where Marx did not repeat his condemnation of Indian mores and Asiatic society but did talk about the immutability of the latter. He did not, however, mention irrigation in this connection.

23 *MEW*, 31:44. Interestingly, shortly after this, on 23 Feb. 1865 Marx and Engels sent a joint declaration to the paper refusing further collaboration because it refused to attack the ministry and the feudal-absolutist party as frequently as it did the Progressives. See *MEW*, 16:79.

24 *MEW*, 31:45, 47.

25 Ibid., 63.

26 *MEW*, 16:41–78.

27 *MEW*, 31:64.

28 Marx frequently used this derogatory epithet in private references to Lassalle, even after the latter's untimely death. It is but one of many comments that allow scholars like Kunzli (*Karl Marx: Eine Psychographie* [Vienna, 1966]) to argue he was an anti-Semite despite his own Jewish ancestry.

29 *MEW*, 31:67–68.

30 *MEW*, 16:57, 68–69.

31 McLellan, *Karl Marx*, 338–339.

32 *MEW*, 16:84–85.

33 In this connection, Helene Demuth reportedly told Eleanor Marx that Engels

had "burnt lots of letters referring to himself" after Marx's death (Kapp, *Eleanor Marx*, 1:278), but that would not explain the gaps here, which are in Engels' letters to Marx, not Marx's letters to Engels, unless Engels wanted to destroy evidence of his contributions to *Capital*, vol. 1, out of false modesty. If the latter was the case, he did not do a thorough job, but the most likely explanation for the missing replies is simply the loss of letters in the normal course of events.

34 *MEW*, 30:223–224.

35 Ibid., 225.

36 See *MEW*, 23, esp. 362–390, 483–489, 494–504.

37 *MEW*, 30:263–268. For an interesting discussion of these issues, see Robert Paul Wolff, *Understanding Marx: A Reconstruction and Critique of* Capital (Princeton: Princeton University Press, 1984).

38 *MEW*, 30:273.

39 Ibid., 274–275. For Engels' rejoinder, *MEW*, 1:509, where he said Ricardo's view was correct in practice, if one assumed that a fall in demand momentarily reacted upon ground rent and thereby forced the removal of a proportionate quantity of the worst cultivated land from use. This was not what happened, however, so Ricardo's conception was insufficient.

40 *MEW*, 30:280–281.

41 Ibid., 284.

42 Ibid., 287, 288, 729n301.

43 Ibid., 288–289, 303, 731n322.

44 Ibid., 315. As the name would suggest, a self-actor was any self-acting (automatic) machine, especially a self-acting mule, which was a device with a moving carriage for simultaneously drawing and twisting fibers into thread.

45 Ibid., 309–312, 317, 319–320.

46 Ibid., 326–327, 329.

47 Or at least it does not appear in the published correspondence.

48 *MEW*, 23:457–458n, 89, 166, 178, 259, 269, 283, 308, 320, 421, 445, 448, 468, and 683; 31:274–275. Also, on 20 November 1865, Marx had asked Engels to get from Alfred Knowles, a Manchester cotton spinner, some data on average weekly wages, prices, etc., that he needed immediately to write the second chapter. Again, the reply is missing from the correspondence, but Marx apparently did use the data in the first edition of *Capital*, only to find it was factually in error. In the second edition, he replaced it with more accurate information supplied by an unnamed manufacturer. *MEW*, 31:157–158; 23:232–234. Just who this manufacturer was is not altogether certain, but on 7 May 1868 Marx asked Engels for further information on the same score to use in discussing the rate of profit in the second volume of *Capital*. He said that the data used in volume 1 (to illustrate the rate of surplus value) had come from Engels' factory. Engels said Marx had gotten the data directly from Henry Ermen. It had to do with Gottfried Ermen's spinnery, with which Engels was not connected in any way. Marx needed to write to "Henry Ermen, Bridgewater Mill, Pendlebury (private)" to get further information. Perhaps it was Henry who gave Marx the more accurate data used in the second edition of volume 1. For other examples of Marx's consultation of Engels in connection with *Capital*, see Henderson, *Engels*, 2:393–394.

49 *MEW*, 31:128, 132.

50 The agreement with Meissner provided for the simultaneous publication of two

volumes of *Capital*, the entire length of which would not exceed sixty proof sheets. Meissner later agreed to change those requirements. Ibid., 288, 636n173, 134, 137.

51 Ibid., 174, 179, 287–288.
52 On this matter, see esp. Henderson, *Engels*, 1:205, 219, 222–225; 2:559–560.
53 *MEW*, 31:296–297.
54 Ibid., 662n341, 301.
55 Ibid., 303–304.
56 Ibid., 305.
57 Ibid., 305–306, 662n347. Marx wrote Engels on 27 June, "So that you see how exactly I have followed your advice in the treatment of the appendix, I am copying for you here the divisions, paragraphs, titles, etc." There followed a nearly two-page outline. Ibid., 314–316.
58 Ibid., 308, 310–312, 314.
59 Ibid., 320.
60 Ibid., 321–322.
61 Ibid., 323.
62 Ibid., 324.
63 *MEW*, 23:18.
64 *MEW*, 31:327.
65 Ibid., 328. I must say the logic behind Engels' comments is not entirely clear to me.
66 Ibid., 329–332, 333; *MEW*, 24:169–182.
67 *MEW*, 31:334, 664n360.
68 McLellan, *Karl Marx*, 341.
69 *MEW*, 31:360, 669n397.
70 Ibid., 362; *MEW*, 16:207–218, 226–242, 288–309.
71 *MEW*, 28:323. In the same letter, Marx commented that the pawn shop resource was exhausted and asked Engels to send him one pound (p. 322).
72 *Marx and Engels*, 52.

Chapter 9   Conclusion

1 Letters to Bertalan Szemere, 22 Nov. 1860, and to Engels, 4 July 1864, *MEW*, 30:573, 418.
2 Alvin W. Gouldner, *The Two Marxisms: Contradictions and Anomalies in the Development of Theory* (New York: Seabury Press, 1980), esp. 252. This is a thoughtful book that, among other things, supports basically the same argument as I am presenting here. This argument is, however, interwoven among a number of others and is not, as a result, developed as systematically as it could be. Also, Gouldner did not always document his insights fully, although he did provide many citations to Marx and Engels' writings. As the title suggests, however, he did recognize the many contradictions in Marx's writings, which were carried over into conflicting interpretations of his canon.
3 "Engels and the History of Marxism," in Eric J. Hobsbawm, ed., *The History of Marxism*, vol. 1, *Marxism in Marx's Day* (Brighton: Harvester Press, 1982), 292.
4 For a similar interpretation, see Robert C. Tucker, *Political Culture and Lead-*

ership in Soviet Russia: From Lenin to Gorbachev (New York: W. W. Norton, 1987).

5   *MEW*, 13:10. Engels' "sketch," of course, was his 1844 article "Outlines of a Critique of Political Economy." Gouldner (*The Two Marxisms*, 255) quoted part of this passage.

6   See chapter 3 above. Both comments, incidentally, date from 1890.

Bibliography

Primary Sources

The Betrayal of Marx. Ed. Frederick L. Bender. New York: Harper and Row, 1975.

Birth of the Communist Manifesto. Ed. Dirk J. Struik. New York: International Publishers, 1971.

Born, Stephan. *Erinnerungen eines Achtundvierzigers.* Ed. Hans J. Schütz. Berlin and Bonn: Verlag J. H. W. Dietz Nachf., 1978.

Easton, Loyd D., and Kurt H. Guddat. *Writings of the Young Marx on Philosophy and Society.* Garden City, N.Y.: Doubleday, 1967.

Engels as Military Critic: Articles by Friedrich Engels Reprinted from the Volunteer Journal *and the* Manchester Guardian *of the 1860s.* Ed. W. O. Henderson and W. H. Chaloner. Manchester: Manchester University Press, 1959.

Engels, Friedrich. *The Condition of the Working Class in England.* Translated and edited by W. O. Henderson and W. H. Chaloner. Stanford: Stanford University Press, 1958.

Feuerbach, Ludwig. *The Essence of Christianity.* Trans. George Eliot. New York: Harper and Bros., 1957.

Gerlach, Hellmut von. *Von Rechts nach Links.* Hildesheim: Gerstenberg Verlag, 1978.

Gespräche mit Marx and Engels. Ed. Hans Magnus Enzensberger. 2 vols. Frankfurt a. M.: Insel Verlag, 1973.

Gründungsdokumente des Bundes der Kommunisten (Juni bis September 1847). Ed. Bert Andreas. Hamburg: Dr. Ernst Hauswedell, 1969.

Hegel, G. W. F. *Logic.* Trans. William Wallace. 3d ed. Oxford: Clarendon Press, 1975.

———. *Phenomenology of Mind.* Trans. J. B. Baillie. New York: Harper and Row, 1967.

———. *The Philosophy of History.* Trans. J. Sibree. New York: Dover, 1956.

Hyndman, H. M. *The Record of an Adventurous Life.* New York: Garland, 1984 (facsimile of the original 1912 edition).

Lancashire Record Office:

  DDX 358/1: Agreement, 25 Dec. 1862 between Godfrey Ermen, Cotton Spinner, Thread Manufacturer and Bleacher, and Friedrich Engels

  DDX 358/2: Articles of Partnership, Ermen & Engels, 30 June 1864

  DDX 358/3: Dissolution of Partnership, 18 Aug. 1869

  DDX 358/4: Letter, Engels to Godfrey Ermen, 1 June 1874

Marx, Karl. *Capital.* Trans. Eden and Cedar Paul. 2 vols. New York: E. P. Dutton, 1962.

———. *Texts on Method.* Translated and edited by Terrell Carver. Oxford: Basil Blackwell, 1975.

Marx, Karl, and Friedrich Engels. *Collected Works.* 35 vols. to date. New York: International Publishers, 1975–.

———. *Gesamtausgabe (MEGA).* Berlin: Marx-Engels Verlag, 1927–1934.

———. *Gesamtausgabe (MEGA).* Berlin: Dietz Verlag, 1975–.

———. *Selected Correspondence.* Moscow: Foreign Languages Publishing House, n.d.

———. *Werke.* 41 vols. Berlin: Dietz Verlag, 1956–1979.

Reminiscences of Marx and Engels. Moscow: Foreign Languages Publishing House, n.d.

Steinberg, Hans-Joseph. "Freiheit und Notwendigkeit: Aus einem verlorenen Brief von Friedrich Engels an Ernst Belfort Bax vom Jahre 1886." *International Review of Social History* 18 (1973):276–280.

———. "Revolution und Legalität: Ein unveröffentlichter Brief Friedrich Engels an Richard Fischer." *International Review of Social History* 12 (1967):177–189.

Secondary Sources

Adamiak, Richard. "Marx, Engels, and Dühring." *Journal of the History of Ideas* 35 (1974):98–112.

Adamson, Walter L. *Marx and the Disillusionment of Marxism.* Berkeley: University of California Press, 1985.

———. "Marx's Four Histories: An Approach to His Intellectual Development." *Studies in Marxist Historical Theory.* Supplement 20 of *History and Theory* (1981):379–402.

Althusser, Louis. *Pour Marx.* Paris: Maspero, 1965.

Ashton, Rosemary. *Little Germany: Exile and Asylum in Victorian England.* Oxford: Oxford University Press, 1986.

Avineri, Shlomo. "The Discovery of Hegel's Early Lectures on the Philosophy of Right." *The Owl of Minerva* 16 (1985):199–208.

———. *The Social and Political Thought of Karl Marx.* Cambridge: Cambridge University Press, 1968.

Axelos, Kostas. *Alienation, Praxis, Technē in the Thought of Karl Marx.* Trans. Ronald Bruzina. Austin: University of Texas Press, 1976.

Ball, Terence. "Marx and Darwin: A Reconsideration." *Political Theory* 7 (1979):469–483.

Ball, Terence, and James Farr, eds. *After Marx.* Cambridge: Cambridge University Press, 1984.

Baritz, Moses. "Friedrich Engels in Manchester: His Relations with Marx." *Manchester Guardian,* 14 March 1933:18.

Berger, Martin. *Engels, Armies, and Revolution: The Revolutionary Tactics of Classical Marxism.* Hamden, Conn.: Archon Books, 1977.

Bleuel, Hans Peter. *Friedrich Engels, Bürger und Revolutionär: Die Zeitgerechte Biographie eines grossen Deutschen.* Bein and Munich: Scherz Verlag, 1981.

Bünger, Siegfried. *Friedrich Engels und die britische sozialistische Bewegung, 1881–1895.* Berlin: Rutter and Loening, 1962.

Cadogan, Peter. "Harney and Engels." *International Review of Social History* 10 (1965):66–104.

Carlton, Grace. *Friedrich Engels: The Shadow Prophet.* London: Pall Mall Press, [1965].

Carver, Terrell. *Engels.* New York: Hill and Wang, 1981.

———. *Marx and Engels: The Intellectual Relationship.* Bloomington: Indiana University Press, 1983.

———. "Marx—and Hegel's Logic." *Political Studies* 24 (1976):57–68.

———. "Marx, Engels and Dialectics." *Political Studies* 28 (1980):353–363.

Cohen, G. A. *Karl Marx's Theory of History: a Defence.* Oxford: Clarendon Press, 1978.

Colp, Ralph, Jr. "The Contacts between Karl Marx and Charles Darwin." *Journal of the History of Ideas* 35 (1974):329–338.

———. "The Myth of the Darwin-Marx Letter." *History of Political Economy* 14 (1982):461–482.

Cornu, Auguste. *Karl Marx et Friedrich Engels: Leur vie et leur oeuvre.* 4 vols. Paris: Presses Universitaires de France, 1955–1970.

Demetz, Peter. *Marx, Engels und die Dichter.* Stuttgart: Deutsche Verlags-Anstalt, 1959.

A Dictionary of Marxist Thought. Ed. Tom Bottomore. Cambridge, Harvard University Press, 1983.

Draper, Hal. *Karl Marx's Theory of Revolution.* Vol. 3. *The "Dictatorship of the Proletariat."* New York: Monthly Review Press, 1986.

Easton, Susan M. *Humanist Marxism and Wittgenstein in Social Philosophy.* Manchester: Manchester University Press, 1983.

Elliott, Charles F. "*Quis Custodiat Sacra?* Problems of Marxist Revisionism." *Journal of the History of Ideas* 28 (1967):71–88.

Fetscher, Iring. *Marx and Marxism.* New York: Herder and Herder, 1971.

Findlay, J. N. *The Philosophy of Hegel: An Introduction and Re-Examination.* New York: Collier Books, 1966.

Frey, Susan Thornton. "Friedrich Engels' *Dialectics of Nature* and Nineteenth-Century Science." Ph.D. diss., University of Washington, 1978.

Friedrich Engels, 1820–1970: Referate, Diskussion, Dokumente. Ed. Hans Pelger. Hanover: Verlag für Literatur und Zeitgeschehen, 1971.

Frow, Edmund, and Ruth Frow. "Frederick Engels' Association with John Watts." Typescript seen in the Working Class Movement Library, Manchester, n.d.

———. *Frederick Engels in Manchester: Two Tours with Maps.* Working Class Movement Library, Manchester, n.d.

———. *Karl Marx in Manchester.* Manchester: Manchester Free Press, 1985.

———. *The New Moral World: Robert Owen and Owenism in Manchester and Salford.* Preston: Lancashire Community Press, 1986.

Gallie, W. B. *Philosophers of Peace and War: Kant, Clausewitz, Marx, Engels and Tolstoy.* Cambridge: Cambridge University Press, 1978.

Gemkow, Heinrich, et al. *Karl Marx: Eine Biographie.* Berlin: Dietz Verlag, 1968.

Goode, Patrick. *Karl Korsch: A Study in Western Marxism.* London and Basingstoke: Macmillan, 1979.

Gouldner, Alvin W. *Against Fragmentation: The Origins of Marxism and the Sociology of Intellectuals.* Oxford: Oxford University Press, 1985.

Gouldner, Alvin W. *The Two Marxisms: Contradictions and Anomalies in the Development of Theory.* New York: Seabury Press, 1980.

Hammen, Oscar J. "The Marx-Engels *Briefwechsel.*" *Journal of the History of Ideas* 33 (1972):77–100.

Hammen, Oscar J. "The Young Marx Reconsidered." *Journal of the History of Ideas* 31 (1970):109–117.

Hammen, Oscar J. *The Red '48ers: Karl Marx and Friedrich Engels*. New York: Charles Scribner's Sons, 1969.

Henderson, W. O. *The Life of Friedrich Engels*. 2 vols. London: Frank Cass, 1976.

Henderson, W. O. *Marx and Engels and the English Workers and Other Essays*. London: Frank Cass, 1989.

Henry, Michel. *Marx: A Philosophy of Human Reality*. Trans. Kathleen McLaughlin. Bloomington: Indiana University Press, 1983.

Hillman, Gunther. *Marx und Hegel: Von Spekulation zur Dialektik*. Frankfurt a. M.: Europäische Verlagsanstalt, 1966.

Hodges, Donald, and Ross Gandy. "Marx and Economic Determinism." *The Review of Radical Political Economics* 14 (1982):33–41.

Hook, Sidney. *From Hegel to Marx: Studies in the Intellectual Development of Karl Marx*. Ann Arbor: University of Michigan Press, 1971.

———. *Reason, Social Myths and Democracy*. New York: Humanities Press, 1940.

Hunt, Richard N. *The Political Ideas of Marx and Engels*. 2 vols. Pittsburgh: University of Pittsburgh Press, 1974–1984.

Hyppolite, Jean. *Etudes sur Marx et Hegel*. Paris: Editions Marcel Rivière, 1965.

Ilychov, L. F., et al. *Friedrich Engels: A Biography*. Trans. Victor Schneierson. Moscow: Progress Publishers, 1974.

Jenkins, Mick. *Frederick Engels in Manchester*. Manchester: Lancashire and Cheshire Communist Party, [1951].

Jordan, Z. A. *The Evolution of Dialectical Materialism: A Philosophical and Sociological Analysis*. New York: St. Martin's Press, 1967.

Kägi, Paul. *Genesis des historischen Materialismus: Karl Marx und die Dynamik des Gesellschaft*. Wien: Europa Verlag, 1965.

Kahan-Coates, Zelda. *The Life and Teachings of Friedrich Engels*. London: Lawrence and Wishart, 1945.

Kain, Philip J. "Marx, Engels, and the Dialectics." *Studies in Soviet Thought* 23 (1982):271–283.

———. "Marx's Dialectic Method." *History and Theory* 19 (1980):294–312.

———. *Marx' Method, Epistemology, and Humanism: A Study in the Development of His Thought*. Dordrecht: D. Reidel, 1986.

———. "Marx's Theory of Ideas." *Studies in Marxist Historical Theory*. Supplement 20 of *History and Theory* (1981):357–378.

———. *Schiller, Hegel, and Marx: State, Society, and the Aesthetic Ideal of Ancient Greece*. Kingston and Montreal: McGill-Queen's University Press, 1982.

Kapp, Yvonne. *Eleanor Marx*. 2 vols. New York: Pantheon, 1972–1976.

Kaufmann, Walter. *Hegel: Reinterpretation, Texts, and Commentary*. Garden City, N.Y.: Doubleday, 1965.

Kelly, Donald R. "The Science of Anthropology: An Essay on the Very Old Marx." *Journal of the History of Ideas* 45 (1984):245–262.

Kluchert, Gerhard, *Geschichtsschreibung und Revolution: Die historischen Schriften von Karl Marx and Friedrich Engels, 1846 bis 1852*. Stuttgart: Fromann Holzboog, 1985.

Kolakowski, Leszek. *Main Currents of Marxism: Its Rise, Growth, and Dissolution*. Vol. 1. *The Founders*. Trans. P. S. Falla. Oxford: Clarendon Press, 1978.

———. *Positivist Philosophy from Hume to the Vienna Circle*. Trans. Norbert Guterman. Harmondsworth: Penguin, 1972.

Köllmann, Wolfgang. *Sozialgeschichte der Stadt Barmen im 19. Jahrhundert*. Tübingen: J. C. B. Mohr, 1960.

Korsch, Karl. *Marxism and Philosophy*. Trans. Fred Halleday. London: NLB, 1970.

Krader, Lawrence. *The Asiatic Mode of Production: Development and Critique in the Writings of Karl Marx*. Assen: Van Gorcum, 1975.

———. "The Works of Marx and Engels in Ethnology Compared." *International Review of Social History* 18 (1973):223–275.

Lamb, David. "Hegelian Marxist Millenarianism." *History of European Ideas* 8 (1987):271–281.

Levine, Norman. *Dialogue within the Dialectic*. London: Allen and Unwin, 1984.

———. *The Tragic Deception: Marx contra Engels*. Oxford and Santa Barbara: Clio, 1975.

Lichtheim, George, *George Lukács*. New York: Viking Press, 1970.

———. *Marxism: A Historical and Critical Study*. New York: Praeger, 1961.

Lukács, George. *Geschichte und Klassenbewusstsein: Studien über Marxistische Dialektik*. Berlin: Der Malik Verlag, 1923.

MacGregor, David. *The Communist Ideal in Hegel and Marx*. Toronto and Buffalo: University of Toronto Press, 1984.

———. "Marxism's Hegelian Blind Spot: The Theory of the State in Hegel and Marx." *Current Perspectives in Social Theory* 9 (1989):143–175.

———. "The State at Dusk." *The Owl of Minerva* 21 (1989):51–64.

Macháčková, Vera. *Der Junge Engels und die Literatur (1836–1844)*. Berlin: Dietz Verlag, 1961.

McLellan, David. *Friedrich Engels*. New York: Viking Press, 1978.

———. *Karl Marx: His Life and Thought*. New York: Harper and Row, 1973.

———. *Marx before Marxism*. New York: Harper and Row, 1970.

———. *Marxism after Marx: An Introduction*. London: Macmillan, 1979.

———. *The Thought of Karl Marx: An Introduction*. New York: Harper and Row, 1971.

———. *The Young Hegelians and Karl Marx*. London: Macmillan, 1969.

McMurtry, John. *The Structure of Marx's World-View*. Princeton: Princeton University Press, 1978.

Maguire, John. *Marx's Paris Writings: An Analysis*. Dublin and London: Gill and Macmillan, 1972.

Mayer, Gustav. *Friedrich Engels: Eine Biographie*. 2 vols. 2d ed. rev. Haag; Martinus Nijhoff, 1934.

Mehring, Franz. *Karl Marx: The Story of His Life*. Trans. Edward Fitzgerald. Ann Arbor: University of Michigan Press, 1973.

Messinger, Gary S. *Manchester in the Victorian Age: The Half-Known City*. Manchester: Manchester University Press, 1985.

Moore, Stanley. "Marx and the Origin of Dialectical Materialism." *Inquiry* 14 (1972):420–429.

Neumann, Sigmund. "Engels and Marx: Military Concepts of the Social Revolutionaries." In Edward Meade Earle, ed. *Makers of Modern Strategy: Military Thought from Machiavelli to Hitler*. Princeton: Princeton University Press, 1943, pp. 155–171.

Neumann, Sigmund, and Mark von Hagen. "Engels and Marx on Revolution, War, and the Army in Society." In Peter Paret, ed. *Makers of Modern Strategy: From*

Machiavelli to the Nuclear Age. Princeton: Princeton University Press, 1986, pp. 262–280.

Nikolaievsky, Boris. "Toward a History of 'the Communist League,' 1847–1852." *International Review of Social History* 1 (1956):234–252.

Nikolaievsky, Boris, and Otto Maenchen-Helfen. *Karl Marx: Man and Fighter*. Trans. Gwenda David and Eric Mosbacher. Bungay, Suffolk: Penguin, 1976 (first published 1936; revised 1970).

Nordahl, Richard. "Marx on the Use of History in the Analysis of Capitalism." *History of Political Economy* 14 (1982):342–365.

Ollmann, Bertell. *Alienation: Marx's Conception of Man in Capitalist Society*. Cambridge: Cambridge University Press, 1971.

O'Malley, Joseph. "Marx's Economics and Hegel's *Philosophy of Right*: An Essay on Marx's Hegelianism." *Political Studies* 24 (1976):43–56.

O'Neill, John. "The Concept of Estrangement in the Early and Later Writings of Karl Marx." *Philosophy and Phenomenological Research* 25 (September 1964–June 1965):64–84.

Padover, Saul K. *Karl Marx: An Intimate Biography*. New York: New American Library, 1978.

Peters, H. F. *Red Jenny: A Life with Karl Marx*. London: Allen and Unwin, 1986.

Plant, Raymond. *Hegel*. Bloomington: Indiana University Press, 1973.

Powell, Michael. "Chetham's Library." *Manchester Region History Review*, 2, no. 2 (1988):25–31.

Pryor, Frederic L. "The Classification and Analysis of Precapitalist Economic Systems by Marx and Engels." *History of Political Economy* 14 (1982):521–542.

Reipricht, Kurt. *Die philosophisch-naturwissenschaftlichen Arbeiten von Karl Marx und Friedrich Engels*. Berlin: Dietz Verlag, 1969.

Ritter, Harry R. "Friedrich Engels and the East European Nationality Problem." *East European Quarterly* 10 (1976):137–152.

Rjazanov, D. *Marx und Engels: Nicht nur für Anfänger*. Trans. Rainer Traub. Berlin: Rotbusch Verlag, 1973.

Sanderson, John. *An Interpretation of the Political Ideas of Marx and Engels*. London: Longmans, Green, 1969.

Schmidt, Alfred. *Der Begriff der Natur in der Lehre von Marx*. Frankfurt a. M.: Europäische Verlagsanstalt, 1962.

Seigel, Jerrold E. "Marx's Early Development: Vocation, Rebellion, and Realism." *Journal of Interdisciplinary History* 3 (1973):475–501.

——. *Marx's Fate: The Shape of a Life*. Princeton: Princeton University Press, 1978.

Shaw, William H. *Marx's Theory of History*. Stanford: Stanford University Press, 1978.

Sherwood, John M. "Engels, Marx, Malthus, and the Machine." *American Historical Review* 90 (1985):837–865.

Stedman Jones, Gareth. "Engels and the End of Classical German Philosophy." *New Left Review* 79 (May–June 1973):17–36.

——. "Engels and the Genesis of Marxism." *New Left Review* 106 (Nov.–Dec. 1977):79–104.

——. "Engels and the History of Marxism." In Eric J. Hobsbawm, ed. *The History of Marxism*. Vol. 1. *Marxism in Marx's Day*. Brighton: Harvester Press, 1982, pp. 290–326.

Stepanova, Yelena. *Frederick Engels*. Moscow: Foreign Languages Publishing House, 1958.

Suchting, W. A. *Karl Marx: An Introduction.* New York: New York University Press, 1983.

Thomas, Paul. "Marx and Science." *Political Studies* 24 (1976):1–23.

Toews, John Edward. *Hegelianism: The Path toward Dialectical Humanism.* Cambridge: Cambridge University Press, 1980.

Tucker, Robert C. *The Marxian Revolutionary Idea.* New York: W. W. Norton, 1970.

———. *Philosophy and Myth in Karl Marx.* 2d ed. Cambridge: Cambridge University Press, 1972.

———. *Political Culture and Leadership in Soviet Russia: From Lenin to Gorbachev.* New York: W. W. Norton, 1987.

Ulrich, Horst. *Der Junge Engels: eine historisch-biographische Studie seiner weltanschaulichen Entwicklung in den Jahren 1834–1845.* 2 vols. Berlin: VEB Deutscher Verlag der Wissenschaften, 1961–1966.

Wallach, Jehuda L. *Die Kriegslehre von Friedrich Engels.* Frankfurt a. M.: Europäische Verlagsanstalt, 1968.

Wessel, Leonard P., Jr. *Prometheus Bound: The Mythic Structure of Karl Marx's Scientific Thinking.* Baton Rouge: Louisiana State University Press, 1984.

Whitfield, Roy. *Frederick Engels in Manchester: The Search for a Shadow.* Manchester: Manchester Free Press, 1988.

Wolff, Robert Paul. *Understanding Marx: A Reconstruction and Critique of Capital.* Princeton: Princeton University Press, 1984.

Index